Bismillāhir-Rahmānir-Rahīm.
In the name of God,
the Most Compassionate, the Most Merciful.

THE CHOICE

M. R. BAWA MUHAIYADDEEN ﷺ

THE CHOICE

FELLOWSHIP PRESS
Philadelphia, PA

Library of Congress Control Number: 2013957594

Muhaiyaddeen, M. R. Bawa.
  The choice / M. R. Bawa Muhaiyaddeen.
  Philadelphia, PA: Fellowship Press, 2014
  p. cm.
  Includes index.

  Trade paperback: 978-0-914390-95-4
  Hardcover: 978-0-914390-96-1

  1. God. 2. Sufism. 3. Islām. 4. Shaikh and disciple. 5. Truth and falsehood. 6. Natural and artificial. 7. God's creation and man's creation. 8. Justice and injustice. 9. *Dhikr*. 10. Peace of mind. 11. Bawa Muhaiyaddeen Fellowship and Mosque. 12. Muhammad ⊖ foretells the future. 13. Causes of destruction. 14. World war III. 15. Jesus ⊖ and the antichrist. 16. Conception. 17. Organ transplants. 18. Chemicals and food. 19. Intoxicants. 20. Causes of diseases. 21. Burial in earth vs. cremation. 22. Angel of death. 23. Balance. 24. Positive and negative. I. Title.

Copyright © 2014
by Bawa Muhaiyaddeen Fellowship
5820 Overbrook Avenue, Philadelphia, Pennsylvania 19131

All rights reserved. No portion of this book may be reproduced in any manner without written permission from the publisher.

Printed in the United States of America by FELLOWSHIP PRESS
Bawa Muhaiyaddeen Fellowship
First Printing

Muhammad Raheem Bawa Muhaiyaddeen ☙

CONTENTS

INTRODUCTION
    To Save the World from Destruction   xv

PROLOGUE
    The Last Discourse   3

PART ONE: IN THE WORLD OF THE SOUL
    1. The Great Kingdom Within   9
    2. The Clay Pot & the Copper Pot   17
    3. When God Created Man   27

PART TWO: IN THIS WORLD
    4. Which Story Shall We Tell   33
    5. The Light Speaks   45
    6. The Light Continues to Speak   69
    7. The Story   95
    8. Our Thoughts   119
    9. Faith   137
    10. Balance   145
    11. Purity   163
    12. Peace   171
    13. Two Words   197

PART THREE: DESTRUCTION
    14. Whatever Comes   215
    15. Kali Yuga   231
    16. Tampering with Nature   245
    17. The Limit   269
    18. The War   293
    19. Jesus ☮ & the Antichrist   309
    20. What's Gone Is Gone   321

PART FOUR: IN GOD'S KINGDOM
    21. The Night Is Finally Over   333
    22. Taking the Children to Heaven   339
    23. What Form, If Any, Will He Take Next   343
    24. Can He Still Instruct Us   347
    25. What Will Happen to the Fellowship   357
    26. How Can We Help   361

EPILOGUE
    Protect My Mosque and My Words   379

GLOSSARY   385

INDEX   407

Verily never will Allāh change the condition of a people until they change it themselves (with their own souls).

—*Holy Qur'ān, Ar-Ra'd:11*

INTRODUCTION

A'ūdhu billāhi minash-shaitānir-rajīm.
I seek refuge in God from the accursed satan.
Bismillāhir-Rahmānir-Rahīm.
In the name of God, the Most Compassionate, the Most Merciful.

TO SAVE THE WORLD FROM DESTRUCTION

*Thursday, April 1, 1982, 9:05 A.M.
Colombo, Sri Lanka*

"Why did you create me in this *dunyā*, O God?" I asked. This was a huge question I had for God.

Then the sound came into my *qalb*. The answer was, "O *insān*, O Man, I did create you, so there must be a reason for it. I created the *ambiyā'*—the prophets, the *aqtāb*—those beings who have attained the power of the light of discerning wisdom, the *auliyā'*, the saints, and the guides. I have sent them down since the time of Adam ☮. Do you not know this?

"It is through them that I demonstrated My qualities, My actions, and My conduct. Through them, I revealed My creations and the explanations of My creations, the *dunyā* and the *ākhirah*—this world and the kingdom of God, the *rūhs* and the *ruhānīs*—the pure souls and the impure souls, the good and the evil, the hell and the heaven, the judgment and the Day of Judgment, the day of *maut*—the day of death, and the Day of Qiyāmah—the Day of the Questioning. I had also given explanations regarding judgment and justice earlier.

"It was in this manner that I gave many explanations to each *nabī*, each prophet, as I sent him down. The prophets then brought My words to the people of the world and explained the teachings. Do you not understand that?

"All of them were called miscreants by the world. The community of mankind said malicious things about the *ambiyā'* and called them miscreants behind their backs. They were called sorcerers and magicians, thieves, murderers, and necromancers. They were insulted. They were berated and rejected. Some were murdered, some were hung, and some were made to die by other means. The people did many things like this to them.

"Up until the time of Muhammad Mustāfār-Rasūl ☮, My words and actions were revealed by the *ambiyā'*, and there was also a section I Myself revealed directly. At that time, many people rejected, insulted, and cursed the *ambiyā'*. They spoke against them, and insulted them. They insulted My words and they insulted the *ambiyā'*.

"But a few who perfectly realized and clearly understood the teachings developed between the two, between the truth and those who insulted the *ambiyā'*. They existed between the truth and the opposition to it, and those few grew in clarity and truth. Just a few developed between the two. After the Rasūl ☮, no more *ambiyā'*, no more prophets, were sent down. They were no longer sent down after Muhammad ☮, the final *nabī*, the final prophet. They stopped being sent down.

"After them, the world again forgot the words I spoke. The words were forgotten. Those who had disparaged and berated the *ambiyā'* forgot to do so. That ceased. Those who disparaged and berated the *ambiyā'* and the *auliyā'* disappeared. There were also no people who stood between the truth of My words and their insulting talk, no people who were clear! Those people did not come either.

"In the past, there had been a few clear people who stood between the two, but because those two things—the truth and the insults—had disappeared, the clear people did not come to search for Me either. They did not come because neither the truth nor the insults were being demonstrated, because neither was being demonstrated or explained. If it had occurred, a few would have come.

"Someone was needed to hear the words—to hear them. Some people were needed to hear the words and to find comfort in them. Others needed to find comfort through insulting the words—those who were insulting the words needed to find comfort in doing so. Those who listened to the words were born in order to receive comfort from the words. I have to find comfort in understanding My creation in this state—that will comfort Me. Those who come to this world amidst these circumstances in order to know Me must be comforted. They must also obtain peace.

"But at one time there was not even one of them left. I created you because there was no one left. I created you, and you must now listen. You must finish listening to the sadness and the happiness of those words. You must hear all that the prophets heard. You must hear out all of it, and with certitude and strength, demonstrate and explain what I said before. You must remind the people. They have forgotten what the *ambiyā'* said, but the *ambiyā'* are not here anymore, so now you are the one who must show them, remind them, and tell them. They have forgotten the words. You must speak to them and remind them of the old words.

"You must tell them what I have said and you must listen to them. Those who want to have peace will have to come between the two. It is for this reason that I created you: to listen to the insults. I created you to experience all the happiness and the sadness. I sent you down for this. You were the one who was born in order to hear the insults. You were born to experience all of that.

"Therefore, do not ask Me why I created you! You have to get peace from what comes between you and My words, they have to get peace from insulting you, and those few coming towards Me who listen to My words have to find the peace in those words.

"This is why I created you. This is your story. This is why I created you. There are no more *ambiyā'* now. This is why I created you. This is your purpose. You must create a connection between your brethren: this is the story. Remind them!

"If the insulters and the listeners stop, the world will be destroyed. There will be no one left to remember and the world will be destroyed. It will come to the point of having to be destroyed. The world will be destroyed.

"Therefore, there must be a person who speaks the words and who reminds the people. There must be someone to reveal the old words, the fundamentally deep words.

"They must be revealed. They must be remembered.

"The *ambiyā'* spoke the old words and reminded the people. Saying those words brought them peace. They obtained peace and those obscure few who heard the reminders and wanted to come to Me also got peace. This is the reason.

"Because it is like this, if one, two, or ten people come to Me because of that reminder, it will save the world.

"It is to save the world from destruction that I created you to remind them yet again.

"You must listen to the insults and remind them at this time. You must remind them of My words. This is why I created one human being for this time and said, 'Now go and do this!' Therefore, you were born to listen to the insults. Hear them out and finish. Tell them what I tell you to say, and then leave. Tell them the deep things.

"In addition to that, you are a human being and I am the Rabb. You are a human being and you must make your brothers and sisters human. The other group who are also your brothers and sisters—let them finish insulting you. Listen to their insults and comfort them. Let them get peace from insulting you. You will get peace from telling them. Say the words and be peaceful. Those few who listen will understand and get peace from listening. I will have peace if all of you have peace. When all of your needs are fulfilled and you finally have peace, that will be My peace. Peace for Me is when all of you get the needs of your minds fulfilled.

"Someone is needed to do this. That is why I created you as a human being. I sent you down just as I sent down all the rest. I created you as a human being. If you had understood this, you would not have asked, 'O God, why did You create me? Why have I come into this world? Why do I have this suffering?' You would not have asked this. You would not have asked this. If you had understood, you would not have asked Me why I created you. You would not have said, 'O God, why did You put me into this?'"

These were the sounds that came into my *qalb*. Then I thought, "All right, this duty can be done for a certain amount of time—but He has certainly placed a limit on it. It will go on until the limit. I will listen, I will tell them, and then I will go."

PROLOGUE

PROLOGUE

A'ūdhu billāhi minash-shaitānir-rajīm.
I seek refuge in God from the accursed satan.

Bismillāhir-Rahmānir-Rahīm.
In the name of God, the Most Compassionate, the Most Merciful.

THE LAST DISCOURSE

*Monday, November 17, 1986, 7:50 A.M.
Philadelphia, USA*

All praise and glory belong to Almighty God, to Allāhu ta'ālā Nāyan. We dedicate everything we seek to Him.

We must put everything we look for and everything we do into His hands. Then we can be given the appropriate qualities, deeds, love, and tranquility. Then we can be given His qualities and His wealth. If we give Him what we earn, He will give us the wealth that He has, the wealth of His *mubārakāt*. Then His good qualities and good deeds will come to us. This is how it must be. This is what an *insān kāmil*, a perfected human being, will look for and how he will conduct his search.

My love you.

All praise is for Him. Do not look for anything for yourself. Do not try to obtain anything for yourself. In any point that you seek—seek God alone. When you go to pray in the Mosque, do not think, "I am going to pray. I am looking for something for myself." Do not take anything for yourself. You must go there to see if there is anything you can do for the Mosque. If you see something that is dirty or that needs to be done, you must help. That is the truth—it is for you.

We should never think of what someone else can do for us. Instead, we must think, "What can I do for him? What kind of help can I offer him?"

The Fellowship is the same. We should not think, "What help has the Fellowship given me? What has the Fellowship done for me?" We must think, "What help can I offer the Fellowship? What can I do to show the way, in order to help it succeed and progress?" Think of this.

Some of you have come here to learn from the Shaikh. That is all right. But you must think, "What have I done for the Shaikh? What help can I give him?" You must do this.

Whenever you begin to do something, you should never think, "I previously did something for that person. I did this! I did that." You must never think in this manner. No matter how much you have done, you must continue to reflect upon your life.

Jeweled lights of my eyes, what should we speak of, what should we do, what answers should we give? If we keep speaking about ourselves and praising ourselves, our achievements will be evil. The bad things will be revealed as our achievements. If we accept praise, we will be accepting a faulty thing.

The makeup of the *dunyā* glitters in ignorance like the moon glitters in darkness. We should not pick up these glitters and think, "I am glittering." Those things will glitter and go. The evil qualities of ignorance, lack of wisdom, pride, envy, deceit, satan's qualities, and vengeance glitter like this.

For us to acquire these glittering qualities and to try to take them into the *ākhirah*, into the kingdom of God, is not the goal. What we must do is discard those qualities. If we want to discard them, we must think of each thing we do. "What are we doing? What is this for? What is that for? What consequences will result? What progress will result? What is it that we should actually do?"

Let us reflect upon and look at *dīn, dunyā,* and *ākhirah. Dīn* is absolute purity. *Dunyā* is what pleases us and what we love— it is beautiful. The *dīn* remains absolutely pure. The *dīn* is absolute purity. The *dunyā* is the beauty and the light within absolute purity that will become the *ākhirah,* the kingdom of God, the world of God.

Look. How can it be found? Islām is the *dīn.* Islām is understanding *halāl* and *harām,* the permissible and the forbidden. Islām is understanding absolutely pure unity and harmony. For a human being, the *dīn* is the sustenance that is *halāl* for him.

That truth is Islām. That is *dunyā.* The *dunyā* in a human being consists of the beauty, the qualities, the deeds, the conduct, the truth, and the ninety-nine *wilāyāt* of God that are His actions— when it is understood, that is *dunyā.* This is what a human being must seek during his life, *hayāh.*

Dīn and *dunyā!* We must obtain God's qualities from the *dīn.* When we assemble these qualities, they become the *dunyā,* the beauty, the house for our life.

If a person is to seek these things during his lifetime, he must look at what a chicken does. It digs into the world in order to obtain the food it needs. Peck, peck, peck, peck, peck, peck, peck! It takes the food and pushes everything else aside. Gems, nuggets of gold, this and that are all discarded. What does it need? Worms, insects, grubs, beetles, larva. Similarly, if a person of wisdom wants to learn from the Shaikh, he must dig into that *dunyā.*

The wisdom of the Shaikh is an enormous mountain. A person of wisdom will come to peck and peck for it. He will peck and peck for every word. Like a chicken discarding things in the *dunyā,* he will take in only Allāh's treasures: the qualities, deeds, conduct, truth, unity, equality, peace, tranquility, justice, integrity, equanimity, the three thousand qualities of grace. He will take in these qualities. He must take in the beautiful qualities of grace, wisdom, and equality, while discarding everything else. That food is the *dīn.*

Dīn and *dunyā. Dīn* is the absolute purity known as Islām. It is the most beautiful food. This sustenance is *halāl.* It is absolutely pure. The beauty it possesses is the *dunyā.* It is a beautiful house. That is how it exists as heaven. If you take in the purity like that, it will be heaven. The *dunyā* will become heaven for you and your house will be beautiful.

The *dunyā* will become heaven. This, your house, will be your state in *ākhirah.* This then will be heaven, and in *ākhirah,* it will become the house of your Father, in accordance with your efforts. *Dīn, dunyā,* and *ākhirah.* Those three are where you gather the materials and assemble your house.

This is what you must dig out of the Shaikh. If you are to get it, you must peck and peck and peck and take it in. That will bring unity and harmony—the unity, equality, peace, tranquility, and serenity that are Islām.

Part One
IN THE WORLD OF THE SOUL

A'ūdhu billāhi minash-shaitānir-rajīm.
I seek refuge in God from the accursed satan.
Bismillāhir-Rahmānir-Rahīm.
In the name of God, the Most Compassionate, the Most Merciful.

THE GREAT KINGDOM WITHIN

*Monday, February 26, 1979, A.M.
Philadelphia, USA*

You are the ruler of everything in your own kingdom. Each person is the ruler of his own kingdom. You are the king. You are all rulers of your own respective kingdoms. You possess the storybook and you act. All of you rule your own kingdoms. Within you is a great kingdom containing eighteen thousand universes that God has given you.

As the ruler of that kingdom, you must study how to be just in that kingdom. You must learn what justice is like and what kind of justice you possess. You must learn what peace exists there, what tolerance exists there, what tranquility exists there, and what judgment you will receive from God. How will you judge others? Will you side with yourself or with others? If you reflect upon these things a little, it will be good.

Until you read your own story, until you discover your own faults, until you find your own peace, and until you find your own unity, your kingdom will be misguided regarding what you do with others. All of the justice with which you act towards others will be wrong. It will be wrong.

It will be called wrong, and the kingdom you rule will be like a bar kingdom. It will be like going to the bartender. When drunkards go to the bar they speak to the bartender about the altercations taking place there. "These people are just drunkards. Pour me a bottle, please. I need a bottle. They are just drunkards and crazy people. Pour me a bottle, please." This is how you will conduct your kingdom. It is not correct.

Nothing you say to others, do to others, or lie about to others will bring you peace until you realize that you are a drunkard as well and that you have also come to the bar. You will not have peace until you know what you come to the bar for, what actions you carry out, why you buy what you buy, what you drink. You will not have peace until you give it up. Thank you.

Wisdom is a treasure of God.

(Bawangal begins to sing)

God gave wisdom.
God gave us wisdom.
He instilled in it the bliss of His grace.
He established within it a state of justice and peace.

He built you a kingdom upon the water.
As its King, He sustained it in the name of His grace.
He formed His blissful actions, qualities, and conduct,
and He made us understand them.
He placed the resonance that is Allāhu there.

He formed and created *insān*, Man, and
placed him into *'ālamul-arwāh*, the world of pure souls.
He set many seasons there, in cycles.
He formed and placed everything
into the form of the embryo for us.
He made us understand it with total certitude.

He told us to develop with determination
the state of all states
that is *īmān*, absolute faith in God.
He served us great quantities of
the treasure that is grace and
asked us to imbibe it.
He told us to reject and discard all things *harām*.
He formed *sharr* and *khair* from Himself and
bestowed them upon us.
He told us to know and to understand right and wrong.
He told us to choose the *khair* and to act accordingly.
He told us to choose the *halāl* and to eat it.
He told us to adhere to the practice of justice.
He told us to live in this manner
without straying for even one minute.

He told us to make the two, *insān* and Allāhu, into one.
He showed us the connection between *insān* and Allāh.
He established the state of compassionate love.
"Discover it and act accordingly," He said.
"Make everything as peaceful as yourself," He said.
He told us to have *sabūr* in those states of peacefulness.
He placed there patience,
sabūr and *shukūr*, inner patience and contentment.

He placed there patience, *sabūr,* and *shukūr.*
He placed *tawakkul,* trust in Him,
into the world to which we go and from which we return.

He told you to choose, and
to be aware of the Wisdom within wisdom.
He told you to demonstrate
the *amānah*—the treasure held in trust—
of nothing other than Allāhu.
"All praise is His," He said.

"My messenger is the one who accepts this and
who acts accordingly," He declared.
"He is all of Allāh's qualities," He said.
"He is the one who accepts them and
who acts accordingly," He said.
"I am the One who does not fail in
the practice of justice," He said.
"My representative is the one
who establishes that state," He said.
"I made him My messenger for *'ālamul-arwāh,*" He said.
"He is the representative who comforts all lives," He said.

"Be as aware of everything as you are of yourself," He said,
as He told *insān* to rule everything in the entire world.
He told him to know Him day and night.

After knowing Him, He said, "Understand yourself."
"When the understanding comes,
it will be resplendent," He said.
"Understand the *furūd,*

the obligations I have ordained for you, and
then pray," He said.

"The body and the life are two," He said.
"Your body is earth," He said, as He formed it.
"Your life is My *dhāt,* the essence of My grace," He said.
"It will always be My treasure," He said.
"I have created it as the *amānah*—a trust—for you," He said.
"If you comprehend this,
 you will intermingle with God," He said.
"If you comprehend this,
 you will intermingle with God," He said.

"Act correctly in the practice of justice," He said.
"Take My qualities and act with them
 without straying for one minute," He commanded.
"Know the five and understand them," He said.
"Know the six and make them resplendent
 within your wisdom," He commanded.

He blessed you with
 the grace of eyes, understanding, and ears.
"Know the sense of smell, the mouth,
 the tongue and taste," He said.
"Discover the house known as the *qalb*," He said.
"This is where I—your Creator—dwell," He said.
"Worship, do the five times prayer and *'ibādah*," He said.
"If you recite and see the connection,
 it will be Me," He said.
"Live with love and kindness," He said.
"See all lives as your own life," He said.

"Have love for all living beings," He said.
"Speak to them of charity, mercy,
 justice, and integrity," He said.

"You too will live alone,
 as I live alone," He said.
"Yet all living beings are within you," He said.
"Know this state," He commanded.
"Do your duty without selfishness," He commanded.
"That itself will be the state of peace," He said.

"Give up earth and gold," He said.
"Cut off the hypnotic delusion that is maya," He said.
"Earth, woman, and gold
 are things that will hypnotize you.
 Cut them out by the roots," He said.
"Stay within the limits, as I do," He said.
"Practice My justice and My laws," He said.
"Do this day and night," He commanded.
"This is the quality of Allāhu," He said
 as He bestowed the grace.
"O *insān*, understand all of this," He said.
"I am the One who dwells in all lives
 as your everlasting glory," He said.

"Destroy the state in which
 one attacks the other," He said.
"I am the State in which everything is seen as One," He said.
"Hunger, illness, old age, and death
 are parts of the state that is the body," He said.
"They are parts of the state that is the body," He said.

"Do not live depending upon that body," He said.
"I am the One who lives within it—
 live depending on that One," He said.
"Know the self and understand it," He said.
"I belong to all the lives in the world," He said.
"Know mind and desire," He said.
"When you comprehend silence, you will be light," He said.
Āmīn.

A'ūdhu billāhi minash-shaitānir-rajīm.
I seek refuge in God from the accursed satan.
Bismillāhir-Rahmānir-Rahīm.
In the name of God, the Most Compassionate, the Most Merciful.

THE CLAY POT & THE COPPER POT

*Wednesday, July 30, 1980, 9:30 A.M.
Philadelphia, USA*

QUESTION

I have heard you say that we come here through our desire and I have heard you say that a human birth, to be born as a man, is the most exalted birth, because it is the only way we can know God. I want to know the connection between those, and also, how did that desire become manifest?

TRANSLATOR
(speaking to Bawangal)

Bawangal, you have spoken about birth. You have explained it in two or three different ways. Could you please explain that? First, you have said that we were with God before. Then you said we came here through our own desires. Third…

(the translator turns to the person asking the question)

One is we came through our desire, first thing we were with God, third is what?

M. R. BAWA MUHAIYADDEEN

Where did I say that?

TRANSLATOR
(speaking to Bawangal)

You said that in your talks and discourses.

M. R. BAWA MUHAIYADDEEN

I might have spoken of it in the *Resonance of Allāh*.

QUESTION

The fact that we were born, and aside from this birth that we can know…

TRANSLATOR
(speaking to Bawangal)

Ah, she said the third one is that man's birth is exalted and that is why he is the rarest of the rare and that is how we can understand God.

M. R. BAWA MUHAIYADDEEN

Yes. All three are correct. This is a small point.

When God created your soul, the light came from Him and He spoke to you, "I have now created My story, and everything in *ʿālamul-arwāh*. I have created the world of the soul, the kingdom of the soul, the kingdom of the world, the kingdom of heaven, and the kingdom of hell. I have created all the kingdoms in creation. All My secrets are within them. If you are to understand Me in your life, you must understand My secrets. After you understand My secret, you will know Me. When you know Me and understand yourself, you will know My mystery. You will know what

My mystery is like, and then you will understand. This is a secret, and that is a mystery.

"Thus, you will leave the world of the soul and go to the world of creation. Do you wish to know everything about Me and about yourself? Do you wish to know the mystery that is capable of understanding Me? Do you want to do that? Do you want to see all of My creation and My secret arts of creation? It is all a great wonder. Do you want to go see it? The kingdom you are looking at now is a mystery. Here, you do not see Me or understand Me. I have made the kingdom of the world a secret in which to know Me, to understand Me, to understand yourself, and to understand all the creations. The kingdom of creation contains many wonders. Do you want to see it?"

You said, "Yes, I would like to see it."

Then God said, "Since that is so, I will give you two choices. You must understand these two choices. In the first section, there are those who want to control the world: they will endeavor to rule the world. Then, there will be a few who want to rule My mysterious kingdom. They will be somewhat rare, it will be very difficult for them, and they will experience many hardships.

"However, I am you and you are Me. You emerged from Me. The soul is absolute purity. I am giving you the soul as an *amānah*, a trust. I am giving you something that belongs to Me. In addition to giving you My belonging as an *amānah*, I am giving you My qualities: *sabūr, shukūr, tawakkul,* and *al-hamdu lillāh*—patience, inner patience, contentment, trust in God, and giving all praise to God. I am giving you assessment, subtle wisdom, discerning wisdom, and Divine Luminous Wisdom—*madi, nupa arivu, pahut arivu,* and *pērarivu*. I am giving you peace, tranquility, serenity, compassion, and mercy towards other living beings. I am giving you My treasure as an *amānah*.

"Do not lose it. This treasure belongs to Me. You must bring it back to Me. This is the treasure of goodness, the wealth of the kingdom of heaven. You must bring it back to Me. You must bring back the absolute purity that is the soul, and these absolutely pure treasures.

"If you leave the *amānah* somewhere, or put it down somewhere to be ruined, you will be subject to The Questioning. You will have destroyed My earnings and My faith in you. If you do not return the treasure I entrusted to you in good faith, you will become a debtor. Live carefully, and return this treasure to Me. Then you will not be in debt.

"Use that treasure to run your business after you get there.

"I will give you a house that will be built of earth, fire, water, air, and ether. You can live in that house and do your duties; however, you must clean that house every second because it is not a reliable house. Dirt will take hold of it every moment! It will change, and mold will grow on it. It will change every moment, changing as the air changes and as the seasons change. It can change with the wind and with the rain, with water, with fire, and with movement. Therefore, you must constantly polish that house, keep it clear at all times, and control that house. If you control it and correctly use the goodness and the treasures I have given you, that house will be clear for you. Do this. You must do this.

"Keep it clear and then read My story. As you research My story, you will know your story. When you know your story, you will begin to build yourself an appropriate house. When you build the house, you will be My child—you will change. Then you will understand the value of this mysterious kingdom. When you understand, you will obtain My kingdom. Would you like to do that? Would you like to go see it? There is a lot to learn and many secret things to study. Would you like to go?"

"Yes, I would like that. I would like to go see it once."

"Then you may go. This is the story. You can go. However, I do need to tell you one thing. When you go there, it will not be like it is here. Hunger will come to you; lust will come; anger will come; sin will come; foul-tempered impatience will come; haste will come; falsehood will come; envy will come; jealousy will come. You will be confronted by many things that will come to you. As I told you previously, you will have to make all these things peaceful with these treasures. You must instruct all the things that come to you, in a manner that is appropriate for them, and make them calm.

"You must give them each a place and make them have *sabūr*. Show them right and wrong, show them love, make them stop, make them stay where they are. Hunger, illness, old age, and death will all come to you there. You must control them with the wealth I gave you before you arrived there. This is what you must do. Then you will be My child.

"If you spend from the treasures I gave you, you will have no enemies. If you lose this treasure, you will have many enemies there.

"There are two pots I can give you from My kingdom. Two pots. One is a copper pot. The other is a clay pot. The clay pot has no value, but if you are not careful and you let it fall to the ground, it will break.

"The world does not see the value of the clay pot—it does not shine. I gathered earth and made this pot of clay. The other pot is made of metal—it shines. Yet it will regularly tarnish and change. If you stop paying attention to it for a little while, it will darken, and develop a blue, poisonous color. It will become poisonous. It will look green and then it will look blue. It will develop a patina, and it will constantly change. Although you polish and polish it, it will continue to change afterwards. Yet, if the copper pot falls to the ground, the dents can be hammered out. It can be beaten and hammered and repaired. When you carry it, it will look attractive to all eyes, and they will call it valuable. If you have a copper pot, the creation-world will consider you to be extremely valuable. They will call that pot wealth. 'This is wealth!' they will say.

"They will value it and they will grab you and lift you up to the treetops. They will lift you up to the tallest treetops. However, you will not be able to climb down. You will fall. They will all praise you but you will fall. Celebrity will come. Praise will come. Respect will come. Honors will come. The 'I' will come and the 'you' will come. That is what will happen to the copper pot. One who has the copper pot will be comfortable anywhere. He will be happy anywhere. Everyone will praise him. Everyone will invite him, saying, 'Come.' He will get what he requires at all times.

"However, if the clay pot falls to the ground, it will break. If it falls to the ground, it will break. If you do not take care, it will break. If you put it down too quickly, it will break. No one there will value this pot. It has no value in the world.

"The value of the clay pot resides with Me. The value of this pot exists within Me. I am the only One who knows the worth of this pot. You must be very careful with this pot. One who chooses this pot when going to the creation-world will have many difficulties, many hardships. He will not have water to drink. He will not have a house. He will not have rice for his hunger. He will be exposed to the sun, the rain, the water, and the wind everywhere. They will all fall upon him. No one will respect him. The entire world will drive him away, all living beings will drive him away. They will not accept him. He will be a clay pot—a beggar. 'This beggar is destitute. He is not useful for anything,' they will say as they describe the clay pot.

"And if he is not careful, it will break. The world will not comprehend the value of that pot, but I will know. One who chooses this pot will have no peace there. He will have difficulties and many hardships. No one will accept him; he will have only difficulty. He will have to dry up in the sun, get wet in the rain, and become lean from hunger. He will have to search for water. He will have no place in which to live. He will have no place in the world.

"His only place is the place in which I dwell. He will abide wherever I abide. But there will be no place for him in the world. This is the value of that pot: he will live wherever I live.

"The one who chooses the copper pot will be in all the places I am not. He will have peace in the world. He will be tranquil in the world. He will be praised in the world. He will be valued in the world. He will have titles in the world. He will receive honors in the world. He will obtain great quantities of praise.

"The world will not accept the clay pot. Therefore, I alone know the value of the clay pot. Carry it carefully, and bring it back to Me. You will go for only one week to the world-kingdom, to the creation-kingdom. You will be here for many millions of years. The journey there will be for one week. If you bring that pot back in good condition, you will be here for many millions of years with Me. Such is this kingdom.

"Look over here at the honey. Look over here at the fruit. Look over here at the *houris* and celestial maidens who will serve you, who will do *khidmah* for you. Look around you, they will all accept you, everyone in this kingdom will accept you. No one in that kingdom will accept you. This is My mysterious kingdom. The other is a show-kingdom.

"The place to which I am sending you is a show-kingdom. It is a show of sexual games, arts and sciences. I have made it, but I do not exist in it. I am here. Those are just My arts.

"I do not exist in them and they do not exist in Me. I do not exist in the arts that I created. I am watching them. They do not exist within Me. I have expelled them, and they are outside of Me. I have sent them out and am presenting the show. However, the good things here are within Me. If you can exist within what is within Me, it will be all right.

"There will be many difficulties for the clay pot. You must decide which pot you want. I will present you with two pots. Some people will ask for this one, some people will ask for that one. Those who choose to take the clay pot are very rare, extremely rare. Almost everyone else prefers the copper pot. Yet, very few of those who choose the clay pot will see the kingdom of hell.

"Very few of those who choose the clay pot will see the kingdom of hell. It is very rare for them to go to that kingdom. Very rarely do people ask for the clay pot. It is very rare here. It is also very rare for those who choose the clay pot to go to the kingdom of hell. Most of them will not go there.

"However, those who choose the copper pot will be the majority in the kingdom of hell. Look over there at them. Listen to their sounds."

Those who prefer the clay pot will say, "O God, I do not want that! Please give me this pot. I will go to learn Your secret and come back. No matter how difficult it is going to be, somehow I can spend a week there and come back. It is just for one week."

Others will say, "It is not just for one week. I like this pot better—it has ethnic groups, religions, scriptures, I am great, I am a poet, I am a *gnāni*, I am a great man, I am a king, I am a ruler, I am a renunciate." They will be comfortable: they will have all the comforts of the world. When the copper pot falls to the ground, no matter how many dents it picks up, those dents can be straightened out. It is done with money. It is done with the mouth, with words, with clothing, with beards, with mustaches, with *jubbahs*. That is how they straighten out the dents. Dress! Money and dress. They can be great people with those tokens.

However, one who chooses the clay pot will have many difficulties. The world will not accept him. He will undergo many difficulties. He will not have water for his thirst. He will not have food for his hunger. He will not get a job. He will not have proper clothes to wear. He will say, "O God! O God! O God! O God!" He will hold the clay pot in his hands and say, "O God! O God! *Al-hamdu lillāh! Al-hamdu lillāh! Shukūr! Al-hamdu lillāh! Tawakkul-'alAllāh! In shā'Allāh! Ma shā'Allāh!*" as he performs his duties. He will experience hardship that week, but then he will obtain his Father's kingdom. In that kingdom, he will have a house, property, and everything.

God will say, "Look. These are the two pots, the two choices. You have come here to ask for the pot you require. Choose the one you prefer. Do whatever you want. The state you choose is the state in which you will live. I have given this choice and this treasure to everyone."

God has given the treasure that is the *amānah* to every human being. He has given patience, *sabūr, shukūr, tawakkul,* and *al-hamdu lillāh,* compassion, love, truth, tolerance, peace, serenity, and the ability to do selfless duty to every human being. God has given His qualities only to man. He has given the soul to him as absolute purity. It is because you turned your back on it and failed that He sent His representatives, that He sent His men of wisdom, that He sent the *aqtāb* to explain to you about the treasure you had forgotten. "Change. Change. Come over here," they said. He sent the *rusul,* the *ambiyā',* the lights of God, the men of wisdom, and the *aqtāb* to remind you. If you understand, it is possible that you will turn away from this show.

If you throw away the copper pot, you can change. If you throw it away and choose the clay pot, you can still change. You can still say, "O God, I do not want this." You can make an exchange. If you say, "O God, give me the other pot, I do not want this one," you can change.

If you choose the copper pot, you can discover the kingdom of hell in that state. If you choose it, you can reach a state consistent with it. These are the Laws of God.

That is what you might have been given there when you asked for it. He will have given you the one you chose. If you arrived here and then asked for the other pot, He would have given you that. If you ask for the clay pot, that is what you will have. It is what it is. All right. Thank you.

A'ūdhu billāhi minash-shaitānir-rajīm.
I seek refuge in God from the accursed satan.
Bismillāhir-Rahmānir-Rahīm.
In the name of God, the Most Compassionate, the Most Merciful.

WHEN GOD CREATED MAN
*Friday, November 30, 1984, 10 A.M.
Philadelphia, USA*

A'ūdhu billāhi minash-shaitānir-rajīm. Bismillāhir-Rahmānir-Rahīm. I seek refuge in God from the accursed satan. In the name of God, the Most Compassionate, the Most Merciful.

Allāhu ta'ālā Nāyan made the intention to create Man after He created the world and the creations for him.

None of the *malā'ikah*, the *jinns*, or the celestial beings thought good thoughts about that which was about to become Man. "Man is going to be an evil being. He will be an evil being. He will not be someone with a connection to God." The heavenly beings, the *jinns*, and the fairies had this thought.

Abu, satan himself, was the leader of the *jinns* in the heavenly world, the leader for the section of the *jinns*. There were leaders for each section of the *malā'ikah*, and he was the leader of the *jinns*. The fairies and the others had other leaders. The prophets, the *ambiyā'*, had others.

At this time, God heard them and said, "Regarding the words you have been speaking—yes, I have created everything. I have also created you. Now I will create Adam out of a handful of earth. I am going to build him out of earth. I am going to place five of you within him and give him life. However, he will know things you do not know. Man will know things earth, fire, water, air, and ether do not know. He will know the secrets of the heavens. He will know your secrets and the secrets of the heavens. I will give him all ninety-six abilities, *tattwas*. You have thirty-four; he will have ninety-six, sixty-two more than you.

"Adam will be very exalted. Adam will be the exalted one who will understand Me and be the one who is joined with Me. I will show you an exemplification."

He showed them this exemplification before the creation of Adam ☺. He showed this exemplification of His new creation to all the heavenly beings, the *jinns,* and the fairies before He actually created *insān*. He showed them the four hundred trillion forms of man—his animal forms, his human forms—all the forms within Man. He showed them the freedom of the world. He showed them all the happiness and the freedom of the world.

He summoned all of them and told Man, "Look over there. Everything you need is there. Money, gold, silver—everything is being distributed. All among you who need those things, go there, and get them. They will give you whatever you need there—money, cash, houses, properties, inheritances. They are handing them out there. Whoever among you needs those things, go."

God then went to the other side where they were telling the people, "Bring your own pots. Everyone must bring his own pot." There God told them, "If you want the treasures I have, you must bring your own pots. You must bring them if you want to get what is here. However, you must come alone. Those who come here, must come alone. They cannot come here with other people; they cannot bring other people. They must come alone and be clear. Clear. If you come to Me with absolutely pure clarity, you can take whatever you need."

As they were being shown this, they began to ask, "If we come to You, will we get wealth? Will we get houses? Will we get properties? Will we get this? Will we get that? Will we get this? Can we not be given all of it?"

They were told by those handing out the things: "It does not work like that. What you get will be known only to you and to Him. If you go with clarity, you can get whatever you need there. You can decide what to get, what you can carry and what you cannot carry.

"If you go there, you can get all those other things. If you come here, you must come alone and you must be clear. We do not know what He will give you. It will be known only after you take possession of it."

As you go towards it, you will say it is beautiful. But when you actually get there and look at it—*(Bawangal laughs)*.

So everyone went over there. No one came here. God came here, but no one else. Finally, three people came. Only three people from this world came. The others did not.

God showed them, "This is how it will be in the *dunyā*. Those three people will understand through the ninety-six abilities. They will control those abilities and they must also control you. They will understand. They will know Me. Those who know Me will be able to control everything.

"I am a Treasure. Whoever takes possession of Me will never lack anything. I am a Treasure, an inexhaustible Treasure, an everlasting Treasure. Whoever takes possession of Me in his heart, and keeps Me there in his bank, will not lack anything of any kind. He will never lack anything at any time ever. Whatever he needs will be given to him at the time he needs it. Look at this. Only three people have come to take possession of this. The others are people too, but they will not know."

God spoke to the heavenly beings, "You will not know yourselves and the animals will not know themselves. The animals all have thirty-four abilities and so do you.

"You have only perception, awareness, and intellect. You understand only as much as intellect understands, you do not understand anything beyond it. The others are the same.

"Yet Man has four additional levels of wisdom. Those four levels of wisdom were bestowed upon him for the purpose of understanding truth. Therefore, he will choose Me and place Me within himself. One who chooses Me will have all things: he will possess My entire kingdom. He will rule My entire kingdom." That is what God said.

As a result, it is not merely a matter of reaching God. It is not a simple matter to become worthy of His property. We must seek and obtain that Treasure with great effort. We must work hard to reach it.

If you want to get something easy, you should go to the other side. It is easy. They have religions, ethnic groups, scriptures, and doctrines. Those things are easily obtained. However, it will be like throwing a lighted match into a beautiful house. A tiny match can ruin all of it. If we collect all the things that are there, that match will light the fire of hell and then the fire of hell will burn.

It was in this manner that God gave this explanation to the *malā'ikah,* the *jinns,* and the fairies. "Therefore, Adam will be a being more exalted than you. Man has so many abilities. He can ascend as much as he can descend. He has the remedy that will enable him to rise to the greatest height. He also has what it takes to reach the lowest depths."

Part Two
IN THIS WORLD

CHAPTER 4

A'ūdhu billāhi minash-shaitānir-rajīm.
I seek refuge in God from the accursed satan.
Bismillāhir-Rahmānir-Rahīm.
In the name of God, the Most Compassionate, the Most Merciful.

WHICH STORY SHALL WE TELL

Wednesday, February 17, 1982, 10:40 A.M.
Colombo, Sri Lanka

Which story shall we tell?

Shall we tell the story of this body, the sinner
that was born and that traveled
all around this desolate world?
Or shall we tell the story of the Supreme Being
who placed it there, and
protected it while it spent ten lunar months in the womb?

Shall we tell the story of our mother and father
who danced together and formed us there?
Shall we tell the story of how we took the birth of a sinner,
how we sang and roamed the world?
Shall we tell the story of how we became an eight span body,
how we grew and lived and wandered and died?

Shall we tell the story of the body's hunger,
how we roamed and
ran for the sake of the hunger of the one span stomach?
Shall we tell the story of the body's hunger?
Shall we tell the story of being born on the earth,
of being later buried in the earth, and burning in the fire?

Shall we tell the mesmerizing story of the maya-mantras,
the sexual games of those mantras?
Shall we tell the mesmerizing story
of the maya-mantras,
the sexual games of those mantras?
Shall we tell all the stories we have hidden away,
the story of the sixty-four sexual games,
the hidden story,
the whirling story of the sixty-four dances?
Shall we tell of the dance that is a story,
the dance of the karmic story that gives us form?

Shall we tell the story of how great the world is,
how permanent our relatives and relationships are,
the story of the wandering mute who holds on to his kin?
Shall we tell the hypnotic and distressful story of our bondage
to the blood ties who stalk us and seize us?

Shall we tell the confusing story of dancing and singing and
how one man becomes a slave to another?
Shall we tell the story of how there is One for meditation,
how there are two for increasing the world, and
how it ends with four people at the cemetery?

Shall we tell the sad story of how
we became subject to this birth,
trembling, trembling with the difficulty of
being bewitched by desire?
Shall we tell the story of the monkey that is maya,
that dwells in mind, desire, and intellect,
that dwells in the mesmerism of the mind, and
the story of the dog of desire that roams and
wanders throughout the world?

Shall we tell the crazy story of wife, child,
puppy, calf, cow, and house
that have been possessed by a wandering demon,
that intermingled with
the ninety-six obsessions arising from bile,
that control us, and make us insane?

Which story should we tell in this birth?
Which story, which meaning should we describe in this birth?

Shall we tell the story of God who
created all the things that move and
all the things that do not move,
who first created all the seeds and then their resultant forms?
Shall we tell the story of the eternal, great Meaning
intermingled with the divine grace of the Creator,
that exists as the Heart within the heart,
that feeds us little by little with memories and warns us?

Shall we tell the eternal story of the One
who dispenses and demonstrates justice,

who opens and demonstrates the eternal way,
the story in which God and we
are united as fragrance is united with a flower?

Or shall we tell the story of being dressed in this sinner's body,
developing in grievous sin,
becoming an embryo in the earth,
taking shape in water,
forming relationships in blood,
flying in the air,
blackening in the fire of anger, and
roasting in the fire of karma?
Which story shall we tell in this birth?
How shall we finish it?

O creations born with me,
O true friends of my life,
O brothers and sisters who are the love to my love,
O beloved who are the wisdom within my wisdom,
O true-hearted wondrous creations of the Almighty One
who knew the seed, but created without seed.
O rare and wondrous creations
who have received grace, effulgence, life, light, and
who live as the loving ones.

O creations born with me.
When we clearly understand the story
of the *'arsh*, the throne of God,
that is within the story of
the *ākhirah* of the *dunyā*, God's kingdom of the world, and
when we clearly understand the meaning

of the desire known as hell,
that will be a good story.
If we clearly understand,
that will become a good story in this birth,
O you who have been born with me.

The Trusted Friend is the story.
The Creator is the story.
The story of the One who gave birth to us,
the One who created us,
the One who named us and raised us,
the Trusted Friend,
the One with whom we are united,
the Heavenly One in the exalted state
that cannot be enclosed by anything,
the One who is filled with compassion itself,
the Creator who exists as the Protector who created us—
if we discover that and comprehend that,
if we comprehend His objectives,
and know them, then that,
that will be a good story.

As the Body within the body, inside, outside and inside,
the One who exists as discernment and right judgment,
the One who does only what is good,
the One who speaks only truth,
the One immersed only in wisdom,
the One who cultivates only love,
the One who cultivates only love,
the One who feeds us with the milk of grace—
shall we tell the story of that Father?

When we know the history of that Father,
we will know the story of the Pure One
who stands beyond all purity and impurity.
When we know it as truth and comprehend it,
that story will be a good story.

Know this, O my trusted friends,
O children of love,
when we know the story of the Good One,
we will be liberated on that day,
we will attain a life of grace, and
riches without end,
the riches of God, the Khudā.

O please know this in detail,
O my real creations born with me.
This is the authentic story
of His words, His actions, and His conduct.
The Truth is the Truth,
that One is the Master,
we are all from One Creator,
creations born with one another.
When we obtain His birthright and rejoice,
that will be a good story.

May we become aware of this good story,
may we be clear,
may we know it with wisdom.
May we know it clearly with wisdom,
and love all living beings.
May we do His duty,

at this good and opportune time,
and perform good deeds.

On the day we know the story of God, the First Cause,
and tell it day and night, every hour and every minute,
with our words, actions, breath, and speech, on that day there
will be good speeches, good stories,
good words, and good actions.

This is the story of the Real One within us.
This is the wealth of our birthright.
This is the way to goodness.
May we realize that this inheritance is our only inheritance.
The riches of wisdom
belong to Him who is filled with love.
If we live as people with good manners and customs,
we will receive the wealth of the Supreme Being.
We will reach the Light of grace,
the Divine Luminous Light, the Light of love.

We will be a trusted friend
who will end the suffering of the world.
What path do we need to reach
in order to end the suffering
of all living beings as much as we can?
Helping all living beings is a good story.

May we become aware of this story, and
know the truth.
This is God's story and it belongs to us.
It is our story too in the end.

Even if we travel everywhere in the village,
even if we travel everywhere in the nation,
even if we travel everywhere in the jungle,
even if we travel to every shore,
even if we travel to every ocean,
even if we travel everywhere in the sky,
even if we travel to every sun,
even if we travel to the underworld,
even if we travel throughout the *ākhirah,*
the story is simply about knowing.
May we know the conclusion to this story in our hearts.

When we begin to be clear in our hearts,
we and the One to whom we belong will have the same story.
When we understand that story,
that will be the heaven we will be able to know.
We will be able to know the history
of the conclusion of the story,
and that He Himself is the history.

When we read His history and become His child,
when we become the child
who does the research and understands His history,
we will be able to discover that what we study is the wealth.
When we become His student and His child,
when we become His friend
without mixing anything else into it,
we will be able to understand
as one who has received His Light in this story.

You will know,
brothers and sisters,
loving children,
creations who have been born with me,
true friends to my life, that
this is the goodness in the story,
the story we have come here to read.

To know this is His history.
To know this and to be clear is
the good quality of the students that we are.
The good qualities are the duty.
We must travel throughout all the villages,
know what exists in all the lands,
understanding the body,
and knowing everything within it.
The soul is within the body.
We must know and choose the One who owns it,
and share with all lives
the good qualities that originate from Him.

This is simply a story of helping others.
We must be aware of this,
O brothers and sisters.
We must stand in His grace
village by village,
country by country,
heart by heart,
as the inner awareness within the self,
as the wisdom within wisdom,
as the awareness within awareness,

as the conscience within conscience, and
as the justice within justice.

If we understand this and act according to our destiny,
if we understand and act according to His qualities,
if we know and act according to His actions,
if we reflect, know, and act accordingly,
if we understand the meaning
of His treasury of grace, and act accordingly,
it will make us free.
It will free us from the thoughts of maya in which we dwell.
We will understand that everything is
in the hands of He who is One.
We will pass over all of it,
acting while leaning on the hands of that One,
and we will reach Him,
the rare Treasure, the wisdom, and the qualities.
This is the rare and marvelous wonder we must understand,
O brothers and sisters.

O you who wish to understand and know this story in detail,
to know this history, the history of your Father.
When we see it as the good duty,
it will be the only truth in our lives.
It will be the only exalted state and wealth in our lives.
It will be the only goodness in our birth,
the blessing of our Lord, the grace.

May we know this in clear detail, and
be aware of the Truth in wisdom.
Everyone must endeavor to clearly know this as wisdom.

With perception and with awareness,
existing as faith, determination, and certitude,
we must establish the absolute purity of *īmān* in our hearts.

God's wondrous fragrance
that exists there as the King will then appear.
When that fragrance emerges from the *qalb,* the inner heart,
what will we lack in the world?
We will exist as the *qalb* that exists as Him,
and the two will be experienced as One.
When we exist as
the blissfully developing blossom and its fragrance,
what affliction can we have?
What sorrow can we have in our birth?
We will have no confusion, no sorrow,
no death and no birth.
We will have no hours or minutes
in which to wander about pursuing what we see.

This is the explanation.
These are brief details of the story.
This is the explanation,
this is the story, and
these are brief details.
Yet if you become even a little aware of it, you will know that
this is the state of peace, and that
this is the unparalleled and unequaled splendor
of the Rabb who is our King.
This is the origin and the objective
of all the stories we have studied.

After the bondage of having been born is understood,
this is the nature of our Father,
this is the nature of our Father's history.
This is the story of the One who brought us up.
This is the meaning
that belongs to the One who enables us to live.
This is the explanation of the Lord, the Good One, the Teacher.
This is a true story that has actually occurred.

All of us must join together as relatives and
understand the story we are studying.
Then the entirety of our karma
will be understood and dispelled.
We must be aware of and
reflect deeply upon the history of this story.

When we understand it,
there will be no danger for us in the world, no birth-sin.
Shall we understand this, O creations born with me?
These are the details, this is the story of this history.
Āmīn. Āmīn.

A'ūdhu billāhi minash-shaitānir-rajīm.
I seek refuge in God from the accursed satan.
Bismillāhir-Rahmānir-Rahīm.
In the name of God, the Most Compassionate, the Most Merciful.

THE LIGHT SPEAKS

*Wednesday, June 22, 1983, 7:48 A.M.
Philadelphia, USA*

This is a story of a man who was thinking about God with wisdom.

He was a man of faith, thinking about God. "Why has this world come to such a state of destruction and hostility? Why has man become subject to so many difficulties and hardships? Why does man appear to be in such a sad state today? O God, what is the reason that man's life has come to this state in the world today? The difficulties of a life without peace have appeared among humankind. What is the cause of this?" He was thinking inside himself to God. "Is there no rule for this? O God, is there no protection for this?"

He was at the foot of a tree, thinking about this, when a beautiful light, a soul-light radiating from the earth, rose up to the sky and returned as two lights, transformed into a man and a woman. They had no form, just an aspect of light.

The two of them stood before him and asked, "Do you know who we are? Son, do you know us?"

"I understand a little. Because you emerged from the earth at first, I believe you are our Mother and Father."

"Yes, in the beginning Allāhu ta'ālā Nāyan created us of earth. We were made of earth and we received this blessing because we worshiped Him. We have been blessed with this form of light because of our faith. We are Earth and called *pār*. Now look at us, *pārungal*. We are the Mother and Father who, as Earth, sate the hunger of your soul and of your stomach. We exist as the wisdom that sates the hunger of your soul and the hunger of your *qalb*. Look at us. This is the good fortune God has given us. This is the result of our faith. This is the reward we have earned from this earth.

"We are just one handful of earth, yet we are Mother to the creations, to humankind, to everyone who bears a form. We are Mother to the animals and we are Mother to humankind. We are Mother to anything that takes form from earth. We are Mother to all energies that can speak, that can make sound, that are alive. We are Earth, the Mother who assists them all silently. To those who are human beings, we are a Mother and Father they can recognize.

"To him who has the wisdom and the qualities to understand the Lord who is my God, we exist as a liberated state of light that satisfies the hunger of his soul and the hunger of his stomach. Like us, he will be capable of bringing peace to all living beings. He will be the one who has received the grace of God and the peace of God, and he will be the one who can also bestow that peace upon others. Although he is mere earth in the world, he will be earth as we are earth, and benefit others as we do. He will be light as we are light, and benefit others as we do. Just as we were bodies and gave birth like human beings and increased, he will be human and increase the truth.

"He will unite the true brothers and sisters. He will embrace them with love and unite them. He will make them happy with all living beings. He will unite them all. When he is transformed into this state of light just as we were transformed, he will do duty as we do and make all lives peaceful. If he lives as the child of Man, if he becomes like this, he will do this work. He will live his life in peace and impart that peace to all lives. Although he is earth, he will impart peace and tranquility to all lives; he will make them peaceful. If he develops from there and transforms himself into a pearl, he will be light as we are, and impart peace to the soul-pearls. He will impart peace to all souls. He will teach peace with God's Laws. He will be the one who gives peace to wisdom and to the soul. God will stand before Man in this state.

"God has also given our children the good fortune He has given us. Yet, look here: our children have lost their love, their wisdom, and their faith. They have lost it. They have forgotten God.

"They have lost love, wisdom, the purity of the soul, and faith in God. Look here: Who is enemy to whom? There was never any enmity whatsoever against my children. There is no enmity from earth towards them. There is no enmity from the purity of the soul. There is no enmity from wisdom. There is no enmity from God. There is no enmity from truth.

"If any enmity were to develop within man, he would be his own enemy. The one who is an enemy to himself has the form of a snake. He creates the poison in himself, the poison that is for biting others and for killing others—it develops from that. If no one falls victim to the bite, and if the poison of the bite remains inside the snake, when the thunder and lightning come, when the sky rumbles, the poison bursts forth because the membrane is thin, and kills the snake. The teeth rupture from the thunder, and its own forces kill it. Only the snake dies.

"Similarly, man dies from his own enmity. He kills himself. He kills those who were born with him, he murders them, and then dies from the same thing. The reason for this is that not earth, nor fire, nor water, nor air, nor ether, nor sun, nor moon is his enemy. They are all his siblings.

"Look at me. They have all emerged from me. God made them appear from within me. God made water come alive within me to sate the thirst of my children, to wash away their dirt, and to make them happy. The air removes the fatigue of all lives, makes their breath clear, and makes them happy. Both of them are your siblings. Look, both of them are your siblings. We are the Mother and they are siblings. The fire warms you, soothes you, and makes you peaceful. The sky brings you beauty and happiness: it openly displays its colors and hues and makes your mind peaceful.

"The sun exists in a state in which it bestows its light and makes the creations, the plants, and the seeds grow through certain means. The moon dispels the darkness, and creates the circumstances in which embryonic forms can take hold, flowers and seeds can grow, and buds can form. These are the circumstances manifested from the moon. All of them are your siblings. They are not flawed. They bestow peace in the same manner to everything. They exist in the form of peace to the trees, to the flowers, and to the shrubs. None of them bear any enmity. The earth bears no enmity.

"Look here. I am showing you everything.

"They display only unity and love. They bear no enmity to any life. They have only love. Do they have any hostility?

"The men who are my children see this as divisiveness. They see differences in colors, ethnic groups, languages, and other things. They see differences in justice; they see differences in love; they see the soul as different and God as different; they see truth as different, and through this they violate the honor of women.

They convert justice into injustice. They ruin the course of integrity. They alter a life of truth and turn it into a life of ignorance and lack of wisdom.

"They see sin as goodness and goodness as sin. They act as if truth were falsehood and falsehood were truth. They are all actors. They act as if patience were poison and poison were patience. We can see that the world is like this. Look here. I will show you. They are all siblings. There is no evil in the earth. The heavenly beings, the *ambiyā'*, God, and the souls have no evil of any kind. Look here, come, I will show you."

(The light of Mother Earth begins to sing)

In the heart of one who has lost truth,
in the heart of one who has lost truth,
in his heart dwell wolves, jackals, dogs, cats, and snakes.
In the heart of one who does not know goodness,
there are dogs, jackals, tigers, lions, and
elephants that dwell in his *qalb*.

In the heart of one who does not know love,
the evils of arrogance, karma, and maya rule his life.
In the heart of one who has no compassion,
karma, sin, and anger enter and grow ripe.
Murder and sin mingle with the blood in his heart.

In the heart of one who does not understand himself,
Allāhu's warnings enter into his life and ripen there.
One whose life has no unity, exalted qualities,
or developing wisdom
falls and burns every second into
the fire of the qualities in his own heart.

"This destruction is sought by each person for himself. It is the selfsame fire his own heart, his wisdom, and his intellect have sought. Every person seeks his own fire in this manner. In his own life, he searches for the fire and he falls into it. He is the one who blackens and burns in it. He reaches this state of evil because he has forgotten truth in his life.

"If it were not for those few in the world who love God, who trust God, and who bear true hearts, this world would burn in fire and sin. It would burn in the fire of sin. Everything would burn in the fire of man's arrogance and be reduced to ashes. It is only because of the existence of those rare few good people, those wise people with God's qualities and intentions, that the world has been protected even to this extent today.

"Come here, let's look. Look over there. There is a church, there is a mosque, and there is a temple. Have you looked at all three of them? This city is the world. Look at what we are looking at. The light will guide you. Look. What are the people doing? Where are they going? Look. They are worshiping God. They are going to worship what they call God.

"Is it God to whom they pray? Look over here. White, black, rose—all are here in separate sections. However, their clothes are of mixed varieties; they wear black, white, and many other kinds of clothing. Their hats are also like that. Do you see? What are they worshiping? Whom are they worshiping? They call this a Christian church.

"When I emerged from the earth, I knew God alone, I knew only Him. I received this light through Him. We became the original Mother and Father to all the children I bore through the acquisition of my goodness and through my actions. We suffered six hundred years of hardship for one sin. The two of us were separated and suffering, one in the East and one in the West. For six hundred years, we asked God to lift us up again, until we came together in Jiddah where God reunited us. For our one mistake, we suffered for six hundred years.

"Now look over here. God changed my earth-form and I became formless, in the way that you see me now. The earth that I was changed, and I have now been transformed into light. When the heart turns to light, the form will no longer exist. The *qalb*, the wisdom, and the soul of such a person will become sheer light. When his wisdom becomes complete and his soul emerges, only light will remain. Worship is light. That is worship. Faith is worship. Whom does that light worship? Worship means the earth must be transformed. The earth-form and its qualities must change. When that transformation occurs and reaches that state—that is worship. Then he can receive the light, the absolutely pure light of the soul.

"God has no form, no shape. Your qualities must change, just as we changed, in order to see Him. We must turn into light, our qualities must be turned into light, we must see Him, and worship Him.

"Look over here, there are so many statues, so many forms. Have you seen them? Look, are the candles being lit for the statues or are the candles being lit for the people? They are lighting candles for the statues. The statues have no eyes. The statues and their house have no eyes. The people put the eyes on the statues, place the candles in front of them, and then try to dispel the darkness. Yet, they remain in darkness.

"That earth will never change, it will always exist in darkness. Those statues will never turn into light. They will always be earth connected to earth. Therefore, how can the people change in that unchanging place? This is ignorance, is it not? God is a power, a Light. The house of God is a house of fraternal unity, a house in which to think about God. It is a place where all of us can unite and think, unite and pray to Him, think of Him, and worship Him. It is a place in which to unite without color, hue, ethnic group, religion, and separation, where each person can think, one by one. As they think, all their *qalbs* will be formed into one and be given to God as one unit. That is prayer, worship, unity, and love.

"Look over here. Do you see what is happening? When you look over here, they are all statues. When you look at them, they have many kinds of colors. Yet, for the people there is a place for the black, a place for the white, a place for the poor, a place for the rich. These places must be bought with money. Those who pay more money sit closer to the front. Those who give less sit in another section. Those who give the most are at the very forefront. Those who give less are here, here, and there. If they are black, they are further back, arranged by color and hue. If they are white, but have no money, they are in another section, near the black section.

"Do you see this? It is God's house. What is going on? Is this prayer? Is this a place of worship? Look at that, each one of you. There is a minister, reading the Bible and reciting. Some of the people in the church are bowing while others are looking around. They are looking around and around. Some are bowing down and looking, others are standing and looking, some are looking out of the sides of their eyes. What is this? They are not praying. What are they looking at? Some people look at the beauty of the clothing of others. Some people's coats are nice. Some people's pants are nice. Some people's saris are nice, some people's hats are nice, or the style is nice. This is what they look at and that is where their thoughts go. What can we do about it? Is this worship? Is this a place in which to pray to God? Look at that. The service is over and someone is coming with a box, asking for money. Look here. It is a business. They collect the money, they take it, and they keep it.

"A church is a place in which to dedicate the soul, a place in which love is given and wisdom is received. It is a place in which to offer love to God and to receive wisdom and the absolute purity that is the light of the soul. It is a place in which to give Him this birth, mind, and desire and to receive the blessing of the absolutely pure and divine wealth of the soul for this world and for the *ākhirah*. We come to this great place to receive the blessings for the duties we must develop and perform. Look. Do you see?

"But now it exists in this state. People do not come to get these things. Some of them are even being forced to come. Other people are making them go, saying, 'Come, let's go to church.' Some people would prefer to play, some people would prefer to go dancing, some people would prefer to go to other places. Some want to go to the bar; each one of those people is being forced to go.

"They have not absorbed the lesson that this place is a place that is a foundation for them; they have not learned good qualities, good conduct, virtue, and faith in God at home. They have not learned this. In the same vein, they have not taught this remembrance to their hearts, they have learned only enough to go to church for the sake of the world. The children, the husband, the wife, and others in the family do not carry that one thought, that experiential thought, into their lives. They go only to promote their own particular religion and ethnic group. That is why devotion is not growing. Only destruction is growing. In that state, they will be gathering only sin. They will be gathering separation, terrible sin, divisiveness, colors, hues, and business. Will these things become worship? No.

"Observe it, and then let it be. Come, let us go this way.

"Here is a Hindu temple. Look, the people have come to worship God. Some have great devotion and tears are flowing from their eyes. Some are there in wet clothes, they have immersed themselves in water, cried, and rolled on the ground. They have rubbed ash onto themselves. Some have rolled on the ground to get there, reciting names. They arrive like this and like that in many ways. Some arrive well-dressed, wearing watches and bracelets; some come as business owners, some are big rich people. They arrive rank after rank.

"See how many kinds of statues there are around the temple. There are cows, there are demons, there are some like devils with long teeth; there are vampire-demons, and there are some holding tridents. A *kāli* is there, a *vairavar* is there, lions are there, tigers are there, so many, so many. They are like cows, like horses, like people, like beautiful forms. How many decorations there are. How many statues there are. Many statues from rats, to elephants, to birds, to vultures, to crows are all around the outside of the temple. They are all there. So many snakes. Everything is there. Inside are certain other more special statues. The statues inside are greater than the statues outside. Some of them are simply stones, some have three-pronged tridents and some have spears. Some have forms while others are just one stone placed upon another. The people are praying to all kinds of things. They have all been given different names.

"Look, the people are standing outside. One person is standing inside the temple, and he is the *pūjari*, the one who pours the milk the people have brought onto the statues and stones. He takes the fruits and coconuts the people have brought as offerings. He takes a portion for himself, he puts aside another portion for something else, and he gives another portion to the idols. Out of three portions, he keeps two, and gives one to the idols. He pockets any money that comes with it. There are millions and millions of gods. Millions of names have been given to these gods. There are so many gods.

"The people believe in these gods. 'Āndavā! Kadavulay!' they cry out each name. 'Āndavanay! Kadavulay! protect me,' they say as they surrender to the idols. They give them candles. They pour oil and ghee into lamps and they place the lamps in front of those statues and hold the lamps up to them. No one is holding the lamps up for the people. The people give light to the statues, but no one gives light to the people. How are the statues going to give light to the people? The people do everything themselves. They have to do everything; the statues do nothing for them. The statues do nothing! The people have turned the earth into many kinds of statues. They have created many idols that are opposite to God.

"The gold and the silver were things that came from me. The water was from me, the earth was from me, the gemstones were from me, the gold was from me, the silver was from me, and the iron was from me. All the metals came from me. All of this came from me. When I was earth, these substances were all within me. I did not receive the light from these energies.

"I drove out all of them and I embraced the qualities of God. I attained that peace. I depended upon the beauty of compassion, peace, tranquility, and truth. With faith, I embraced the qualities that could give peace to all lives.

"I surrendered to God and then received this state. I discarded everything else because I did not find any value in it. I found value only in God. I found no value in any of those statues. When I was in that state, God gave me this beauty, this loveliness, this completion, the greatest *daulah* of the three worlds, the wealth of grace, the wealth of *gnānam*. I have lived for all this time to share that wealth with my children. Yet, instead of obtaining it, they worship in order to have statues.

"Some of them surrender to snakes. To surrender to a snake, one has to take the form of a snake. He will get the poison or the form of a snake. To surrender to a cow, one has to wear the form of a cow or the qualities of a cow. To surrender to an ass, one has to wear the qualities of the ass or the form of the ass. Either the form or the qualities will exist in every section they bring into being. They will be given whatever they craft in their minds. If someone crafts a monkey, he receives the attributes of the monkey, and he will be given the body of a monkey or the qualities of the monkey. That is all they will be given.

"The millions and millions of qualities and actions they craft with their thoughts are represented by the forms. These are the thoughts crafted by the mind. These are the energies that arise in the mind. They are the thoughts and energies and qualities that emerge from their minds. These are the statues they sculpt from the earth and that emerge from arrogance, karma, and their qualities. They are all creatures that catch and eat one another.

"The snake can catch the rat. The eagle can catch the snake. The vulture can eat the dead. The lion can catch them all: it can catch the horses, the goats, and the cows. The tiger can catch the monkeys, and this and that. The elephant can destroy the jungle. Each one of these creatures is capable of attacking the other. One runs away in fear as another attacks. Nothing that can safeguard anyone is there. They are capable only of attacking one another. If this state comes to him, he will also attack others. These qualities and this form will enter into him. He becomes subject to those actions when he externalizes his internal qualities as he crafts the outer forms inside himself. One will attack another. One will kill another. One will drink the blood of another. One will take vengeance on another. One will deceive another. He will change into a bloodsucking vampire demon, a *kāli*, a *vairavan*. There are so many forms within him. This destruction begins as soon as these qualities take form within him.

"The world exists silently without saying anything; man is the reason for destruction. He is responsible for destroying devotion, for destroying God and for destroying truth, for destroying goodness and cultivating evil, for turning justice into injustice and for turning injustice into justice, for twisting truth into falsehood and for twisting falsehood into truth. He is responsible for doing all these things, for acting with all these qualities. He thinks, 'This is worship of God. This is life.'

"This is where destruction begins. He himself creates the divisiveness and the destruction. Is this God? Is this the truth? No. It is his own ignorance, lack of wisdom, arrogance, karma, maya, *tārahan, singhan, sūran,* the lechery, hatred, miserliness, greed, fanaticism, and envy that are the six evils, and the intoxicants, lust, theft, murder, and falsehood that are the five crimes. With those many qualities, he destroys the earth, his good heart, his good qualities, and the Light and the beauty of God. He destroys his own life.

"Man is the cause of it all: the hurricanes, the fires, the earthquakes. The earth quakes because it can no longer bear his crimes and his sins, his ignorance, and his transgressions. The hurricanes strike because the air can no longer bear the blood and the hatred. The fire of his own injustice emerges from the earth and causes fiery destruction. Earthquakes, hurricanes, tsunamis, the fire and the rocks that blast out of the volcanoes, and the fire that can make rocks explode are all the result of the injustice and sins he has committed. He has forgotten God, he has lost his devotion, and he has acted with a heart entirely lacking in compassion. This is not God's fault.

"God is unity. He is entirely kind. Everything came from the kindness that came from God's true-heartedness. He is simply kindness, loving kindness. Man looked upon this loving kindness as separation and created divisions. And now, that is what has seized him.

(The light of Mother Earth begins to sing)

Love is kindness
in the body and in the heart of a person with wisdom.
In his heart, grace itself is true-heartedness,
in his heart, grace itself is true-heartedness.

His heart itself will exist as the fragrance of God.
The truth of the One Who Is Complete Everywhere
is the fragrance that is his life.

The kindness of his life will be such that
all lives will become his own life.
The state of his life will be fragrant
with the qualities of God with which he leads his life.

In those lovers who have formed a relationship with
and who have united as One with wisdom,
the grace for those lovers, the kindness for those lovers,
the grace for those lovers, the kindness for those lovers,
the true-heartedness for those lovers,
the true-heartedness for those lovers is
to embrace and form a relationship bosom to bosom,
to jubilantly attain oneness,
and connect one to One.

This is the state that lives in the Form of Love as
the Friend of the absolutely pure heart.
This is the state that lives there, God's state.

Only because there is such a heart in the world in which
God's state, His qualities, God's state, His qualities,
these qualities, wisdom, and truth exist,
only because it has appeared in a few,
is the state of wisdom able to hold back
the destruction and the end.

"This wisdom is the reason destruction has been limited. Otherwise, the fire that the evil ones have cultivated would already have destroyed the world and the lives within it. The reason the state of destruction has been limited even to this extent is because there are a few like this somewhere in the world. The truth is holding it back. You must realize this.

"Look at that. Over there is a mosque of what is called Islām. Look at it. Everyone is coming to it. They are performing their ablutions, the *wudū'*, with extreme haste and impatience, and going inside very fast. As they enter, some people look for the *imām*. If the *imām* is leading the prayer, the people who have come late stand at the back, and quickly, quickly pray. Some join the congregation and pray, while others stand alone and pray. It is all done quickly, with haste, very fast. Everyone is there together. When we look at them, they appear loving. The king and the beggar are the same. The rich and the poor are the same. Their clothing is also similar. Giving the *salāms* and the love are all done in the same manner. That is all fine.

"But after the prayer, some of the people are giving *salāms* selectively: who is more important, who works abroad, who is rich. That is who they select. They are not giving *salāms* in the way they prayed. They are merely going through the motions. They run and run, looking and looking around while giving *salāms*. They even run after those who have gone outside, but only if they are important. If they are poor, they just glance at them, giving *salāms* to a few of them. Have you seen this?

"This is the house of God, and we cannot see any forms or statues here; the unity is good and the love is good, but it is good only here in this situation. As soon as the prayer is over, divisiveness arises amongst them. Then 'big man' and 'little man' arrive. There is no equality. Their clothes are similar; everything is fine there. The prayer is the same. The *'ibādah* is the same. However, as soon as it is over, the differences arrive. They have to find and catch a rich man and give him *salāms*. They go very fast, saying, 'I have to go to work. I have to do this. I have to do that.' The differences exist.

"They are all one, but as soon as they leave that place and go outside, as soon as the prayer is over, they are no longer one. The differences have appeared in their hearts. The differences are there, not the unity. The poor are in one section, the rich are in another. Sadness is in one section, happiness in another. Their states can be understood there. This is God's house, everyone has gathered here, everyone is equal, everyone prays together as one, but in their hearts, that state does not exist correctly. Here there is separation of how much someone earns, and such differences—their state exhibits the differences. It resembles neither unity nor God's qualities. They have not drawn closer to God's state.

"The words of God have been revealed by the messengers and the prophets, the *rusul* and the *ambiyā'*. From the time I was created by God, He sent His words, pearl after pearl. He sent and sent down grace and Light. Finally, before the Light known as Nūr Muhammad was impressed upon my forehead, Allāh spoke as He was embracing me: He asked me to recite the *Kalimah*. He asked me to say the *Kalimah* through the Light as a witness.

"I told Him then, 'I am a little person. I am a low person. I am not someone who has great *daulah*. I am poor in *daulah*. I am very low.'"

Earth said the *Kalimah* to the Light known as Nūr Muhammad with extreme humility, *"Lā ilāha illAllāhu."* Fire, Water, Air, and Ether all said the *Kalimah* with pride, but Earth said it with extreme humility. It was then that the Light known as Nūr Muhammad came to embrace Earth, to hold it tightly and to kiss it, saying, "You are the Mother to everything. God will create everything with you. There will be no place in which you do not exist. All that is good will come through you. Allāh will bestow all things through you. He will create all the things to eat from what comes through you; He will bestow the *rahmah* through you. All the wealth, all the *rahmah*, everything will proliferate from within you. Allāh has bestowed this exaltedness upon you with His grace." Such was the Earth which the Light known as Nūr Muhammad embraced and kissed.

"The exaltedness of that kiss brought me to the state in which I exist today. The reason was that I annihilated pride. I annihilated the pride of having been given so many riches. Allāh gave me the Light of the *mubārakāt* because of my love and humility. That is the reason He gave me this *rahmah*. That is the reason I gave birth to so many children. He gave me the exaltedness of existing as the Mother and the Father to all lives. He gave me the exaltedness of *sabūr, shukūr, tawakkul,* and *al-hamdu lillāh*, love, compassion, unity, kindness, the quality of embracing with love. Although I had so much wealth, it was through these qualities that I obtained this blessing. That is what Allāh gave me.

"But these people—no matter how much they congregate—

have not given up these things. Although Allāh has taught them so much and they come to this mosque, they do not manifest the unity that exists during prayer in their qualities or in their *qalbs*. Each person attacks the other. Each person separates the other. As soon as each person leaves the mosque and goes outside, his qualities and his divisions come into being, separate, separate. One person has good food while another person has poor people's food. One person has beggar-food while another has food that is not alms. One person is rich while another is poor. Islām is not like this.

"Allāh has said, 'Islām is Light.' The relationships between people in Islām and the unity of Islām mean that if a lamp burns in one place, there will be lamps everywhere. When the light of the sun dawns, the whole region will be light—there will be light. Islām is exactly like this. The kindness of Islām is such that if there is food in one house, people in all the houses will eat. If there is sadness in one house, there will be sadness in all houses. If there is peace in one house, there will be peace in all houses. They will be united.

"When a crow dies, how many crows gather around it. Groups and groups of crows gather. *'Kaa, kaa, kaa!'* they say even if they see only a piece of black cloth. The kindness of Islām is such that if they see harm or goodness has come to someone, all of them will come, *'Kaa, kaa, kaa, kaa!'* They will gather. They will gather in order to help. That is Islām.

"Without that state, it is a tainted Islām. Tainted. The words of Islām are tainted and turned into forms. Those tainted words will have many forms, many colors. Those tainted words will turn into many differences. Those words will turn into many divisions and operate in a section that is opposite to the actions of Allāh and Rasūl ☮.

"Everything everywhere is Islām. However, the proof of the state known as Islām has been given through my son Muhammad who emerged from me. He brought the final proof. As long as the *Kalimah* is said to the Light without seeing the proof—the unity—that *Kalimah* will be said incorrectly in each mosque, each church, and each *qalb*. Until unity develops correctly, the *Kalimah* will not be said correctly. We must gather together in the *qalb* just as we gather together in the mosque. We must give *salāms* in our *qalbs* just as we give *salāms* in the mosque. We must have the same happiness in our *qalbs* that we express there. The unity in each *qalb* must be like the unity in the mosque. To gather together in each *qalb* and unite just as we gather together in the mosque is Islām. The state of those whom I showed you in the mosque is not honest.

"Each *qalb* is a mosque. A *qalb* in which good thoughts are cultivated is a mosque. When the good qualities that do *tasbīh* to Allāh come into someone's *qalb*, it is a mosque. A *qalb* in which someone does *taubah* for the sake of Allāh to ask pardon for his mistakes is a mosque. A *qalb* in which someone knows himself and does *taubah* to ask pardon for his faults, a *qalb* in which he does *tasbīh* to Allāh is a mosque. A *qalb* in which someone dispels his own faults, gives love to others, and shows compassion towards them is a mosque. Wherever the wellspring of the thought that remembers Allāh in a meditation that never forgets God for even a second flows in someone, that is a mosque.

"The service and duties in that mosque are to show empathy and generosity towards all lives, to be full of care for them and focused on them, to respect them and to endeavor to help them. The *qalb* of such a person will be the means for countless numbers of similar actions: it will be the Ka'bah. It will be Allāh's kingdom, a mosque, a place of prayer and worship. It will be a place that proves the state of the unity of Islām.

"If this state does not exist in someone, it will be a place of separation. In it will be many separations, many differences. In it will be many paths to destruction. It will display destruction.

"Islām does not destroy. Christianity does not destroy. Hinduism does not destroy. Destruction comes from the qualities that each person has, his divisive thoughts, his separations, the many murderous thoughts of the forces within him. His crimes and transgressions, his divisive thoughts, his sins are destroying the world. Man has changed. He is destroying himself and others with those thoughts. That is why he is suffering. That is what will bring destruction.

"A fruit will not cling to the branch after it ripens. It will fall. Similarly, when a man's karma and sin ripen and mature, they will have a limit; they will not stay where they are, they will fall upon him. They will fall upon him and kill him. There is a limit for all those things. They will not exceed that limit. They will fall back upon him. There is a time limit for the rock that a man can hold above his head. He cannot hold it up past that limit; he cannot support it. It will fall on him.

"When that time comes, his qualities, his actions, his behavior, and his sins will all fall upon him. They will all be capable of striking him. This is the only thing that will strike, and it will strike everyone. What humankind has created through a state of self-destruction will destroy each person in the world. This is the destruction now. Everything everyone does exists in this state. It is not God's fault. It is not the fault of truth." This is what the light explained and demonstrated to that man of faith.

(The light of Mother Earth begins to sing)

The abundant wisdom of the One who is filled with beauty,

the qualities of the One who is complete
exist in the open space of the soul.

For one who exists with these qualities,
one who exists with this beauty,
one who exists with this love,
one who exists with this grace,
existing blissfully in God's qualities,
no destruction will come to his world or his body,
no destruction of any kind will occur.

Nothing that opposes goodness will come.
Many things that oppose evil will come.
Many things that oppose evil will come in many ways.
Nothing that opposes goodness will come.
Nothing other than God will come.

To the lover, to the true-hearted one, to His servant,
to the one who worships Him,
to the one who bows down before Him,
to the one who believes in Him,
to the one who worships Him,
to the one who bows down before Him,
love will have one form.

His shape will be beauty,
his resplendence will be light,
his *sūrah*, his form, will be truth itself,
his beautiful *sūrah* will be truth itself.
His kingdom will be justice itself.
His *rūh*, his soul, will be conscience itself.

He will be the witness in every life,
He will exist as their life.
His power will exist as justice.
His power will exist as justice.

All his actions will be performed with love.
He will hand feed them with wisdom.
He will hand feed them with wisdom.
He will act with love and hand feed them with wisdom.

He will act with beautiful justice.
His *rūh* will be conscience,
it will be the *rūh* in his *qalb*.
Anyone who acts in this state
will never experience any destruction.
Although he lives in the world, he will have no enemy.

Whether he has appeared or disappeared,
heaven will comfort his life, it will be the comfort in his life.
His *qalb* will be his comfort, a beautiful heaven for his life.
In his life he will live happily in heaven and in *dunyā*.

He will reach God.
He will reach the grace of God.
He will receive the crown of *gnānam*, of divine wisdom.
That crown is the qualities of Allāhu.
That crown is the actions of Allāhu.
Allāhu's truth is the crown of divine wisdom in His kingdom.
He will reach it.
He will live simultaneously in the world and in the *ākhirah*.
He will live only in that one state.

"This is the path for those who have received that truth. For such a person, the world and *ākhirah* are not far from one another. *Awwal, dunyā,* and *ākhirah*—creation, this world, and the kingdom of God—are not far from him. All three exist in his life and in his *qalb* as heaven. All three exist in the same place, the heaven in which God, he, and those three sections live.

"We are capable of understanding this. When we understand, the destruction will stop. One who does not understand will create the destruction in himself. This is not God's fault. One who does not understand will be the one who takes that form; he will be the one who destroys, he will be the antagonist."

We must think of this. My love you. I will tell you more later, I will tell you the other half later.

A'ūdhu billāhi minash-shaitānir-rajīm.
I seek refuge in God from the accursed satan.
Bismillāhir-Rahmānir-Rahīm.
In the name of God, the Most Compassionate, the Most Merciful.

THE LIGHT CONTINUES TO SPEAK
Thursday, June 23, 1983, 8:00 A.M.
Philadelphia, USA

As light, Adam ☉ and Eve ☉ stood without bodies before that man of wisdom and said, "Son, look over here. Come here, look at this. These are my children. This earth is a child to whom I gave birth, as are fire, water, air, and ether. They exist in the sky and on the land, in all the multitudes of things that appeared from within me. The place in which those five elements gather is the mind. Mind is the ether, the bondage to kinship. In a human being, the mind exists as ether.

"A human being has two parts. His body is connected to earth. There are two parts within him: he needs the outside and he needs the inside. He needs the water inside his body and he needs the water outside his body. He needs the heat inside and he needs the heat outside. He needs the earth inside and he needs the earth outside; he needs food and nourishment. He needs the air inside and the air that exists outside. The ether that is the mind also exists inside for his desire. The mind needs all those things. No damage comes to him through those five things. The damage comes to him through his own mind.

"Look over there at the riches the earth has shared. Look at the seeds God has placed there, seeds created by Him. God lovingly cares for the seeds He has sown and does the farming. He has said, 'Whether you are good or evil, I will grow this produce.' God has made this the Law: if a person's mind burns when he looks at another, if he experiences jealousy or if he tries to take revenge, if he aims his thoughts at someone else, if his mind aims jealousy, revenge, and slander in this state at someone else, his own crop will burn. He will burn the very thing that was meant to benefit him. The fire of his own poison will burn him. If he cultivates the section that belongs to the state of attacking another, his own possessions will burn. His own earnings will burn.

"Look. Is there a flaw in the water, is there a flaw in the earth, is there a flaw in the air, is there a flaw in the heat? No. Look over there at that mountain. Let us say a man is jumping from the top of the mountain. But the air is exerting pressure on him, so that he does not fall with full force. It is supporting him.

"Look at the air, it is supporting him. It supports him until he is about to hit the ground. He is supported by the air pressure. He does not strike the ground with the force with which he jumped. The air supports him. The air supports seventy-five percent of the fall; he falls with only twenty-five percent of the force because of the pressure. Therefore, the air is not the reason the man was killed. It is not the guilty one. The reason for his suicide is his thoughts and the thoughts of another—he is injured between the two. The reason for his suicide is how he hurt another person or how another person hurt him. There is no use blaming the air, God, or the mountain. His own ignorance, lack of wisdom, and arrogance attacked him.

"Look, he has fallen to the ground, and now he is diving into the water to kill himself. The water supports him. Because the air thwarted him, he dived into the water. The water does not kill him as soon as he dives in. It brings him up to the surface. His own weight, the weight of the *dunyā*, the weight of his *nafs*, the weight of his desire, the weight of his hell, the weight of the hells he carries inside himself are pushing him down. The water is bringing him up. The water brings him up three times, saying, 'Escape, escape.' The water helps him escape.

"If he does not escape, his own weight will push him down. That is the *dunyā*. The weight of the *dunyā*, his thoughts, all his sections, his connections to the many, many evil sections will push him down; then he goes under. After the weight leaves him, three days, seven days after his death, he will rise to the surface as a corpse. Until then, he will lie on the bottom. He will be heavy. After he gives that weight back to the earth, he will float to the surface.

"Similarly, if someone who has the section of God does not give the burden of the earth to the earth, his thoughts and all the heavy things his mind has gathered will be the karma that pushes him down. This is the weight that pushes him down. It pushes down his life, his limit, all his sections. His behavior and all the sections of his life push him down so he cannot ascend by even a hand-span. He cannot fly up. No matter how much you give him, even if you give him wings, he will not be able to fly because he will be too heavy.

"Look over there. You are a man of wisdom, a representative of God. Look over there at those people. Endeavor to think of this. Some people, some *gnānis*, some gurus and their disciples are walking over there. Look, they are going to a huge ashram. Do you see them? One of the men is a big guru. Something has been smeared onto his entire body. He is wearing so many things. His hair has been styled and tied up and he has decorated himself head to foot; he is wearing all kinds of ornaments, beads, gem-studded earrings, and jewelry. He is carrying several bags and holding a staff. He is wearing many layers of clothing; he is wrapped in these things inside and outside.

"His disciples are joining him. Look at what they are doing. They are meditating. They went to the ashram and began meditating and worshiping. Look. They are meditating. Now look, some of them are leaving to get tea and coffee, going to the shop. Some are going to steal. Some are going towards the jungle. Each one has something to do. Some are going to steal from the shop. Some are going to steal in the jungle. Some are going to steal from homes. They will collect everything and bring it back to the ashram. Then they can eat regularly and on time. When we look at their meditations and all that they do, how can they put down their burdens through this kind of theft?

"If their intention is to become God, but they collect theft, jealousy, deceit, treachery, vengeance, and such things, and they accumulate even more burdens than they had to begin with, their burden becomes karma. So many sins are joined together in that karmic burden. The weight of the earth, the weight of the water, the weight of the air, the weight of the fire, the weight of the connection to mind and desire are all there. Man carries such a burden within himself. Look at him. He has to push himself up with his hands in order to stand. See how heavy he is as he stands.

"Look how quickly a cow gets up. Look at the cows over there, look at the goats. They stand twenty minutes after they are born. But man carries the weight of the connection to the earth. Look at the child over there. Look at a calf and look at a child. Look at the goat, the cow, and the elk. Look at the huge elephant and its calf, how it stands right away. It takes a year for a person to stand. It takes twelve to fourteen months before a person can stand and walk.

"What is this? It is the world. The world is heavy for him. As long as he carries this burden, he cannot leave the earth and stand. This is the weight. As long as he keeps this burden, he will not leave the earth and stand up. The earth is pulling him down. The air is spinning him around and pulling on him. The water is striking him and carrying him away. Fire is burning him. His mind is trying to make him fly.

"Air is striking him and whirling him around. Water is eroding him. The earth is pulling him down, holding him so he cannot stand. Why? He carries the weight of the earth. His mind is making him dizzy; it is a tornado, spinning his life. In this state, he is spinning and he is heavy. Is this God's fault? He is trying to reach God while he is in this state. He is so heavy. The disciples and the guru are trying to reach God's state. How can that occur? If they are trying to praise God and attain His grace and His *rahmah*, how can they attain it like that? They cannot attain it.

"God is sharing half of everything in their lives. If their eyes are blind, God will take half of that blindness. If someone is hungry, God will take half. If he is sick with a headache, God will take half. If he is having trouble breathing, God will take half. If he is suffering, God will take half. If he has a toothache, God will take half. If his ears do not hear, God will take half. If he has chest pains, God will take half. If his legs are crippled and the nerves are failing, God will take half. Half of whatever he has is taken into God's section. God shares in everything that comes to him.

"Allāh is the Glorious One. One who reaches this state is indeed a Guru, a Shaikh.

"One who has not reached this state wants to obtain the praise that belongs to God, to obtain God's title, the pride known as the 'I,' and God's *daulah*. He wants only the praise—look over there, they are searching for praise. In the world, they need the people's praise, the people's adulation, the people's titles. 'I am God. I am a great *gnāni*. I am a great pundit. I am a singer. I am a songwriter. I am a philosopher. I am someone who can fly in the sky. I am a *munivar*. I am a *siddhan*. I am a miracle worker. I can do all this. These are my titles for these things.' This is the praise he expects. However, he knows nothing except the weight. He cannot carry that much weight.

"'Oh. Good, you are good now,' God will say as He leaves. Until then, God has carried half the weight. 'Oh. Have you become Me now? From now on, you can do your own work. You have taken the praise that belongs to Me, so now work for it!' He says.

"Such a person has taken the praise that belongs to God. What can he do then? His eyes were going bad and now his eyes are gone. His ears are gone. His nose is gone. All the lights that are disappearing, disappear and go. He is having trouble breathing. He is short of breath. *Epp!* In the end, he will jump off the mountain, like this. He will dive into the water and fall to the bottom. He will kill himself. He will take pills. He will take tablets and kill himself. In this state, he is the one who will be doing everything.

"He has forgotten God and attempted to take the praise that belongs to God. He has forgotten God's actions, and has begun to think he is God. He has forgotten God's truth and has begun to say, 'I am the one who is doing this.' When the thought, 'I, I,' arrives, this is the state to which he will be subjected. He is burning himself. He is killing himself. He is the cause of everything that is happening to him. That is how he goes to his end.

"Did you see this? Son! You asked, 'O God, what is the reason for all this destruction? What is the cause of it? Why the earthquakes? Why the volcanic eruptions? Why the hurricanes?' That is what you were asking.

"Man has commenced to do all these things. Man is acting as if he is running the world, acting as if he is feeding the world, acting as if he is the creator of the world. He is blocking God's state. Now man has come to God's state. He is attempting to create a sun and a moon. He has begun to create living beings. He is feeding them, creating their lives.

"God has said, 'Man has even come to remove and replace his own parts, taking them from others. Look here, he has come to a point where he is selling human parts. He has learned how to remove the parts I have created and how to put them into someone else, how to remove those and put them into someone else, and how to remove those and put them into someone else. This is what he is doing. He is doing all these things, and attempting to do My work.

" 'What can I do? In that state, after each of his attempts, I just say, "All right, do it," for whatever he wants to do. If My control goes to him, I say, "Do it." But he will not be able to be in control, and he will be destroyed. He will not be able to control the land, the earth, the hurricanes, the winds, the sun, or the moon. He cannot stop their movement. They will do what they do. They will move. His karma, his arrogance, his jealousy, his pride—all the things he gathers will destroy him. These are the only causes of what is happening.'

"Man has changed. Truth and the world have not changed. The qualities of God, wisdom, and the light of His truth have not changed. They still exist in a few good people. They exist in good people. It is because of them that the movement of the elemental forces has been lessened a little.

"After the prophets, the *ambiyā'*, certain hidden *gnānis,* and lights of God did their duty; they did their duties to God in an unseen manner. They did those duties in an unseen, unseen manner. They performed those duties while hidden in the midst of the demons and malignant spirits.

"They are the reason this world has been spared from the fire, the water, the hurricanes, the winds, and the tremors in the earth. Destruction has been eighty-five to ninety percent held back. Only five to ten percent has been occurring. In a little more time, at least fifty percent will begin to occur. Then only a state of fire will exist. In those times, the truth and those people of wisdom will decrease. Those who possess and love the treasures of God will look at the injustice and change their state; they will change, and they will disappear into God. Those times are coming now. Man's state is like that.

"Look here. Justice has changed. Look here. A new thing is happening. This is the world. It is called the world. In this world, God made women very beautiful. He created a beautiful Eve from Adam. He created that beauty and He made that beauty into women. He fashioned their voices and their sounds from His own essence, the *dhāt*. He formed those sounds from the *dhāt*. He gave them soft voices, soft sounds, soft words, soft demeanor, gentle qualities, speech, and behavior. He gave them soft bodies, bodies without strength. God created them beautiful in form. Women have earth-like qualities, earth-like peace, earth-like beauty. They must bear everything.

"Earth is a woman. Like a woman, the earth contains so many gemstones, gold, silver, and all the precious metals, does it not? Look here. Look at the beauty of the earth. Look at its form. It is a woman. Have you looked at her face? Gold, gemstones, cinnamon stones, nine kinds of precious gems are there. She is adorned in so many, many ways with pearls, with lapis lazuli, with rubies, and with green emeralds. This woman that is earth has been decorated with all these beautiful things. There is no beauty that does not exist in the earth. She possesses colors and hues of so many varieties. Look.

"God has said, 'Earth is a woman, a beautiful woman. It is from this gentle beauty that I created woman. A woman is a beautiful thing and I have formed beautiful qualities for this woman—forbearance, peace, patience, compassion, a soft heart, and empathy. No matter how much has happened, the empathy comes instantly to her and the love. So much compassion, empathy, and generosity come to her.'

"Man is the one who deceives that empathic heart. Women live in a state in which it is easy for men to deceive them. The reason is their empathy and compassion. The reason a man can deceive a woman is her compassion and love. It is her compassion and love and her trust that fall victim to his deceit. She has been created in this state.

"Look here. Look how many women have been violated and deceived by men. Each man has one woman here and another woman there; he leaves her and goes to another; then he leaves her and goes to another place; after that he leaves her too and goes to still another place. He has a woman everywhere he goes. He has four children there, four children here, four children there, two children there, and two children here.

"Look at his qualities: intoxicants, lust, theft, murder, and falsehood. He has many of them. That is how he turns women into demons. He takes their beautiful forms and turns their lives into spirits, demons, and wraiths. He subjects them to suicide and murder. The men make some of the women commit murder, they make some of them commit suicide. They hunt down their honor and subject women to that state.

"There are some men who are like women, but they are very few. There are good and gentle men. Yet if such a man goes to help a woman, he is killed as well. They destroy him as well. If he tries to protect her, they destroy him too.

"Look at this, look at this, look at this. How many. This is how the world is run. This is how those men are running it. They do not obey God's commands and God's words. They do not act with God's actions, truth, justice, conscience, peace, or tranquility.

"These are God's Commandments:
> Know the lives of others as your own life.
> Know the hunger of others as your own hunger.
> Know that any sister is your own sister.
> Know that any brother is your own brother.
> Know that any creation is part of your own family,
> your own lineage.
> Know that any man is from your own lineage,
> your own family, and that he has been born with you.

"Has man forgotten God's Commandments? Has he forgotten that God created the children of Adam, and that I am his Mother? He has forgotten that they are my children. He has lost that justice and he is raping women. Because he is raping women and because of the atrocities he has committed, millions and millions of women have died from jumping into the sea, jumping off mountains, diving into ponds, and falling onto the ground from trees. Look at the dead. They died protecting their honor. Some of them killed themselves in order to protect their honor. Some killed themselves after they were raped, saying, 'I cannot live anymore.' Some women were raped and the children were murdered along with their mothers. Men have done many millions of things like this.

"Are they animals? Men have turned into animals. However, elephants, tigers, pigs, and rhinoceroses do not act like that. Man has changed into that state. Have you thought about this? Men are like demons, ghouls, malignant spirits, and devils. Man has changed at this time. He has no justice. Look here. His state has changed, becoming the cause of the suicides, murders, killings, crimes, and rapes.

"They destroy anyone who can come to her rescue, men and women, even children. Look here. How many houses they are burning. They are burning their harvests. They are burning their possessions. They are burning everything in that state. They are burning and destroying everything, are they not? They are leading evil lives with evil actions on an evil path. Look here. The state of their minds is that of theft, murder, rape, and grievous sin. The state of their minds is that of separation, ethnic group, religious prejudice, color, hue, language, my land, your land, my house, my property, your property, my land, the place where I was born, the place where you were born, my river, my well, my pond, my tree, my bush, my park.

"What do they use to divide these things? They use the 'I.' This is the cause of the murders. 'My kingdom, your kingdom, I am the king, I am the president, I am the minister, I am the man, I am the judge.' They speak in many ways. 'I am a lawyer. See what I can do.' This is how they run the world. This is the reason destruction has arisen. Look over here. They have destroyed so many women and men, so many human beings. Look at the justice of it: the men who tried to save the women died, the women who tried to save her honor died, the children and their beautiful section are all dead.

"Those who sacrificed their own honor for others are dead, and those who tried to save them are dead. They killed everyone who tried to help the women. This is the karma and these are the sins in the world. Horrible things are happening in the world. That is the reason the destruction of the world is coming closer. Look at this," said the light of Adam ☻ and Eve ☻, as they showed him those things.

"Is this God's fault? Man has become an animal.

"God has reserved a beautiful heaven for my children. He has reserved a beautiful kingdom for them. A garden that is a world of flowers awaits them. He has given them the beautiful kingdom of God that is the life known as the *qalb*. He has given them bodies. The life known as the *qalb* is a beautiful kingdom. The kingdom known as the *qalb* is a kingdom of grace, a kingdom of love. It is a flower garden.

"The world is a beautiful flower garden, a kingdom that God has created as a wondrous show for man to watch. The extent of the kingdom known as wisdom, the kingdom of *gnānam*, cannot be described. Allāh, God who is our Father, has created paradise. His kingdom is a kingdom of justice. How beautiful it is. He has created and reserved a paradise in which everyone can live forever without dying.

"God has made such beautiful kingdoms. Man has come to live in them in order to understand this secret: we have come here to know the state of our Father, to know this section. God has sent us here to acquire understanding from all these things, all these beautiful kingdoms. He has sent man here to know this kingdom of the *qalb*, to understand himself, to understand wisdom, to understand the treasure of wisdom, *'ilm*, and the *wilāyāt* that are Allāh's qualities. He has sent us here to understand them, to understand His state, and then to obtain the bliss of the thrones in those kingdoms.

"God has created everything. He has provided the food, the water, and the protection. He has provided the eyes, He has provided the tongue, He has provided the taste, and He has provided the ability to speak. He has provided the ears to hear the sounds, He has provided the hands, He has provided the *qalbs*, and He has provided the feet. He has made the body beautiful and has placed the appropriate faculties there. He has sent man everything.

"But man is not aware of this.

"Look here. Some of them have become judges. Man has begun to dispense God's justice. God is the One who is aware of justice, conscience, love, unity, and compassion when He gives the verdict. The life of another is His own life, the hunger of another is His own hunger. He is aware that the life of another is His own life, the body of another is His body, the eyes of another are His eyes, and the ears of another are His ears. He safeguards others with awareness: He knows the ears of others hear like His own, the eyes of others see like His own.

"He safeguards the vision of others just as He safeguards His own vision. He makes the breath of others flow just as He safeguards His own nose and the manner in which the breath flows inside it. Just as He controls His own tongue and makes it say good things, just as He gives it blissful words and sounds, He shows them to others, and teaches them. Just as He knows the good taste on His own tongue, He gives that good taste to the tongues of others. Just as He takes and gives good things with His hands, He also teaches others to do this. He is the One who displays this state.

"He has made His *qalb* a vast open space. He has made His *qalb* resplendent by looking at the *dhāt*. He has created a resplendence of love there. He exists similarly in the *qalbs* of others in a state of love as the Resplendent One who embraces them. His justice investigates what is within Him. He investigates others in the same manner: He investigates with that knowledge. He safeguards the legs of others just as He safeguards His own legs and how they move. He is the One who dispenses justice while protecting others with the three thousand divine qualities. He dispenses justice through the ninety-nine *wilāyāt*. Allāh is the King who dispenses justice in this manner. He can be called Āndavan, Allāh, God, Rahmān, Rahīm, Rabb, Yahweh, SubhānAllāh, Al-hamdu lillāh, Kadavul, and many other names. That is what He is. He is the Complete One.

"If man tries to take over God's state and to dispense justice, how can that be? Look over here. They are bringing the people who have been accused of murder. They destroyed the possessions of the people they killed, they burned their houses, and no one is left to care for the children. They are orphans. They have no relatives, they have all been destroyed.

"The murderers are wealthy. Some of the murderers escaped without being able to take anything, others are coming with the money they stole after having killed others. What about justice? They have lawyers, they have proctors, they have brokers, they have the judge, they have the court. They have everything. Look over there. They have many relatives, they have friends, they have everything.

"So then, shall we speak of justice? Justice. Now the poor, look at the justice that comes to the poor. They are not allowed to speak. They have the truth, but they are being questioned about something else, and something else. They do not allow the poor to tell the truth, they are being questioned about something else and something else and something else and something else and something else. The witnesses who are questioned are prompted to describe other things. They have brought bystanders, someone who fled from the murder scene, someone who did not commit the murder, and the actual murderer. They are all there. They have even brought someone who was not there at all.

"Now they are focused on the alleged murderer. Is he from the East? Is he from the West? Is he from the North? Is he from the East, the North, the South, or the West? Where does the murderer come from? Is he black and African? Is he American? Is he European? Or Asian? What is his country of origin? Even before the questioning, they have noted where he is from, and his color. 'Yes,' they will say. If he is black, they have noted that. The judge, the lawyers, and all who are there have noted that. They have already seen that. That is justice: color, hue, country of origin, language. They have seen that. 'All right, it is finished,' they will say.

"After that comes the questioning. The lawyer speaks and the judge listens. Justice: no matter how much truth is presented to them and no matter how much they understand that it is the truth, they focus on language, black, white, yellow, country of origin, rich man or poor man.

"A rich man does not understand a poor man. What is the justice between a rich man and a poor man? One is high and the other is low. Justice cannot be done like that. The titled are above and the untitled are below. It cannot be done like that. There is no justice in that.

"If an important man commits murder, he is high; the little man will be blamed for the murder. This happens according to rank. Money does all the work there. The title does all the work. Fame does all the work. The positions and titles of one's ancestors do all the work. Someone who does not have those things is a 'murderer.' He is called a murderer. The actual murderer is too high up, so a man who did not commit the murder is designated as the murderer.

"They call him the murderer and they sentence him to prison. 'He is the murderer, how many years should he stay in prison? One hundred years, fifty years, sixty years. Hang him, shoot him, or put him in prison!' He might not have been involved in this case at all, he might not have been at the scene of the crime, he might not be a murderer, but black and white, and a different language or country of origin can put him in prison. 'You have no lawyer, no nothing, so there is no justice for you, go! That is the verdict, go! Go!' they say to him.

"The verdict was decided the moment they saw him. The verdict comes before they question him. The lawyer, this man, that man, all who are there, will judge him. That is the verdict. The lawyer they get for him will stand with them. He will not say anything. 'That is the law. He is just acting according to law,' they will say. This is what happens in some countries. This is what is happening in the world.

"Ethnic group, religion, and scripture make things work there. If he has a great title, if he follows the dominant religion or scripture, if he has those things in that country, he is pardoned. He is a great person, so he is pardoned. He is pardoned even after he is convicted. This is not done for the others.

"Look at this state. The murderers are all outside. Those who are not murderers—the innocent—are in jail. Whoever has been singled out, whether black or white, is inside. The innocent are inside. The guilty are outside. Innocent good women and men all go inside. Good people are being killed and the innocent are being put into prison. Twenty percent of the prison population are guilty while eighty percent are innocent.

"The prisons are overflowing. All the sections of the jails and prisons are overflowing. Yet eighty percent of the criminals are here, outside! Those who committed the crimes are outside; those who did not are inside. They have filled the prisons with the innocent. The guilty are walking free, everywhere in the land. If they commit crime after crime while the prisons are being filled with the innocent, destruction will come to the nation. Murder, killing, terrible crimes, theft, rape, and grievous sins are being committed. This is destroying the world.

"It is a fear-producing destruction, an intimidating destruction. People cannot leave their homes. They cannot go here, they cannot go there. If they go here, they will be mugged. If they go there, their pockets will be picked. If they go there, they will be killed. If they get lost, they will be raped. If they go to a certain place, they will be hung. If they go over there, they will be buried in a pit. If they go here, they will be thrown into the river. They cannot walk about. So then, there is no case. This is the nature of what is occurring in the world. The world is behaving in this manner.

"Justice does not work in the world. Injustice works in the world. Justice does not work in the courts. Only injustice works. Justice fails and injustice decides the verdict. When a virtuous woman is raped and murdered, they lose their consciences regarding her honor, call her a prostitute, and say that she killed herself. This is what they say as they pass the verdict.

"God's verdict will come for this. God's verdict! The world is behaving like this, no matter where we look.

"They say there is no God. They have made men into God. Even animals and snakes trust in God. The sun, the moon, and the stars believe in Him. If a good man walks on the earth, the earth itself will protect him. If a snake sees a good man, it will shrink back and move away. If a dangerous animal sees a human being in the jungle, it will not kill him. It will look at him and turn around.

"However, should a man see such a person on the road, he will chase him down and kill him. No matter where he goes, he will follow him and kill him, or else he will trick him, find out what he has, hit him, and take his possessions. This is how they act. When a dangerous animal sees a human being, it will give him room. The world has come to this state.

"As a result, the destruction man has cultivated is burning the world. The fire he has started is burning. The fire of injustice is blazing. The fire of all the women who have been violated is burning brightly.

"There are no other demons and devils. Look here. Although they have altered justice, there is still such a thing as conscience, is there not? Conscience has taken a new form in man. Conscience has taken a new form for this type of justice. He has a form and his conscience has a form. 'You will burn, you will burn!' one says. Both forms speak to him. 'Have you done this? Did you judge in this manner? Did you say this about the murder?' Both forms speak to the advocate, the lawyer, the man who paid him off, the man who took the money, the one who spoke, the one who watched. They are like a demon to him. They do not leave him alone when he sleeps, they do not leave him alone when he sits, they do not leave him alone when he walks. The argument occurs between the two of them, between his mind and his conscience.

"The two of them possess him like a demon. Then he runs away, he drinks, he sleeps somewhere else, he throws things. He takes drugs and he takes LSD. When that does not work, he tries drinking some more. When that does not work, he goes somewhere else or back to the bar. The demon accompanies him wherever he goes. His conscience goes with him. The two lives within him are like a demon. He has one form and his conscience has another. Justice and injustice. If he has been unjust, justice awakens and speaks as his conscience. Again and again, again and again, it troubles him, and does not let him sleep.

"The violated women are burning him like this. They are burning his life. They are not allowing him to sleep, not allowing him to eat, not allowing him to be. He runs. They do not leave him when he goes somewhere as a tourist, they do not leave him when he goes to the seashore. They do not leave him whether he sits or whether he sleeps. They continue to do this. This is the demon. This is the demon within each one of them. The karma he gathers by acting in a manner opposite to justice turns into a demon that possesses his conscience.

"It is a battle between justice and injustice. Both come to him and speak with him. They speak in his dreams. They speak in his memories. They speak as if he could see them right in front of his eyes. He hears the sounds in his ears. He hears their conversations within himself. The reels keep turning and they make him insane. They are creating madness.

"He might be going out to commit another murder. He runs in the street, but the two forms, his conscience and his mind, justice and injustice, follow him. Justice has appeared because he has been unjust. Justice comes as his conscience to punish him. That demon seizes each one of those unjust people. When the demon of injustice exists within him, justice comes to destroy that form.

"No one has a remedy for it. There will be no refuge for him even in an old age home. There will be no room for him even in a pit of fire. There will be no comfort for him even if he enters a palace. The fire will continue to burn him even if he immerses himself in water. He will feel it. He will die without being able to die. That is his punishment. He cannot hide from it anywhere.

"It exists in each man who goes astray; this state arises in him. Conscience. The women he violated will turn into demons. Their spirits will turn into demons and follow him. They might take the forms of beautiful women and converse with him. They will approach him as beautiful seductresses. Then, they will change into huge black forms that put their hands around his throat to strangle him. Then, they will turn to skin and bones. They turn to skin and bones as soon as they grab him. Then, they will have ten or twenty hands. Later, they will burn him with fire. They will attempt to do as much to him as he did to them. *Takk!* They will quickly remove his manhood.

"The demon will chase him the way he chased her. It will run after him with ten or twenty hands. '*Aday!* Stop!' it will say. The *rūhānī*—the spirit—will chase him just as he chased this woman. It will make him run in the same manner. It will try to catch him in the same way and do to him what he did to her. '*Aiyō, aiyō,*' he will shout as he runs, but it will not let him go. It will try to force him to jump into the pond the same way he forced her into the pond. Those spirits will try to do this to all of them—anyone who helped him, anyone who held her down, all of them.

"It will come into his dreams and his thoughts. It will drive him mad. He can actually see it coming towards him as a woman. So many hands! He will see it in the daylight and in the darkness. It will walk with him. It will torment his thoughts and his dreams. The punishment for the crimes he has committed will come to him. The *rūhānī* will come to him in the same manner, cut him down, and kill him without killing him. It will remain with him until he is destroyed. It will remain with all who joined him in the crime until they are destroyed.

"A place has now been made for them. Such a person has discarded God. Now God can punish him through his own conscience with certain things He has created—earth, fire, water, air, and spirits. Conscience begins to work in someone who has lost justice. If he has no justice, conscience will begin to work. Justice has to come to that place. Conscience must come.

"Such a man has said, 'There is no God, there is no God.' But the miraculous actions and qualities, the *wilāyāt* of the Rabb, the Creator, will work. It is in this manner that demons, devils, and spirits able to destroy the entire world are now working. The conscience in each heart emerges as two forms. It emerges to show each of those men what he has done. Because he has violated women, their forms will emerge from him as the demons of his conscience. 'Justice is in this state. Injustice is in that state. Virtue is in this state,' they will say. His murders will all be exposed.

"This is a cause of the destruction of the world. Insanity has increased. Many people are crazy, and they drink alcohol. They go to the bar. This is the reason. It is because of the crimes each one of them has committed. They go to the liquor store, they go to the casino, and they gamble. They go somewhere, in order to escape from this law. But wherever such a person goes, it goes with him. What he has done and what he has taken come with him. Whether it be a man or a woman, this story follows that person. It follows him and ruins him. It goes with him until he is utterly destroyed. These causes of the destruction of the world have now been produced.

"There is no actual demon. The honor of those violated women takes that form. Those loving qualities take that form. 'Sinners, this is what you have done!' they shout. Justice and conscience take those forms. They have taken those forms and have begun to destroy the sinners in the world. Conscience has now begun to destroy the unjust qualities and unjust actions of those who have lost their justice. It has taken form. The wisdom that is conscience has begun to destroy them.

"On one side, it has begun to destroy those who have violated women. The spirits and the justice are the demons now. The sins become the demons in the mind of someone who acted after losing his conscience, someone who acted after losing his sense of justice, someone who acted after losing his wisdom, someone who acted after losing his loving qualities, someone who acted without compassion.

"Although they do not work through God, they work through the *wilāyāt* He has created. They are carrying out the destruction without Him. These are the demons, these are the malignant spirits, these are the devils in the world now. They are not actual devils, but miracles that have come to destroy the evildoer. These are miracles in God's creation. They have come to destroy the evildoer—they come as conscience, as wisdom and conscience. Justice is the honor of the violated women. They have taken forms, they have taken the forms of *rūhānīs* and spirits.

"They are impure spirits. They are not the pure spirit. The pure soul is there, but the impure spirits have emerged from those women. They are the demons and the devils. This is working in everyone, wherever you look in the world. They go to those people because of the things they have done. Look at this. It will never stop.

"It will not cease until he becomes a human being, until he acts with those beautiful qualities. It will not cease until justice enters into him. It will not cease until God's qualities enter into him. It will destroy him. It will not cease until peace, tranquility, unity, exalted qualities, just laws, love, compassion, and harmony come into him. It will not cease until other lives are like his own life, until everyone is one family, one group of relatives. Until that embracing heart comes to him, until he embraces others to his bosom and shows love, it will confront his evil actions. It will come with him. This is its state. There is much more.

"This is the cause of destruction, destruction by rain, hurricane, wind, volcanic eruption, water, air, earthquake, and many greater kinds of destruction that are yet to come. Destruction will arise through the weapons each person manufactures, through scientific things, through ignorant things, through things mind, desire, and thought manufacture, through each person's own section. This is an indication of the destruction of the world.

"Truth will protect, evil will destroy—each person. Truth will protect everyone. God's truth will protect everyone everywhere. If someone forgets God and thinks that evil will protect him, that very evil will destroy him. Now is the time in which those things are occurring. This time began sixty to sixty-five years ago, basically, in the last hundred years. It started little by little, and began in earnest about sixty-five years ago. Since 1914 until now, the times that belong to destruction have become predominant.

"Man's happy times in the world have changed. All of the good high ideals in a man's life have changed, and man has come to possess degraded ideals. Human qualities have changed and changed, and he has begun to emulate animals and devils. As those qualities grow and grow, as justice changes and changes, destruction will surround him.

"Famine, illness, poverty, difficulty, loss, drought, many new diseases, many new demons and devils, and many new weapons will come to attack him. That is the reason the age of destruction has commenced in the last century. As he continues and continues, he will see only destruction facing him until his clarity grows. He will not see peace with any clarity. Until man is clear in this world, he will see only destruction. That is all he will see. He will not see peace or tranquility. He will not find peace.

"Let us think of this. It is not God's fault. It is the failure of each person's own justice. Destruction has been brought into being because of a failure of love, unity, and compassion, and because of the injustice of the egotism of the 'I.'

"This is not God's work.

"Man has thrown God away. Now he has to bear the weight of it. If man has become God, he must try to bear the hurricanes and the winds that come from doing that, he has to try to carry the weight. If he says there is no God, he must try to bear what comes.

"If he says God does exist, God will share a portion of his life and man will have the necessary strength. If there is no God, he must try to carry it. Those things will come to him. He is the one those things will surround."

My love you, the story is not finished. This is how the destruction of the world is being produced. I have been telling you some of the words that were told to me several days ago. They told me a lot more, but I have forgotten. I was watching as they were speaking and showing me. They showed me the way the forms changed. They showed me each thing I have described. I have forgotten much of it. I have forgotten. I told you the little I remembered.

This is the cause of destruction. Because man carries these burdens, he has come to the state of being destroyed. He has forgotten God, he has forgotten truth, he has forgotten justice, he has forgotten conscience, he has forgotten peace and tranquility.

He has begun to dispense justice with divisiveness, jealousy, envy, vengeance, racial prejudice, black, white, yellow, purple, and colors like them. He is trying to act according to color lines. His conscience and his justice operate according to color. It is because his justice operates according to money, according to cash, according to title, that justice has not grown within him. Injustice has grown. Injustice has become the cause of destruction. This is what is occurring in the world—what man has cultivated is destroying him. This is the reason.

Man will have peace on the day he drives out those evils. The destruction will stop when he accepts God, when he accepts the qualities of God, when God's actions dawn in each heart. God will stop it, and a time of great peace in life will come into the world.

May all of us think of this. May we correct ourselves and endeavor to walk on our respective paths with the qualities of God. May we take the truth into our hearts, and keep the demons from living with us. We must immediately try to stop them. We must try, so that justice and truth grow within us. We must work hard for this.

Āmīn. Āmīn. As-salāmu ʿalaikum.

CHAPTER

7

A'ūdhu billāhi minash-shaitānir-rajīm.
I seek refuge in God from the accursed satan.

Bismillāhir-Rahmānir-Rahīm.
In the name of God, the Most Compassionate, the Most Merciful.

THE STORY

*Thursday, July 19, 1983, 6:35 A.M.
Philadelphia, USA*

Bismillāhir-Rahmānir-Rahīm. In the name of God, the Most Compassionate, the Most Merciful. My brothers and sisters, loving brothers and sisters, creations who have been born with me, precious jeweled lights of my eyes, my sisters and brothers, my daughters and sons, granddaughters and grandsons, I offer you my love. May my loving *qalb* always serve you and rightfully belong to you.

We need only one kind of wealth, the wealth through which we can reach a good state.

We can attain either exaltedness or degradation. My love you, jeweled lights of my eyes. I was ordered to give this speech at a public meeting, this speech that has now come into my *qalb*. I was told, "Say this. Say this at a public meeting. Schedule a big meeting and say this." That is why these words have come, yet, since you have faith, it is irrelevant whether God told me to do this or whether God did not tell me to do this.

There is Something that exists within you and within me. That Something sometimes speaks from within, and what it says will always be for the good. It speaks of evil actions only so we can avoid them. It will point out what is good. It will speak so we can understand and be aware. That which speaks is a power that exists within Man. That power is commingled with truth, faith in God, certitude, and determination. It exists within justice and conscience and emerges from them.

There is no great distance between Man and God. God is in Man and Man is in God. They are hidden in each other. God is hidden in Man and true Man is hidden in God. There is a reason for this. God is hidden in Man and a true human being is hidden in God. We have the means to see, to understand, to contemplate, and to know this. Man is fully capable of being able to live as a human being.

Man is like a cat sitting on a wall. The world is on one side of it and maya is on the other. The wall is the path that leads to God. The wall is where Man was created and where the journey begins; he can jump off onto either side. Like a cat sitting on a wall, he will jump to the side his mind jumps.

Man can become God or man can become satan. Man can exist like satan or he can exist like God. It is part of his history. When he arrives, he can choose between the two. Man can turn into satan and have the strength of satan or he can turn into God and have the strength of God; both can be seen within him. He may choose either one on the path known as his life.

However, if he has truth, the world will make him out to be a satan and if he has evil, the world will make him out to be a deity. If he has goodness, if he has God's section, if he is on the right side, the world will make him out to be a satan. The world will call him a satan and angrily denigrate him. "Satan, satan," they will advertise. The world will advertise him as such. If he has evil, if he is on the left side, the world will call him a deity, a god; they will call him a god. Both are within him. He has both sections. If he is good, the world will push him away and say he is on satan's side, but if there is evil in him, it will call him a god and accept him.

When the world pushes him away and calls him a satan, his feelings can be hurt, and because of that, he can turn into a satan. If he does change, he will be satan.

When he possesses the truth, the world will hurt him—he will suffer and experience pain. The world, his environment, will hurt him. Everywhere he goes and everything that surrounds him will hurt him. When he possesses the truth, the world will surround him and make him suffer. Everywhere he goes, snakes, scorpions, and humans who are animals will make him undergo difficulties like this and suffer. Water to drink, hunger, clothing, housing, a place to live, a place to sleep will all involve difficulties. During these difficulties, he might forget good qualities, good actions, and God's section, and become a satan. He might forget and turn to satan's side.

However, if he bears all the difficulties and tolerates them, if he lives acting with God's qualities, and if he lives acting like God, he will become God. If he can shake off all those hardships, if his qualities and his faith do not fail, and if he can remain strong, he will become God.

As soon as he gets to the correct place, those troublesome things will turn back; they will not be able to proceed past a certain point. Those troubles will all follow him, but as soon as his *īmān* and wisdom reach the correct place, the place known as Man, all the animals that have been stalking him will turn back. They will not be able to move past that point. The karma, sin, arrogance, and maya will not be able to affect him if he is strong as he moves forward. Poverty, difficulty, and similar things will not be able to affect him if he takes that strength with him.

If he gets past that point, satan and that which is known as the world will not be able to hurt him. All of it will fade away because the power of God will be within him. He will have God's qualities, God's power, and God's faith, and the things following him will have to turn back. After that, he will exist in brotherhood with all lives. He will live in brotherhood with all lives. He will bring them peace and tranquility; he will be the one who can overcome satan, mind, and desire. It is possible. We must think about this.

However, those very troubles can also cause him to turn into a satan. If he is a good person, the world will make him out to be a satan and drive him away. If he is an evil person, they will turn him into a god and accept him. If he is a good person with God's qualities, the world will make him out to be a satan, oppose him, and cause difficulty to him. If his *īmān* and his wisdom change because of the difficulties, he will be given a horrible hell, the hell of fire.

If he overcomes those difficulties with *sabūr*, *shukūr*, and God's qualities, he will become the son of God and be transformed into one who has received the beauty and the Light of God. This is one section.

If he changes, thinking grief and trouble have come to him, if he engages himself in trying to put an end to them, if he thinks he has to end his own suffering, he will reap the fruit of his sin. That is not the way to end suffering, only God is. God is the only One who can heal the pain of the mind. Only He can do it.

My love you, jeweled lights of my eyes. A man in this state can turn to this side or to that side. He can jump down onto this side or he can jump down onto that side. He can do this. We must think of this.

What I have just told you at this meeting is not for any particular religion or ethnic group. It is not for any division of religion or scripture.

The words we are speaking concern Man, the assembly of humankind, and they describe how Man could live. This speech is coming to show us that we can achieve this state in our lives. We are giving this speech about Man, not about religions or ethnic groups. It is not about religions or scriptures or divisions. This speech is about the states in which Man lives and how he changes and becomes satan, Man, or God.

When he is born, he is born as a human being. When he comes to the truth, he can jump down like a cat onto this side or that side of the wall. That is why he is subject to this state. However, if he looks straight ahead at the truth, at the center, a human being can overcome both sides, and proceed in a balanced way. He can remain balanced. This is what we are speaking of here.

The world is a stage. The people are all actors. Man is an actor, a songwriter, a singer, and an artist. He is the actor, the artist, and the one who writes the script. He himself is the actor, he himself is the scriptwriter, and he himself is the artist. He writes his own script. He prepares the arts. He is the choreographer, the one who writes the songs, the one who creates the scenes, and the actor who acts in the play. He is the artist, the scriptwriter, the actor. He is the storyteller. He is the one who makes the preparations, the one who writes the lines, the one who acts and brings the story into being. It is his own story, his story.

The book he writes and the manner in which he demonstrates his story is through verses of karma, or maya, or sin, or any other section. One is the world, another is karma, another is happiness, maya. He himself will write the part and he himself will act it out. He gathers the cast in his mind, he gathers the five elements, he gathers his thoughts, and he puts on his act. Arrogance, karma, maya, *tārahan, singhan, sūran,* lechery, hatred, miserliness, greed, fanaticism, envy, intoxicants, lust, theft, murder, and falsehood, "I," arrogance, pride, jealousy, vengeance, deceit, treachery, anger, and actions like these are written into the lines of his act. He assembles many actors for the supporting cast. Mind and desire create the scenes, the art, and the backdrop. He himself is the songwriter who writes the songs, he himself stands there as the actor who acts and finishes the drama. This is what he does in the world.

The troubles that come into his life depend upon what he writes into the play, the part he reads, and how he acts—it is through them that the troubles and the difficulties come to him. Happiness, sadness, and suffering all appear there. It is like this that a human being writes his own life, adds the flourishes, and exists as the actor.

He is not being attacked by God.

Whatever he prepares, whatever path he prepares, the things that attack him are his own wisdom, his own qualities, his own thoughts, his own mind, his own desire, his own attachments, blood ties, religious prejudices, and so forth. He is not attacked by anyone else. The story he writes attacks him.

He can obtain a good place if he writes a good story about God who is his Father, His qualities, faith, and the lessons he has learned in his life. He can obtain a good place if he writes about the clarity of wisdom and peace, about the powerful and complete kingdom of God, about the beauty, the bliss, the heaven, the happiness, the peace, and the tranquility. If he looks at those things, sees how beautiful those things are, and writes about them, if he is the songwriter, if he writes the play, acts in it, and does the artwork in that good section, he can obtain a good place. He can obtain peace and tranquility in his life. He can make it as beautiful as paradise. He can act like that within himself. Man can act in this way and he can also act on the other side. He writes it all down inside himself.

If a man writes this good story, then the stories of the *ambiyā'*, the lights of God, the *aqṭāb,* the *auliyā',* and Adam, Noah, Abraham, Ishmael, Moses, David , Jesus, Muhammad, Idris, Isaac, Job, Jacob, Salihu, Solomon, Jonah, and Joseph, may the peace of God be upon them all, will be there.

His story will be paradise if he can write and understand their stories, describe the subtleties within them, and present their inner meanings and outer meanings. His story will contain and explain the teachings of God, the words and the actions of God, the conduct and the ideals of God, the ways in which He speaks, the gaze with which He watches, the loving hands in which He embraces, gathers, and unites everything. Then the story of Man's life will be beautiful, healthy, happy, and peaceful.

If a man writes that as his story, his act will be one of excellence. If a man is a writer for this, he will be a *nabī,* a representative, a son, a light, and he will attain the freedom of his absolutely pure soul. He will have no differences, no prejudices of colors or hues. He will have no colors, no hues, no divisions. He will not have them. He will have no divisions, he will have nothing except God and God's children, Adam ☺ and Adam's children, and he will see them as one. The exaltedness of Man will be seen in him.

Man's downfall also comes from himself. His downfall comes about through the story he writes. Man's rise comes about through the story he writes and through his qualities. His ascent comes from his qualities and his story. His descent also comes from his qualities and his story. He does this to himself. He prepares his own descent through his act and he prepares his own ascent through his act. That is how a man can become a satan or God.

If he acts with God's qualities, he can become God, yet if he acts upon this conviction, the world will call him a satan. If he acts with satan's qualities and pride, he will turn into satan, but the world will call him a god. If he acts with God's three thousand blessed qualities, this world and all of satan's qualities will abuse and denounce him, saying, "Satan, satan." They will denounce the truth as satan. They will denounce him as an enemy of God.

However, if he sacrifices his faith, determination, truth, wisdom, and *īmān*, and begins to go to the bar that is called the world, everything he possesses will be a sin. He will have only satan's section. No matter what he does in the bar known as the world, even if he simply puts a drink up to his mouth there, even if he just goes there to drink water, even if he only goes there to eat, even if he merely goes there to look at it, all of it will still be the bar that is connected to hell. He will never get peace from it.

If he does not lose that conviction, he will be able to go beyond the bar. Then he can go on the path of wisdom without losing his wisdom, without losing faith, and without sacrificing his *īmān*. Then he can knock aside all these evils and proceed. As soon as he reaches their limit, everything that was following him will turn back. If they were to go further, they would burn. They could not bear it. That is the state in which man becomes God. It is in this state that his act becomes God. A man can become a satan or God.

Satan can also become a god to darkness through falsehood, jealousy, occult powers, miracles, the world, maya, darkness, hypnotic delusions, the miracles of demons, ghosts, and malignant spirits, the dark miracles of harmful spirits, the miracles of the dark deities, and their glittering and their lights. He becomes a god to the section of hell, and he is raised up there. He will be a god to hell.

If a human being goes to the side that rules heaven, he will be God to the qualities, he will be God to the qualities of God. He will obtain that wealth and become a son to God. He will become God to those qualities. He will become God to that love. He will become God to that compassion. He will become God to that patience, *sabūr, shukūr, tawakkul*. He will change into that state.

Man can become satan, obtain the riches of satan, and obtain that praise or he can obtain the qualities of God, the wealth of the qualities, and become God to the wealth of those qualities. We must think of this. This is the story. These are the stories we write, the stories in which we act, the songs we sing; these are the arts, the songs, and the actors. We act in what we write. Therefore, man can jump to either shore. He can go to this side or he can go to that side. He can act on one side or the other. We must think of this. My love you, precious jeweled lights of my eyes.

When we contemplate this, we see the way in which the world contains many colors and hues—white, black, yellow, purple. No matter how many divisions exist between the religions, whether in Christianity, Islām, Catholicism, Judaism, or anything else, we are all still part of the assembly of mankind. There is no issue with that. Man can be any color. No matter who he is, he still has to write his own story and act in it. It is through this story that he attains exaltedness or degradation. No matter to which section he belongs, the reason for his ascent or his descent is the story he writes and in which he acts. He is the actor; the song is the song he himself writes; he is the one producing the arts.

You yourself are the artist. You yourself are the songwriter. You yourself are the actor. You are the one who will live with the results. My love you, precious jeweled lights of my eyes. When we understand the history of a man, there will be nothing in black or white, yellow or purple, ethnic groups, religions, or scriptures. There is nothing to them.

In this, one is hell, the other is heaven. One is Man, the other is the beast. One can be God, one can be a human being. If that human being changes, he can become an animal. If he goes past even the animal qualities, he can become satan—if his qualities change, he can become satan. If he becomes worse than an animal, he will turn into satan. The first is God, the second is Man. If he remains within God's qualities, he will ascend. If a human being acts with God's qualities, he becomes God.

If a human being turns away from God's qualities, actions, and conduct, he becomes an animal, a *hayawān*. If he turns away from the *hayawān* qualities, he becomes satan, the worst of all. Then hell will belong to him. Without discerning wisdom, *pahut arivu*, he will be worse than an animal. He will defecate where he eats and lie down where he defecates, a *hayawān*, not knowing clean from unclean. He can be worse even than that. Not knowing anything, he can make hell belong to him, and exist as a satan in that state.

God's qualities are the determining factor in man's reaching those states. If a human being assumes and acts with those qualities, he can become God. When his qualities change, he can become *hayawān*. When they change, he becomes *hayawān*. Although the goats, cattle, horses, and asses do not have discerning wisdom, they still serve man. They serve with awareness. They help man by working for him. Even dogs help people. The asses and the horses carry burdens. Cattle and goats give milk. They help man. They have no discerning wisdom, yet they help man as much as they can. They obey him and are subordinate to him. They have no discerning wisdom. They defecate where they eat and lie down where they defecate.

Yet they have faith in God.

Before they sleep, they extend their forelegs in worship, and before they arise, they extend their forelegs in worship. Before a snake sleeps, it raises its head, coils its body, and places its head inside the coils, in worship. A bird is similar. It flaps both its wings, bows its head three times, lowers its head upon its nest, and keeps watch. All lives, even the leaves move once and then they are still. A fruit stops the circulation of the juice within itself and is still. It does not move. Every blade of grass and every weed is like this. Even though they have no wisdom, they have faith in God. They have faith.

The state of satan is worse than that. The state of satan is far worse than that of the beasts that crawl on the ground. Satan cannot tell right from wrong. Through arrogance, pride, and jealousy he works with the forces described earlier. His thoughts are of divisiveness, separation, murder, sin, and of the deluge of blood that arises from wars, differences, and jealousies. His work is revenge, retribution, separating one man from another, and destruction. He works in so many aspects. That is his job. Unity is not his job. Since the time he separated Adam ☪ and Eve ☪ from Allāh, satan's work has been that of devastation, separation, and destruction. He will do whatever it takes.

He has no unity, love, compassion, harmony, equality, peace, tranquility, justice, conscience, recognition of other lives as his own, or solidarity. He simply separates one man from another. These are satan's qualities. This is what is called satan.

Whoever has these qualities will never bring love or unity. He will only divide and doubt, suspect and separate, kill and do the work of a vampire. This is what he will have. He will have only treachery, deceit, jealousy. He will never bring peace nor will he himself have a second of peace either. He will experience torment and torture. There will be no peace within him. He will be tormented when he sits; he will be tormented when he sleeps; and he will be tormented when he eats.

The world will come to bite and pinch him. All the evil things will come to pinch him. He has to run there and do something, he has to run here and do something. Then he has to run to do something else, to run somewhere else to commit a sin. This is what he has to do. These are the conditions under which he operates. He will exist only in this state. He has no time to get involved with the other side. He is on the path of evil, the path of divisiveness, the path of force, the path of ruin. He will never go on the path of goodness. This is the work of satan. His state is worse than that of an animal. That is what is called satan. It is a state of sin, falsehood, jealousy, envy, vengeance, and separation. We must think of this.

Jeweled lights of my eyes, think of this. We must understand with certainty what man needs in order to attain peace. He can find the value of peace only through the qualities of God. You must think.

We are one family, one group. We are the indivisible children of the kingdom of God, the children of Adam ☺ from the lineage of Abraham ☺, creations of God, human beings. We are from the lineage of Abraham ☺, and we must have the same faith in God, *īmān,* and certitude that Abraham ☺ had. We have come from his lineage as a result of his faith. We have come from the children of Adam ☺ because of God's creation. We have come from the lineage of Abraham ☺ as a result of his faith. We become the *ummah,* the followers, of Muhammad ☺ when our faith and *īmān* become correct and clear, and when our wisdom understands.

It is only then that we can be called the *ummah* of Muhammad ☺, or the children, or the disciples. These three become one for we who are human beings—one is to be children, one is to be disciples, one is the need to study wisdom, to know the truth, and to know the qualities of God.

For that, there is no color, no hue, no ethnic group, no religion, no separation at all. The *ummah,* the children, and the disciples exist only within God's qualities, actions, conduct, and grace. We must take on and act with His qualities and His grace, the ninety-nine actions that describe His conduct, and the explanations of His revelations. Acting in this manner is the only thing that will make us valuable. The other side will never elevate us. We will never get a reward from it.

If we want this reward, we must bring His qualities into being. Only His actions, conduct, love, ideals, three thousand divine qualities, ninety-nine *wilāyāt,* justice, righteousness, conscience, love, unity, and one family will guide man. This is what will guide him to the kingdom of God. This is what will guide him to the people. This is what will guide him to the truth. This is what will guide him to justice. This is what will guide him to the path of integrity. This is what will guide him on the path that leads from *insān* to God. We must think. My love you, precious jeweled lights of my eyes.

Unless we realize thoughts like these, unless we know this, unless we are aware of this path, we cannot reach the state known as Man. We can never attain peace, we can never obtain the reward of tranquility, we can never approach the kingdom of God without this wealth. This is the wealth for our lives. We must think of the state in which this wealth exists.

Without this, so what if you are black, so what if you are white, so what if you are yellow, so what if you are Muslim, so what if you are Christian, so what if you are Jewish, so what if you are anything? There is nothing in these divisions. The wealth exists only in this search, only in these qualities. It is only through these qualities that you will be known as a high person or a low person. You must elevate your qualities.

There is no benefit in advertising your blackness, whiteness, yellowness, purpleness, ethnic group, or religion. Even hell will not accept you simply for those things. Hell will accept you only if you gather sin.

Heaven will not accept those things either. Heaven will accept you only if you have goodness. Heaven will accept you only if you have gathered unity and God's qualities. Paradise will accept only these things. Paradise will accept you only if you have gathered God's qualities, the good qualities of unity, peace, tranquility, and serenity. Paradise will accept you only if you have justice, righteousness, conscience, His divine qualities, beauty, light, peace, and tranquility in your life. If, instead, you have the portion of hell, then hell will accept that. Therefore, there is no portion allotted for those things—whether you proclaim yourself black, whether you proclaim yourself white, or anything else.

Develop your good qualities. Develop God's story. You are the songwriter, you are the artist, you are the actor—you must build the good qualities. You must build the kingdom of God. That is why you have the arts and you are the artist. Arrange the decorations of heaven and paradise. Arrange and create your art with the ambrosia-filled qualities, the nine gems, the flowers, the fruit, the flowering trees. Assemble them in your *qalb*. Build them and decide where to place each fruit, each taste, each heaven, each beauty, each *houri*, each *nabī*. Think of the 124,000 *ambiyā'*, and think of the twenty-five prophets mentioned in the scriptures: in the Qur'ān, the Bible, the Torah. You must write about them there, in the *qalb*. This is the song.

You must illustrate the section of goodness. You are the songwriter and the artist. You must bring this art to life, write the story, and act in it. You must act in the act that is known as life. You must try to obtain its benefit and beauty. This is the greatest blessing. These are the riches. Life, *'ilm,* wisdom, courage, God's qualities, actions, light, and completion are all included within those riches.

No such thing as black exists there. No white, no ethnic group, no religion, no color, no "I," no "you." Those things do not exist for paradise. Those things do not exist for truth. Those things do not exist for good qualities.

Water does not act with prejudice. Air does not look at color. Fire does not look at color. Earth does not look at it. The sun does not look at it. The moon does not look at it. The stars do not look at it. God does not look at it. The soul does not look at it. Truth and wisdom do not look at it. Therefore, we too must come to the state in which we do not look at such things.

We must do duty in this manner. The sun belongs to everyone. The moon belongs to everyone. Water belongs to everyone. Air belongs to everyone. Fire belongs to everyone. Earth belongs to everyone—everyone steps on it. Truth belongs to everyone. God belongs to everyone. We must do good to all lives. God's property belongs to everyone. God's wisdom belongs to everyone. Everyone must do God's duty. Therefore, God is the wealth that belongs to everyone. Paradise belongs to everyone. His ninety-nine *wilāyāt,* qualities, and actions belong to everyone. They belong to everyone. There is no division between color, hue, or religion. It is for everyone. These are the things we must gather.

In this story, you will get what you gather.

My love you, precious jeweled lights of my eyes. Think of this. This is the story we write, the story in which we act. We must think about it.

If you want to dispel your suffering and your sadness by the other method, it will only reveal the acts of the ancestors in your life. You must not speak of black. You must not speak of white. You must not speak of Islām either: the Jews are part of it, and Christians are part of it. We must speak only of this: the duty that God does, His blessings, His qualities, and Man.

We must understand the exaltedness of Man, and satan's actions. Man can become God or man can become satan. He can become *hayawān* or he can become satan. Man can become a cruel beast. Man can become the Boundlessly Compassionate One. He can become a loving being able to be a companion to all lives. A human being must be someone who can embrace others with his heart and give them the milk of grace.

A human being can also be someone who can kill all lives, who can separate and divide them all: it is the history he himself writes, and he cannot attain peace through it in that manner.

My love you. If you decrease in wisdom, faith, and strength and imagine you are going to attain peace, if you write the story in a different manner, if you are the actor, the songwriter, and the artist when you act like that, and imagine you are going to attain peace, it will never happen.

Some people act like this with religions, ethnic groups, colors, and hues, filling them with songs, saying, "We are going to attain peace." Some people go to bars to drink. Some go to dances. Some take drugs. Some go to parks. Some go to restaurants. Some go to hotels. Some go to houses of prostitution. Some catch a "friend." Some become tourists. They do countless things like this in order to find peace. Some drink or take drugs or go to houses of prostitution. They imagine it to be the way to peace, thinking, "If I go drink now, my mind will be peaceful."

But you will never get peace. You will never have peace for your conscience. No one has ever found peace in this manner. No matter how much he drinks, his conscience will repeatedly remind him of what he has done. The only thing that will not come to him is wisdom; everything else that happened in the past will join with him. Everything he thought against his wife will come to him. Everything he thought about his children will come to him. Everything he thought about at work will come to him. Any divisiveness he thought of in the past will come to him.

"I had modesty, respect, reserve, and fear of wrongdoing. I am a human being. I was so noble. Now when people see me they will disrespect me." That thought will never come to him. "My dignity and reputation are gone. My life is gone." He will never think that. Such thoughts will not come to him.

Only what happened to him in the past will come. He will think only what he thought before: whether he thought of murdering someone, besting someone, ruining someone, doubting his wife, criticizing his children, or of what happened at work. This is what will come to him. These things will not solve those problems.

Will alcohol solve anything? What will alcohol do? Drugs will simply show him his own history. He cannot attain peace through taking drugs or going to bars.

It will not matter where he goes: the prostitute's house, the bar, the supermarket, the beach, the park, the movies, or even to some rock and roll. There, if he takes drugs or goes to an LSD-roll, that is what will continue to come to him. But his dignity, his family's dignity, and the respect of other people will be gone.

If a human being isolates himself and turns into an animal, if he changes like that, at least his family's dignity will remain intact. His family will be safe. His family's status will not change.

But, if after living with honor he begins to drink in a bar, his dignity will be lost as soon as he enters the bar. The bartender will hold him in contempt. "Oh, he was such a great man, but now he has come to drink." The bartender needs the money, so he thinks,

"All right, I will serve him whatever he requests." As he continues to go to the bar, the bartender will say to himself, "He is just another drunk."

If the man beside him is questioned, he too will say, "He's just a drunk."

If a bystander asks, "Where does he live?"

The bartender will reply, "He had a great position, and was very arrogant. Now everything is finished. His wife left him. His children left him, his son went somewhere else." The bartender will tell him what happened.

"Oh, is that what happened to him?"

"All right, mister, just drink," they will say, as he buys another one.

That is what people who come by will say about him.

After he drinks and shouts and comes stumbling out of the bar, someone else will tell his story, his wife's story, his children's stories, his sons' stories, his daughters' stories, describing the house in which he once lived—his previous job and state will all become public property. Everything he does will bring his family into public view. "He is the son of a drunkard," they will say about his son, "the child of a prostitute—his wife left him for someone else." This is what the public will say. Not only will he make himself public, he will also make his family public. Will he get peace from doing that? That entire family will never get peace. He will use his ignorance and act without ever finding peace.

He will sleep on the street and loiter here and there. His dignity will be gone. If he looks for peace in drugs, LSD, beer, marijuana, opium, alcoholic drinks, and the prostitute's house, he will never find it. Everyone will simply call him a moron. No one has ever found peace in this manner for even one day. No one has ever found peace in a house of prostitution. No one has ever drowned his sorrows in drink or found peace in drinking. No one has ever found it through those things.

People start gambling because of financial difficulties. Or there might be family troubles: a daughter is not obedient, or a son is not listening. "That is why I am drinking." But it will never solve anything. No one has ever achieved well-being from drinking, going to the bar, or here or there.

He will simply make himself insane. He will end up insane, committing suicide, and dying on the street. That will be the extent of it. However, he will not die in peace. He will lack proper clothing. This will be torn and that will be torn. He will begin to beg and steal in order to drink, and this is how he will die: without peace.

My love you, precious jeweled lights of my eyes. No one can benefit from those things. This is what his story will be. This will be the story he writes for himself. This will be his act, his story, and the song he writes for himself. He himself writes it. That is not how to do it.

Only God's qualities will give him peace. As described earlier, God's qualities will bring greatness to him, not blackness or whiteness. God's qualities, actions, conduct, the duty he does, compassion, and unity are the wealth that will do him good. Only this will bring him peace. This story is the only thing that will bring him peace. He cannot find peace in any other story, in anything else he writes. He will find no peace in any other act. He can be a satan or an animal. He can be a monkey, an ass, or a snake. He can descend further and further, but it will give him no peace.

God is the only thing that can bring peace.

We can attain peace only by searching for the appropriate wisdom and qualities. Man must give up jumping from side to side. This is the straight path. One side is maya and the other side is hell. *Dunyā* will pull him. He must balance and stay straight.

A man can be made out to be a satan or a man can live as a satan. The world can make a man out to be a satan and drive him away. If he is good, they can make him out to be a satan and drive him out. All that is evil will complicate his life. When he goes to the bar because he has lost his *īmān*, he becomes sad, depressed, sick, and diseased. He gives up his *īmān*. Because of that he says, "There is no God, there is nothing," as he goes to the bar, to the prostitute's house, and out drinking. He becomes even worse than satan when he loses his faith. His fate will come to this state. His fate will be like the bar, like the brandy and beer store. He will not find peace like this.

One who makes his faith strong, one who makes God's qualities strong within himself will not chase after these things. If he drives them away with determined strength as he searches for wisdom, using *īmān*, faith, and wisdom, and if he arrives at a certain place, these things will not follow him. Then he will have peace and tranquility. He will be a human being and peace will come to him. Then he will be someone who can give peace to all lives. He will become a son of God.

Man can become God or Man can become satan. If a human being lives as a human being, if he acts with God's qualities, if he establishes them within himself, if he makes his story exalted, if he understands and knows it, he can actually become God.

If he changes, and loses God's qualities, he can turn into a *hayawān*, a person without wisdom, a person without discerning wisdom, *pahut arivu*. If he does not act with even so much as the qualities of an animal, if he changes even more, he will turn into satan. He will be someone who does not understand anything. Hell alone will be his. He will have no balance of sins and virtues—his actions will all be sins. We must think of this. My love you, jeweled lights of my eyes.

The state of peace does not come from colors. Peace is not attained through the religions. Peace is not attained from colors, hues, religions, ethnic groups, or disagreements. We will not attain peace through mantras, *tantras*, magic, or divisiveness. We can obtain this wealth only through God's qualities. We can obtain this wealth only through God's actions. When these qualities expand within you, you will climb up. Develop those qualities whether you are black or white. When those qualities arise, you will be a good person.

However, there are two sides to this: if someone comes into money, his ethnic group, religion, black, and white will all be irrelevant. When money comes, those things will no longer matter. He will be a big person. If money comes, he will want to be a big man, his qualities will change, and he will turn into a satan. Satan's section will have come to him. He will descend again correspondingly. The connection to satan will have come to him. As soon as truth leaves him, the connection to satan arrives.

This is not wealth.

If we obtain the wealth known as truth, God's wealth, the wealth of wisdom, the wealth of *gnānam,* the wealth of love, the wealth of compassion, the wealth of patience, the wealth of justice, conscience, God's qualities, and the three thousand qualities of grace, this wealth will never diminish. This wealth will bring beauty, bliss, and light and resplend in the *qalb*. This wealth will free the soul and bring peace and tranquility. It will resplend by itself. It will exist as an ornament in his *qalb*.

When this paradise is built with that beauty, the writer will write the story and produce the arts. The actor will act, demonstrating each thing. This will be peace. His life will be paradise. His duty will be paradise. Everything he does in his life will be the work of the kingdom of God. The qualities, the work, the actions, and the result will be the creation of peace. It will not change. This wealth will not change. No matter how high he goes, it will not change—until he becomes God. His qualities will not change, but everything else will change. Worldly wealth will change. This wealth will not change.

These qualities will lift you up.

If you learn the lessons, the wisdom, and the qualities, this is what will lift you up and make you a good person. You can be black, you can be white, you can be anything. People will say, "He is a good person, a very good person. When we look at his face, he is beautiful. When we look at his qualities, they are beautiful. When we look at his heart, it is beautiful. When we look at his words, they are beautiful. When we look at his actions, they are beautiful." This will make you beautiful. This is the only way to attain exaltedness.

You cannot move up through arguments regarding black and white. We cannot solve problems with religions, scriptures, black or white or yellow. It is only through the qualities. No matter who you are, if you move up in qualities, the entire world will praise you as exalted people. You will be amongst those who have received the wealth from the qualities, wealth that the entire world can praise. If you demonstrate the qualities, the actions, the conduct, the love, and the wisdom, if you put them into action and climb up, it will be good.

Develop these qualities. They will destroy all concepts of miscreants, wicked-hearted people, black and white. These qualities will openly demonstrate the kingdom of grace. They will demonstrate One God, unity, compassion, patience, tolerance, peace, and one family. They will demonstrate completion without any division.

This is the most exalted way we can exist.

Precious brothers and sisters, this is what I was told to say this morning. I have forgotten over half of it. I did remember the other half, and told it to you.

Each human being must think of this. This is the only thing you must hold high. There is no use in arguing and quarreling about black and white, saying, "I. You. My ethnic group. Your ethnic group." There is no benefit in doing so. The benefit of God's qualities comes from obtaining the benefit from the qualities, and climbing up. You must obtain this great wealth in the way God obtained it.

Hold those qualities high. Hold God's qualities and actions high. Hold wisdom high. Peace will come from it. There we can see the peace known as Man, the highest beauty. Work hard for this. My love you, jeweled lights of my eyes.

May God help us all.

Āmīn. As-salāmu ʿalaikum wa rahmatullāhi wa barakātahu.

CHAPTER 8

A'ūdhu billāhi minash-shaitānir-rajīm.
I seek refuge in God from the accursed satan.

Bismillāhir-Rahmānir-Rahīm.
In the name of God, the Most Compassionate, the Most Merciful.

OUR THOUGHTS

Sunday, June 10, 1979, 11:55 A.M.
Philadelphia, USA

Bismillāhir-Rahmānir-Rahīm. As-salāmu 'alaikum. In the name of God, the Most Compassionate, the Most Merciful. Peace be upon you.

May the Fathomless Bestower of Grace, the Incomparably Loving One, the Bestower of Grace who is filled with the treasures of grace protect us and give us His grace. *Āmīn.*

May God who dwells with us every second, every instant of time, every minute, and every moment grant us His grace. *Āmīn.* May He bless us with His grace, His qualities, His actions, and His precious treasures in the inner realm and in the outer realm, in life in this world and in life in the world beyond, and in the life in which the soul is liberated. *Āmīn.* May all praise and glory belong to Him alone.

May our responsibilities, our conduct, our actions, our behavior, and our state all belong only to Him. May we commit our lives only to Him. May we commit the responsibility for our lives only to Him. May He give us the grace to acquire His qualities in this life. *Āmīn*.

May He give us His actions and His conduct. May He remove our qualities and our actions with His grace. *Āmīn*. May He remove the sections of karma and attachment from our bodies. May He remove our arrogance, karma, and maya, our innumerable thoughts, intentions, ideas, divisions, deceits, and separations, all that we hold equal to Him, and all that we depend upon other than Him. May He remove all these millions upon millions of thoughts.

God is the One without these qualities, without these actions, without these snares of desire, without blood ties, without religion or ethnic group, without language, without differences, without colors. He rules alone, dwelling in all lives. He dwells alone, regarding everything from a state of equality. May He give us the rare and great quality of doing our duties in that manner. May He transform our qualities so we act with His qualities and actions. *Āmīn*. May He be the Great King, the Padishāh, for us in death and in life, in hunger and in illness, in old age, in birth and in death. May He grant us His state. May He transform our state and grant us His grace. *Āmīn*.

He is the One who is the Undiminishing Treasure. He is the One whose power is pure and complete. He is the Complete One, unfathomable and undiminishing. He is the One who performs duty and service without tiredness or fatigue. He is the One who performs His duties everywhere without selfishness. He is the One who acts with wisdom and ability.

He is the One who remains pure while intermingled in all things, the One who grants fellowship to them. He is the One who is the sweet taste in every plant, every herb, every shrub, every fruit. He is the One who makes the sparkling light, color, and hue clear in each leaf. He is the Unfathomable Ruler of Grace, the One who is Incomparable Love, the One who bestows the wealth to the undiminishing wealth of life. He is the One who gives us our food and who comforts us. He is the One who tirelessly observes our karma and dispels it. He is the One who bestows goodness upon us. He is the One who lives with us in every second.

My precious children, jeweled lights of my eyes, we must meditate on our precious God who is the jeweled Light within our eyes. He is the only One in whom we must have faith. He is our very life, our *hayāh*, and He is our well-being. We must establish that state within ourselves and live depending only upon That.

All the things we see are changing things. All the things we experience are things that will perish. All the things we think of are things that will die: all the sights we see, the sounds we hear, whatever we see and feel love for, whatever we want, whatever we look at, whatever we gather, whatever we praise, and whatever we criticize. The sun, the moon, the stars, the world, earth, gold, woman, everything that has been created, everything we have seen—all the creations that have appeared—are just God's creations, are they not?

The mind changes as surely as the day turns into night. Everything between birth and death changes. Everything experiences the transformations of ailments and afflictions. Everything appears and reappears and changes. These are the things we see and want. These are the things we yearn for. These are the things that make us happy. These are the things we try to embellish.

Precious children, jeweled lights of my eye, there is so much we have to perceive. We must think about our lives. We must understand: nothing that changes is our wealth. Praise is not our wealth. What we have seen is not our wealth. Our experiences are not our wealth. Our homes are not our wealth. The forests are not our wealth. Money is not our wealth. Riches, properties, and possessions are not our wealth.

Just as every creation in the world changes, everything that dwells within us and everything we want can change. Praise will change, hostility will change, sorrow will change, and happiness will change. We have seen this occur millions and millions of times. We live amongst these things that change.

We live amongst them just as a fish lives in the water. A fish lives in a state in which it cannot leave or avoid water. It thinks its greatest joy is in the water. It loves water. We are attempting to live in each of our sections and thoughts in this same manner. We fall into each intention and try to swim there. We swim in each compliment. We conduct our lives inside karma. We swim in riches, wealth, money, various qualities and thoughts, religions, ethnic groups, and colors. We swim like this in countless, indescribable actions and qualities.

Our thoughts swim within us just as fish swim in water, just as worms and insects crawl on the earth, just as electricity flows between magnetic fields, just as currents, magnetic fields, and whirlpools swirl in water. Our thoughts swim within us, they swim in this body. Every thought swims in our body and in our *qalb*. We love those thoughts. We are immersed in those thoughts, immersed in a force-field we cannot leave.

Avarice, pride, arrogance, anger, hastiness, the separation of "I" and "you," the states of "I am greater than you, you are greater than me," and millions of similar thoughts dwell within us. Each one of us has fallen into them and each one of us is swimming there. We are unable to leave.

Just as the fish cannot leave water, we are unable to leave these thoughts. Once we dive into and swim in various intentions, we are unable to leave these intentions. We are unable to leave our blood ties; we are immersed in them. We are immersed in the attachment to our wives and children, and we are unable to leave. We are immersed in lust, unable to leave. We are immersed in anger, unable to leave. We are immersed in pride, unable to leave. We are immersed in arrogance, unable to leave. We are immersed in religious fanaticism, we swim in it, unable to leave. We dive into our desires and swim in them. We are unable to leave them. We dive into and immerse ourselves in selfishness, unable to leave. We are immersed in attachments to our relatives, unable to leave. We are immersed in land and woman and unable to leave.

Just as the fish cannot leave the water, we cannot leave any of our thoughts. If we analyze every atom of praise and blame, joy and sorrow, poverty and illness, hunger, disease, old age, and death, we see that this is how we steer the boat we call life. We are so immersed that we are unable to change our hearts. We are unable to release ourselves from any of these thoughts. This is what we must reflect upon.

If we live like fish, these thoughts will be the diseases that will kill us. The fish must think about what will happen to it one day. The fish thinks that water is its peace, that water is its life. However, many millions of nets will come, many millions of whirlpools will come, and many millions of waves will come. The fish forgets that there are things that can eat it. It forgets that its own kind can eat it. The fish has forgotten that one fish can eat another and that the small fish become prey to the bigger ones. There are many millions of nets and hooks that can carry us off, capture us, and take us away from where we live. The fish does not understand this. Why? It has only one thought: I cannot leave the water.

In the same way, we too are immersed in the midst of these millions of thoughts, religions, ethnic groups, scriptures, colors, and hues. We cannot leave these thoughts. Like fish, we are unable to avoid this state. We live like fish.

Like the nets, hooks, thunder, and lightning that will strike the fish one day, scattering them and separating them, we too will be scattered in that manner. Poverty, hunger, and disease will come to torture us, but we will be unable to leave. We will say, "We cannot leave our blood ties. We cannot leave our bondage to our earthly attachments." We are unable to leave praise, self-esteem, money, riches, earth, or woman. These are the things we keep in mind.

One day death will come to separate us from all these things. One day God's glance will come to separate us. One day all that we nurtured will eat us. Our relatives will cut us down. Our earthly attachments will kill us. We must try to attain the awareness that everything we nurture in that ocean will kill and eat another. Each thing will kill and eat another. Whatever we nurture will eat us. Whatever we say will eat us. Everything that smells good will eat us. All the thoughts we nurture and in which we swim will eat us. We must reflect upon this.

One day we will be like fish taken out of the water that they relied upon to always be there. We must be aware that we will have to leave everything we consider permanent. The time will come when we have to leave the things we depended upon. The time will come when we have to leave the things we thought were permanent. Precious jeweled lights of my eyes, we must reflect upon this.

We must choose the One Treasure from which we will never be separated. God is demonstrating the principles of everything we say, everything we teach through wisdom, through truth, and through love. He lives with us and within us through the means of *gnānam*, through perception, awareness, intelligence, assessment, subtle wisdom, discerning wisdom, and Divine Luminous Wisdom—*unarvu, unarchi, putti, madi, nupa arivu, pahut arivu,* and *pērarivu.* He lives with us through that wisdom. We do not know that He lives with us—He is with us but we are not with Him.

We live like fish, diving into each thing, swimming along, thinking, "This is permanent. This is our property. This is our glory. This is our value. This is our dignity. This is the connection."

It is because we swim in such thoughts, that the Unfathomable Ruler of Grace, the One who is Incomparable Love, the One who blesses us with the wealth of grace is showing us many things through wisdom and awareness in order to make us aware. Although He is demonstrating this and making us aware, we are like fish unable to leave water, no matter what we hear. We do not leave what is in our hearts. We do not leave what is in our thoughts. We do not leave what is in our desires. We do not leave the sorrow and the suffering in the mind. We do not leave the happiness, the weariness, the profit, and the loss. This is what exists in one section of our hearts. In our lives, we must think.

If each child would only understand that the many dangers that come to a fish also come to us. We must realize this through perception, awareness, and wisdom. No matter how long we live, one day we will have to go. Every created thing must become food for the earth. Everything that grows must become food for something else. Everything that flies in the sky must come down to the earth.

No matter how high they grow, the fruit on the trees will come down to the earth. We must realize that the seeds growing from the earth must return to the earth. All seeds have a connection to earth—no matter how tall they grow, even if they grow to touch the sky, even if they flower and bear fruit in the sky—and must return to earth. Everything connected to earth must return to earth. Even if birds and flying creatures carry the seeds, those seeds will return to the earth through their excretions. We must think of this.

Similarly, knowledge, wisdom, *gnānam*, intelligence, ideas, and everything we study will be like fruit that falls to the earth. All the ties connected to the earth, the karma connected to the earth, the fire-qualities of arrogance, karma, and maya that are connected to the earth will be like fruit that falls to the earth. The water-qualities, the air-qualities, the qualities of maya, the monkey qualities of mind and desire, the qualities of the demonic forces, everything that appears from the earth, even if it grows up to the sky, will be like fruit that falls to the earth. We can do many miracles through the demonic forces. We can accomplish miracles through *jinns*, fairies, demons, satans, and even if we fly in the sky, no matter what branch of knowledge we study, no matter what we do, no matter where we fly, no matter where we go, we will have to fall to the earth like fruit.

When we do not swim in God, when we do not know the truth, when we do not know that He is One, when we do not know where He is, when we do not know ourselves, we will have to fall to the earth like fruit falls from a tree. Whether we fly in the skies or live on the earth or anywhere else, we shall have to fall to the earth as fruit falls from a tree. All the birds that fly in the sky must come down to rest on the earth whether their food is on the ground or in the sky. Therefore, jeweled lights of my eyes, we must realize the meaning of what we swim in, in our studies, in our wisdom, in what we see, and in our thoughts. We must absorb the meaning of what we learn in the time between birth and death.

In every section, we swim in thoughts that we should avoid. The time that we spend swimming in each thought will kill us; it will be an enemy that devours us. Anything connected to earth will eat us. Anything connected to fire will eat us. Anything connected to air will eat us. Anything connected to maya will eat us. We must realize that anything connected to earth will consume us.

God is the One Thing that mind and desire do not see. He is the One Thing that has no beginning and no end. He is the One Thing that has no connection to destruction. We must begin to swim towards That. Until then, all that we do, all that we know, all that we understand, all that we study, all the austerities we perform, all the miracles we experience, all the miracles we perform will be fruit that will fall to the earth. They are fruit that will fall to the earth and perish in the earth.

The shareholders are earth, fire, water, air, and ether. Everything connected to them will become food for the earth. All the creations of mind and desire, all the miracles will become food for the earth. What is food for the earth becomes food for hell. What is food for hell becomes food for the animals we nurture within ourselves. The animals we nurture will eat us in hell. The qualities we nurture will eat us, becoming the animals that greet us in hell. The snakes we nurture will come to eat us in hell. The vultures we nurture will eat us. The demons we nurture will eat us. All the things we nurture will come to life in hell and eat us. That is what is consuming us even now. The arrogance, karma, and maya we create here will devour us there. The pride we nurture will eat us. The selfishness we nurture will feast upon us. All the things we nurture will be the source of the *adhāb,* the torment, in hell for us.

In the pit of hell there are seven qualities: earth, fire, water, air, ether, mind, and desire; these are the seven hells. The qualities we nurture in these seven hells will take form within us. The snakes, the scorpions, the centipedes, the bears, the lions, the demons, and the ghosts that are all living in this cage of the body will be transformed into the animals that will eat us in hell. These are also the things that are consuming us here. What we nurture now will feast upon us on our last day. They will devour us, vomit us out, and defecate us. They will vomit us out, repeatedly, as we take form after form.

Precious jeweled lights of my eyes, we must reflect upon this. Every word we speak here must be reflected upon by every child. This might cause some mental pain. When we tell them to leave those thoughts, it might hurt the minds of the children who swim in their thoughts.

You and we are swimming in religions, ethnic groups, separations, sorrows, self, woman, gold, wealth, lechery, hatred, miserliness, greed, scriptures, colors, hues, and doctrines, and when we speak of the justice of each of these things, when the explanation comes forth, it hurts your heart. It will hurt your wisdom, it will hurt your intellect, it will hurt your desire, it will hurt your mind, it will hurt your color, and cause you many kinds of pain in this way. Yet, each of these words is actually a golden tray bringing you fruit within your body. We must realize this with our wisdom, faith, and certitude. It will hurt until we understand this with certitude and determined *īmān,* and accept God.

Why? The fish cannot leave the water. In the same way, we cannot leave this birth, this body that is intermingled with fire and earth. We cannot leave it. When we tell you to leave it, it will hurt. Why? We are thinking these things are our life and we are swimming in them. The pain will arise because we cannot leave these things. It will cause hurt to the mind. It will cause fatigue. It will cause distress. Therefore, we must think.

We are like fish. We will not be able to leave our thoughts, just as fish cannot leave the water. We cannot leave our earthly attachments, we cannot leave our blood, we cannot leave our birth, we cannot leave our money, we cannot leave our ideas, we cannot leave our gold, we cannot leave the earth, we cannot leave our desires, we cannot leave the monkey mind. In this birth, in this life we are swimming in a state in which we cannot leave our many thoughts. In this life, we experience suffering. We drown in this suffering, we perish in it, and we die in it. This disease is consuming us, like one fish devouring another.

Each quality we nurture will eat another quality. Each thought will eat another thought. Each state will devour a truth. We are subject to states in which all of our good thoughts will be consumed.

Precious jeweled lights of my eye, we have to think. We must think of the fate that awaits the fish—the *mīn*—realizing that we are the letter *mīm* (م). We are the *mīm* in the letters *alif, lām,* and *mīm* (ا ل م). We must think of the way in which we are the letter *mīm* and a fish. Like fish, we swim in the ocean of maya, an ocean that is a *nuqtah*, a dot, a drop. That is a name for us, fish, represented by the letter *mīm*. It is the letter *mīm*, but the name for us is fish.

Therefore, we must think of creation. As we swim through creation, all the time we hold on to any of those things, all the time that we cannot leave those things, the other fish will eat us. Every cell eats another. Every bacteria eats another. One animal eats another animal. One satan eats another satan and attempts to drink its blood. We must reflect upon how every thought is devouring us in this way.

We must endeavor to escape from it. Therefore, precious jeweled lights of my eyes, think with wisdom of each word that has been spoken—that will make you free. If your qualities are the qualities of God, the result will be good. If you bring God's actions into your actions, you will be given the straight path. If your conduct is God's conduct, the way will be open to you and the darkness will recede. If you perform God's duties, you will obtain His palace, His beauty, and His bliss.

Therefore, we should uproot the qualities of the seeds that grow in the earth instead of swimming through everything in life like fish. We must pick up and examine each thing. Desire for land, desire for woman, desire for gold, all these desires are the diseases that are killing us. No matter what education, wisdom, *gnānam*, or miracle we possess, we will fall, just as fruit falls from a tree, and become food for the earth. We will have to become food for the earth and for the demons of the mind. We will have to become food for the thoughts of the mind. We will have to become food for the intentions of earth, and then that will be our fate.

Precious children, jeweled lights of my eyes, we must reflect upon every intention and every thought with wisdom. We must try to escape from the place where we swim in desire, and change. While accomplishing this, we may experience suffering, pain, mental distress, jealousy, envy, vengeance, one person being divided from another, and discrimination. Why? As long as we have that connection, these things will be there. We can obtain God's section only when that connection is annihilated. Then we can go on that solitary path. Then all the evils will be cut away. Then we can have peace and tranquility.

Precious children, jeweled lights of my eyes, every child, please do not subject yourselves to that pain. Reflect on your thoughts. Do not become subject to pain. Think about your thoughts. You must stabilize your minds. You must endeavor to stabilize your minds and escape from that pain.

Precious jeweled lights of my eyes, fish cannot leave the water and live away from it. As long as our lives are attached to the earth, we cannot part from it. Yet we must leave, and it will hurt, but once we break away, there will be no pain. Once we break away from those thoughts, there will be no pain. You must reflect upon this with wisdom. Our attachment causes pain. In every thought, in every word, we must break away to the section of truth. If we realize the attachment, if we understand the connection, if our qualities become the qualities of God, we can extricate ourselves from the places in which we swim.

When we are no longer connected, the fruit will not fall from the tree. If we do not have that connection, we will not fall. We will not come to rebirth. We will not come to hell. As long as we have a connection to hell, even if it is just an atom of hell, an atom of earth, a connection to earthly attachments, or a connection to desire, we will have to fall because of those connections.

Therefore, precious jeweled lights of my eyes, we ourselves must remove the illnesses within ourselves. We can remove them only when we become aware of them. We must remove the diseases within ourselves. We must remove the differences within ourselves. We must remove the arrogance within ourselves. We must remove the jealousy within ourselves. We must remove the millions of thoughts within ourselves. We must remove them one by one and escape. We will be free only when those connections are cut. The meaning of freedom is to have removed those attachments from ourselves. Then the pain will not come, the suffering will not come, the separation will not come, the differences will not come, the colors will not come. When these things have been removed, we will have reached the kingdom of God.

Precious jeweled lights of my eyes, whether told through wisdom or through love, when these things are being said to each section in the heart of each child, pain will come. Why? It is not really your fault. It is not really your fault and it is not really your state. Why? Everything simply swims. Life, the section attached to the earth, is like that. As a result, anger, sin, hell, the sun, the moon, the stars—many thoughts like this swim within us, and that is why they make us suffer. They will all change one day. They will all perish one day. Everything that is born will perish.

There is One Thing that will never perish. We must be aware of that. From all the lessons we learn, we must choose only that One Thing. From amongst all the things in which we swim, we must choose only that One Thing. From amongst all the colors we see, we must choose only that One Thing. There is One and only One Thing we must understand in everything we study here.

There is right and there is wrong. The right is God. The wrong is all that exists in creation as thoughts, desires, and earthly attachments. We must think of this. Whatever we nurture will greet us in hell as an animal, as firewood. There is no fire in hell. Our own anger becomes the fire of hell. There is no firewood in hell. Everything we nurture in our own bodies is the firewood for hell. There are no other creations, snakes, or scorpions in hell. There are no beasts or demons. It is what we have nurtured that appears there as a snake, a scorpion, and a centipede. What we nurture here will become our earnings in hell. We must escape from hell while we are here. We must escape from the things that are eating us here. All the things we think of here will come into being in hell: we are creating those things within ourselves. We must escape.

This is what we must understand now with our wisdom, precious jeweled lights of my eyes. Each child must understand this through learning, studying, and understanding. Unless we undertake this judgment, all the things in which we swim and that we nurture during our lives will become the firewood, the fire, the snakes, the scorpions, the worms, the insects, the demons, the devils, and the malignant spirits.

Precious jeweled lights of my eyes, you must endeavor to escape from them by understanding through wisdom. We must take up wisdom, and free ourselves from slavery to these demons, free ourselves from slavery to these thoughts, free ourselves from slavery to these intentions, free ourselves from slavery to these desires, free ourselves from slavery to the senses, free ourselves from slavery to the world. We must try to be aware of this through wisdom. Precious jeweled lights of my eyes, each child, you must think of the source of each thing. These are the things we have nurtured, and they will be the firewood and the things that will devour us in hell, will they not?

There is something else that we must nurture instead—what is right. God's qualities, God's actions, God's conduct, God's duties, God's service, patience, tolerance, peacefulness, justice, equality, tranquility, compassion, His three thousand blessings, and the ninety-nine *wilāyāt* that are His qualities. This is what exists as heaven. When we acquire these qualities, that itself is heaven. That itself is the kingdom of heaven. In that state, we are in the kingdom of heaven, we are the messengers of God, we have become someone who can rule the kingdom of heaven. That itself will be our heaven. If we nurture that, it is heaven. However, if we nurture the other things, we become subject to hell.

Good thoughts, good qualities, and God's qualities will be our heavenly messengers, they will be the celestial maidens who serve us. They will be the *malā'ikah* who will serve you in heaven. They will do duties towards you. If that state comes into being within you, you will be a king in the kingdom of heaven. Your duties and your service, your good thoughts and qualities will be the children who serve you. When you are in that state, they will be the children who serve you. You will be a king in the kingdom of heaven. May you understand this.

The other states, the poisonous qualities, and changing to the other side will eat you in hell. They will be hell and the things that eat hell. Understand these two things: what are the qualities and duties of God and what are the qualities and duties of satan's demons? Think of this and act accordingly. Precious jeweled lights of my eyes, you must be aware that you are swimming in mind, swimming in desire, swimming in thoughts, swimming in blood ties, and escape from them. All the earthly connections to which we are connected, all of creation will have to change. Yet you are unable to leave them. Why? You are unable to part from them in your hearts because the pain will come. That very pain will be our suffering in hell. Everything that we cannot leave will be the punishment we receive in hell. All that we want and cannot leave behind will turn to hell. Every attachment we love and cannot leave behind will turn to hell in the end. We must think of what these things are.

Jeweled lights of my eyes, my true and loving children, you must think of the two sections and understand them. The actions and the kingdom of God, the Most High, *illAllāhu*, the One who must resonate, are in one state. All creation will change and perish—that is the other state. Just as fish cannot leave water, we are unable to leave what we see. Yet we cannot stay here either, we will have to change. We will perish, be reborn, and die. The end of this is the state of hell. The things we nurture will consume us. The qualities we nurture will be the fires of hell. Our body will be the firewood. Our thoughts will be the demons, the ghosts, and the snakes of hell. Our desires will be the pain that devours us.

If we realize this, children, we can escape from the pain, from each thing in which we swim. We must break loose from each pain, each thing into which the mind dives and swims. You will attain freedom when that wisdom and the correct state arise within you. It is then that you will have good thoughts and good qualities; then God's path will be open. The grace will flow and the darkness will be dispelled. The mind will become a light. The *nafs*, the base desires, will be driven away. Anger and arrogance will all perish. We must think of this.

God is the One who dwells in all lives, in the large and the small, as *hayāh*—as life. We must develop the quality that dwells in all lives. We must stand as the life within all lives, helping them. We must develop that quality. This will not be accomplished through words or through talk, through intellectual acumen or terminology. We must look out from our open hearts and do what is needed. God is looking on as the Peaceful Witness. He is looking at each word we speak. He is looking at every thought, at every intention. His gaze is upon us and we must be in a state of awe. We must be in a state of awe because He is listening to our words. He is looking at us because He loves us. We must know that. We must maintain that state of awe with certainty. We must have the certitude that nothing can move without Him.

If that reverence, that determination, that faith, that belief, and that *īmān* are established within us, we will be able to control our tongue and every word we speak. We will be freed from all the places in which we swam. We will be freed from each sight we saw. We will be freed from every thought. We will be freed from every intention.

Precious children, jeweled lights of my eyes, every child must reflect upon this. All the children must open their hearts and reflect upon this. We have explained and illustrated the two sections. You must be aware of these two parts and look at them.

Primarily, you must understand: What is it that is hell? What are the things that live in hell? Did God create hell? No. God never created anything like it. Hell is what we ourselves nurture. What is it that is heaven? There is no heaven anywhere else. Heaven is simply the qualities we nurture that then become the kingdom of Allāh. That is heaven.

What is it that is judgment? What is judgment? If we can judge ourselves with God's judgment here, that is judgment. There will be no judgment there if we can accomplish this judgment here. If we do not, He will decide to which of the two kingdoms we will go. We must be aware of this. The judgment is within us. Right and wrong are within us. Heaven and hell are within us. If we can accept this and endeavor to understand, we will know that there is only that One and nothing else. We must realize and closely look at this state.

Precious jeweled lights of my eyes, all the children must think. Please do not just talk about it. You must bring this state into your actions and escape from the things in which you swim. You must free yourself from slavery. You are unable to leave and it does hurt. Just as fish are unable to leave water, you are unable to leave your mind and desire, you are unable to leave the connection to life and earth. You need wisdom to escape them. You need faith. You need patience. You must make an effort to be free.

Precious jeweled lights of my eyes, it is God's responsibility to give us His qualities in this way and to make us free. Our responsibility is to make the effort. We must endeavor to bring this into our awareness. May God bless us. May God give His grace, His meaning, and His explanation to every child. May He make you free.

May we give all praise and glory to Him and endeavor to escape. *Āmīn. Āmīn. Yā Rabbal-'ālamīn.*

May He Himself grant this blessing. *Āmīn.*

A'ūdhu billāhi minash-shaitānir-rajīm.
I seek refuge in God from the accursed satan.

Bismillāhir-Rahmānir-Rahīm.
In the name of God, the Most Compassionate, the Most Merciful.

FAITH

Tuesday, September 16, 1980, 11:00 P.M.
Philadelphia, USA

In the presence of the Shaikh, if the first words that come to your mouth are positive, then a positive thing will occur. If a negative word comes, he will block you. "Danger will come from it," he will say. "A loss will occur." He can empower you according to your own words. He can make it all good. If your words are negative, something negative will occur, and it will not be good. Then the Shaikh has to block it.

Therefore, that is why Prophet Muhammad ☪ said regarding one man, "It will be a good day for him," because his first words were positive.

To a second man he said, "It will be a bad day for you." That is how he answered when two men asked him whether it would be a good day or a bad day for them. The second man asked, "Will it be a bad day or a good day? Will it be a bad day or can I go?"

The first one asked, "Will it be a good day or a bad day?" He said it differently.

To the second man, he said, "Your words expressed the positive last. Everything that came first was negative." That is why he told him, "This time is not right for you."

Similarly, the words a person speaks prior to undertaking the journeys in his life will determine their outcome. Whatever he says will end up in his life. If he says, "I am sick, sick, sick, sick!" he will never be well. If he says, "I am poor, poor, poor," wealth will never come to him. If he says, "There is nothing, nothing, nothing in the house," no matter how much comes, he will have none of it. If he says, "I'm poor!" he will remain poor no matter how much comes. If he says, "I'm sick, sick, sick!" no matter how healthy he is, he will not be well. He will be unwell.

If someone says, "What God gave me is enough, enough. He gave it to me. God gave it to me," that is what will be. He will never lack anything. If he says, "I have the wealth that God gave me. I have it. I am not in need," he will not be in need. The words he utters will determine the results. If he says, "This illness has come. That is all right. I am a little sick. But it is nothing, I am well," he will be well. It is according to this state that he will progress.

(Bawangal now begins to address two particular people in the room, but of course, this applies to all of us)

The lesson for you has been that when coming here, you have been saying, "My husband is not well. We have to go," when your husband is here with you. When he comes here, you say you have to leave because he is not well. When he does not come, you say you have to leave because he is not well. It is not a good lesson to repeat.

Look at this professor. He has no job, yet he gives money for charity and does everything he needs to do. He does not have a job right now, but he has never told me that it was difficult for him. He says, "God will give. God knows." That child is managing like that, and therefore, that child is progressing.

Since you got married, when have you ever been well? Your wife has been saying, "He is not well, not well, not well. We have to go. He is not well." When you are here, she says, "He is not well." When you arrive, she says, "He is not well." When you are not here, she says, "He is not well." What kind of lesson is this for you? When are you going to be well? This lesson is not good. Those words are not good. They will never bring the good. They will never benefit you.

A human being must always be well. "It is nothing. I am quite well. I am just a little tired. It is nothing. I am well." In difficulty, he should say, "I have no such difficulty. I will manage with what God has given. There is no hardship. I have everything in fullness. What God has given is complete."

No wife should ever say, "I have nothing in the house. There is nothing to cook." A wife should never say, "There is nothing to cook, nothing to cook." If she says that, then no matter how much there has been, in the future there will be nothing to cook. She must say, "I have the *rizq* that God has given me. I can feed my husband from it too. It is fine." If you are in this state of completion, you can experience completion in your life. If you do not have these qualities, you will have to experience suffering in your life.

What does it take to kill a man? There is no need for one human being to actually murder another. To say, "*Aiyō*, the poison has entered your mouth. *Aiyō*, the poison fell into the water!" is enough. That person will die. "It's poisoned. It's poisoned!" becomes the poison. If you say, "It's nothing to me. It is nothing. What poison? God is here, not poison. There is no poison. I am well," there will be no poison. You must say, "It is nothing to me."

If you say, "*Aiyō*, the demon is coming, the demon is coming, the demon is coming!" the demon will come. The demon will come. If you say, "Whether it's a demon or a ghost, why would it come to me? God is here!" the demon will not come.

What you are doing is *no good*. It is not good to use those words. They will never bring you anything good. You must always have determination, faith, and certitude. Positive words must come from your mouth. Good words. In happiness and sorrow, positive words must come. That will bring success to your life. To anyone. To everyone.

Otherwise, the words are not good. Negative words should not come to you. Negative thoughts should not come to you. Negative intentions should not come to you. Even if you come here a thousand times, what is the use if you are in that state?

Your words must be pure. Your hearts must be pure. Your *qalbs* must be pure. It is only if a honeybee falls into a flower that it can take the honey. It is only if it completely enters the flower and sticks to it that it can take in the honey. It cannot get any honey otherwise. That is how you must be with the Shaikh: if you want to get all that he has, your entire *qalb* must stick to him. Your faith must stick to him. You can get the honey only if it sticks. You will never obtain it otherwise.

In your *qalb*, you must die in his words. No matter what he says, you must die in those words. It is only if you die that you can succeed. If you do not die, you will not succeed.

You must use wisdom. Good words must come to you, good thoughts must come to you, good intentions must come to you, good objectives must come to you, good actions must come to you, and good qualities must come to you. That is what will bring you success. Then no distress can do anything to you.

I will tell you my experience: Long ago, I did not know how to swim. I went to bathe in a pond. Everyone else was bathing, so I too went. It was extremely hot, so I said, "I will also go." When

I went in, I fell into the water. When I tried to stand, there was nothing under my feet. The water had become very deep. *"Ah! Ah! Ah! Ah!"* I shouted.

At that moment, the thought of death came to my *qalb*. All I could say was, *"Ah! Ah! Ah!"* When I realized how deep it was, fear came to me. I was afraid. My certitude was gone. As soon as my certitude left, the water took me down. My arms and legs were paralyzed. The ability to move my arms and legs had abandoned me. My brain had left me. While I was going under, the water entered into me, and I could not breathe.

Suddenly I remembered something. I realized something. My certitude was gone, but I remembered something. *"Ah?"* I said. I could breathe again because I had jumped up. I had realized I did not need to stand. Then courage returned and I was able to swim back. I had come back into balance, I could move my arms and legs, and I could swim. There was no need to sink—I could reach the bank by swimming there. It happened when I tried to stand and it was very deep. I started to sink at the moment I realized how deep the water was. I was immediately paralyzed. My arms and legs were completely paralyzed and I could not stay afloat.

The people on the bank were just watching. *"Aiyō!* A *swāmiar* has gone swimming! He's gone under!" They were all around, but they were afraid. I went down but I jumped back up. That was my experience. My nerves were paralyzed, my strength had left. The fear! "How deep it is!" I tried to stand, but there was nothing for my feet to step upon. I could not do anything the moment I thought, "I am in too deep." When the fear came, everything else left. When I thought, "I can swim. I do not need to stand. I can swim," I came up and swam back.

In two or three minutes, it was all gone. My strength had left. You must never be afraid like this. You must have certitude in poverty and in hardship. If you think, "What am I going to do?" it will be finished. It will be finished. I have experienced so many things like that in the jungle and elsewhere.

In the days when I was a young child, I was unafraid as young children are, but after some time went by, a little fear came to me. When I wandered in the jungle, and tigers, lions, and elephants approached me, I was a little afraid. The fear came when I saw a lion, or even just heard the sound, *"Oooh! Oooh!"* I was afraid. I had no certitude at that time: "If I run, the lion will chase me. Then it will catch me. If I climb a tree, it will climb after me." Bears and tigers too could climb. Tigers can all climb. It was a little difficult. They could all climb. Thus, I was afraid when I saw them. I was not afraid when I was very young; the fear came later.

After that, a little more time went by. Then I said, "My God. When God is with me, what is there to fear?" If a lion came, I stared at it. It stopped, stared at me, turned away, and went back. It left, and I could go on my way. On the roads, here and there, and on the jungle paths, it was the same wherever there were elephants, lions, and tigers. There were huge poisonous snakes and there were pythons. When I stared at the snakes, they put their heads down and left. They left, and I could proceed on my way. Subsequently, I was not afraid of them anymore.

Then came certain demons, all kinds of sorcerers, evil spirits, and ghosts. I was a little afraid. But afterwards, when the demons came, I stared them down. When I stared, they would disappear, or else they would catch fire and burn. Previously, I was afraid, but then the certitude came.

It is in this manner that we have to stare down every evil. Let the poverty come. We simply have to look at it a little. "What can you do? What can you do to me?" Let the demon come. Just stare at it a little. Let the dog come. Let the biting dog come. If you stand without saying anything and stare, it will leave. You do not need a stick, a branch, or a rock for that. Just stare a little. It will leave. Therefore, this is the certitude that you must have.

You should never have vengeance. You should never be jealous. You should never be ignorant. You should never be proud. You should never have what is called the "I." You should never have doubt.

You must have determined faith in God. You must have faith. You must have truth and *īmān*. If we are in that state, we can get through anything in our lives. Let the illness come. You should not let go of your faith until you fall unconscious, until the end. Do not let go of it. You must have that certitude. What are you ever going to do anyway? You must say, "My God. What can I do? Only You can do this." You must have that certitude. That is how you must swim. Then you will be successful in your lives, will you not?

Your words. Positive words must always come to your mouth. Negative words should never come. Negative thoughts should never come. Positive thoughts must come to you. Bad ideas should never come to you. Good ideas must come to you. Jealousy should not come to you. You must be grateful. You should not be envious. Peace must come to you. Contentment must come to you. You should never be vengeful. You must be honest. Then you will have peace and tranquility. You should not be vengeful. Compassion must come to you. You should never have pride. You must praise God. God is the One who must do everything. If you can practice this, it will be very good for your lives. You need this in your lives.

CHAPTER 10

A'ūdhu billāhi minash-shaitānir-rajīm.
I seek refuge in God from the accursed satan.

Bismillāhir-Rahmānir-Rahīm.
In the name of God, the Most Compassionate, the Most Merciful.

BALANCE

*Tuesday, February 9, 1982, 8:30 A.M.
Colombo, Sri Lanka*

Even the nectar of the gods taken in excess is poison.

In the same way, everything we do in our lives must be done only to a certain extent. If we go beyond that, it is poison and that food is not food. Using a stick to beat to ripeness a fruit that has not ripened naturally will not make it taste good. The flavor will not come into it. The taste will be off and it will not be food.

Similarly, when there is no yielding to God, no fear of God, no faith, no melting wisdom in one's own heart—when there is no melting, that worship is not worship. No matter how many duties are done, duties performed without melting and without awareness are like fruit beaten with a stick.

No matter how much is taught, no matter how much love is shown, no matter how much is done for you, wisdom heard without an open heart, service performed without an open heart, worship performed without an open heart will be like fruit beaten with a stick. All the points the *qalb* does not accept, all the points into which the *qalb* does not melt and dissolve will be like fruit beaten with a stick. The taste will not be there.

What is tasty to the mouth is an enemy to the stomach.

Everything a man likes and desires in the world, everything he studies in the world, everything he learns, everything he understands in the section that is the world—every section he gains happiness from is an enemy to his soul, his wisdom, his truth, and his life. They are actually also enemies to his body and his desire—they are diseases. However, these things will be tasty to the desire, the mind, the intention, the body, the eyesight, the eyes, the ears, the nose, and the tongue of one who likes these things and says these things seem like good food. These things will be tasty to one who likes the scenes of the world, the attachments of the world, the sins of the world, the blood ties of the world, and the pleasure that comes from them. Nevertheless, these tastes are all enemies to truth.

What is tasty to the mouth is an enemy to the stomach.

All these tastes are enemies to the liberation of his soul, his life, genuine worship, wisdom, and faith. Enemies. What is tasty to the mouth is an enemy to the stomach. In this way, they are all enemies to truth. They are all enemies. On one side they seem like pleasure, on the other side they are all diseases, birth-karma, diseases that attach themselves to him. The connection is like this: what is tasty to the mouth is an enemy to the stomach.

What is fragrant to the nose stinks to wisdom. Pleasure to the ears is an enemy to the meaning. Pleasure to the mind is an enemy to the *qalb*. All the sections that bring pleasure to the physical body will be enemies to the soul body. We must think of this.

Having thought, we must understand which fundamental things, which attachments, which pleasures, and which kind of learning are intrinsically worthwhile. To understand, we must open and look at each one. Everything has a limit. Our studies, life, love, compassion, all have a limit. Should any of these things exceed the limit, those attachments and that love can cause an accident.

What we know as life has a limit. The law has a limit. Thoughts have a limit. If a person's thoughts go beyond that limit, they will strike his brain and insanity will come, high blood pressure will come, his blood will boil, and many illnesses will affect him in this manner. Therefore, because everything has a limit, this must be understood: "This is the limit. Do not go past that point."

This side and that side must be balanced. There must be a stopping point. If we go beyond it, something will burst. Whether it is a scale, or your conscience, or wisdom, there must be a balance proportionate to your capacity.

There are small scales and large scales. The balance must be achieved in proportion to your wisdom. The balance must be achieved in proportion to each of your actions. The balance must be achieved in proportion to your body. The balance must be achieved in proportion to your own awareness. The balance must be achieved in proportion to your clarity. The balance must be achieved in proportion to your understanding. The balance must be achieved in proportion to your conduct. That is the limit.

In life there are scales that can weigh one ounce, two ounces, three ounces, four ounces, a half pound, three-quarters of a pound, one pound, two pounds, twelve pounds. The weight for a particular scale might come to twelve pounds. We cannot place anything more on that scale or it will break. We cannot place more than one pound on some scales or they will break. There might be a scale on which up to twenty-eight pounds can be placed; no more can be placed upon it, that is its limit. There might be a scale on which up to a half a hundredweight can be placed; any more and it would break. That is its limit. There might be a scale upon which more than a hundredweight cannot be placed. Similarly, there are scales that can weigh one hundred, two hundred, four hundred pounds, or a ton. More than that cannot be placed upon them. We can only place things upon them up to a certain limit. Beyond that limit, the scale would break.

Our wisdom and our life are like this. Our capacities are like this. Our heart must be balanced in proportion to our state. The balance will be shown to you in proportion to your understanding. It will be shown to you in proportion to your qualities; if it goes beyond, it will burst. It will break. The balance in our lives depends on the understanding of the wisdom upon which we stand, on our clarity, on our faith; it all depends upon the extent of the awareness in our lives. If we go to analyze beyond that, our balance will burst. It will burst. The balance will be gone. It will simply break.

Man's entire life depends on being in balance like this. Everything depends on his capacity, and the extent to which he understands the capacity of each thing depends upon the amount of wisdom he has. That is how the balance will be shown. No matter how much he evaluates what is within himself, if he goes past the balance, the balance will be gone. Then there will be disease, illness, poverty, difficulty, and loss. He will have lost his balance. The scale will be broken. That is when danger comes to us. From the time we are babies, the scale continues to show us the balance in proportion to our state.

According to the *najjām*, the ancient astronomers, the scale shows a thousand years for every day of life for some people. For others, the scale shows a hundred thousand years for one day. For others, a *yuga*, fifty million years, is one year. For others, forty million years make them four years old. For others, two hundred million years make them four years old—for them, four *yugas* are equivalent to four years.

The balance is set according to each person's state.

Our capacity, our state, our wisdom, our balance, and our growth exist here in the heart. The scale is here in the heart, and we must think of this state. Otherwise, it will break, and there will be an accident. From the time we are born, everything has a limit. As the weight increases, our lives are lived according to that scale, according to that explanation, as we proceed to each step and each place: "This is the limit." The limit will show us the balance. We must use conscience, justice, compassion, and God's qualities in proportion to our capacity, according to the scale that the Bestower of Limitless Grace has given us. We can only place onto the scale an amount that is dictated by the place in which we stand.

It is easy to talk about, difficult when weighed.

We can talk: we can talk scripture, we can talk doctrine—it will all sound the same. We can talk *gnānam*. The speeches will all sound the same, but the balance will be exceeded. The scale will break, or else the needle will go to the other side, all the way around and back, and break. It is not like that. You must calculate the amount. You must correctly watch over the scale as you do the weighing, making sure that it is within your capacity, within the capacity of your wisdom and ability.

What the scale shows us depends on the state in which we exist in our lives. God's scale shows the balance, the balance for our lives, in proportion to our wisdom. It will even show us grace in proportion to our state. We must know this in our lives. We must understand that the balance must not be neglected.

Each thing must be assessed. Before something is weighed, the scale must be assessed, wisdom must be assessed, and the thing to be weighed must be assessed, "This is how much there is." The limit must be evaluated in life: "That is the limit."

Unarvu, unarchi, putti, and *madi*—perception, awareness, intellect, and assessment—that is the limit. You must calculate the limits. *Nupa arivu*—subtle wisdom—is the balance. *Pahut arivu*—discerning wisdom—shows us what each thing is and how much the scale can bear. *Pērarivu*—Divine Luminous Wisdom—subtly provides only as much as grace can support: "There is only so much that can be placed here. Beyond that, it cannot be weighed. This thing cannot be weighed here."

Balance. You and we must think of this. This is life. If we do not think, all of it will end up going against us, against our intentions, and against our lives.

These miracles, this flying, and this sitting may all be pleasing to the eyes, but they will be enemies to the meaning. They will be tasty to the mouth, but enemies to the stomach. They are all limited. They are all things that break, things that are here and physically pleasing. Religion, ethnic group, scripture, philosophy, doctrine, color, and hue all bring physical pleasure. Illusory pleasure. They are like salty, dirty sweat oozing from the mind. Dirty sweat. The mind's sweat.

What oozes from the mind? Arrogance, karma, maya, *tārahan, singhan, sūran,* lechery, anger, miserliness, greed, fanaticism, and envy, intoxicants, lust, theft, murder, and falsehood, desire for land, desire for woman, desire for gold, "I" and "you," "mine" and "yours," religions and separations, ethnic groups, blood ties, gold, property, salaciousness, desires, sexual cravings, and things like this ooze from the mind. They are the bodily fluids. What comes from the mire of the mind? Stench. These springs ooze from blood, from water, from air, from exhalations, from desires, from attachments, from the embryo, from fire, from anger, from sin. They are the springs of maya, the springs of karma.

What arises from these springs? The mire of the mind. This mire of ignorance is destroying us, destroying the limit. All of these things are like the things that appear pleasing to the mouth, but are actually enemies to the stomach. Pleasure to the mind is an enemy to truth. Pleasure to desire is an enemy to wisdom. Pleasure to the eyes is an enemy to the meaning. Actions such as these are the dirty mire, the mire of hell, the mire of karma. These things are destroying us. You must think of this.

However, the spring that flows from wisdom; the spring that flows from truth; the spring that flows from the *qalb* within the *qalb*; the spring that flows from His qualities; the spring that flows from the soul; the spring that flows from faith, certitude, and determination; the spring that flows from lack of any attachment; the spring that flows from duty, patience, tolerance, peace, *sabūr, shukūr, tawakkul,* and *al-hamdu lillāh* is a spring of grace. That spring is an absolutely pure spring. When that spring is enlarged, all the other springs will be blocked.

The mire of the mind will be blocked because it comes from below. All the eyes of those springs will be blocked and the eye of the soul's bliss will be opened. The eye of this spring must be opened. Then life will be peaceful. This is how we must understand the limits.

It is a spring that transcends prejudice and scripture, and finds equality, peace, tranquility, serenity, and unity. It does not see separation. It is the highest of all springs. May we reflect upon this. We can understand the kingdom of God, God, and ourselves according to this limit. We can understand our lives.

Within this physical body there is the soul body. The scale—justice—is within it. The justice of life is the scale of justice. We must weigh upon it what is known as the world and what is known as the self. Then we can understand how the balance is shown to us according to this limit. The balance is shown to us in proportion to the state in which we exist.

This scale will show us the balance from the time we are babies until our final hour. This is why we must not think, "We have learned *gnānam,* we have learned wisdom, we have understood." Those things are all the mire of the mind. Everything you understand through the mire of the mind emerges from those springs. Accidents will occur when balance is lost. When your life is out of balance, it will break you. The scale and the balance will break when the limit is exceeded. You must understand this in the knowledge you have learned. Understand your state, and determine how much your scale can bear.

This is how we must understand wisdom and ability. Then we can understand our state, the state of the mind, the state of our lives, the state of our soul, the state of our wisdom, the state of our attachments and blood ties, and the states of attachment and non-attachment. When you understand these states, the scale will show how far away you are standing. It will tell you, "You will not be able to go beyond that, into what lies beyond."

The mind is *rounding,* the world is *rounding,* and maya is *rounding* without balance. You seem to be holding the reins, but the horse will not move. You suddenly discover that the horse you have mounted is a horse without reins. You cannot find your balance, the mind cannot conceive of it. You are holding on to that horse, but you will not complete the ride successfully upon it as it will not go beyond the limit. It will break. This is life—balance. If you mount the horse of the mind without knowing how to grab the reins, you will try to fly. When you lose your balance and drop the reins, your life will break.

Whether this is applied to lust, to desire, to marriage, to sexual cravings, to gold, or to possessions, the size of the scale will be determined by where you stand. The capacity of the scale will be determined by your life. If your mind flies beyond this, it will break. Your balance will be lost. You must think of this.

In order to think of this, to understand this, to understand the scale, and to understand our own state, we must find a good human being, a Shaikh of wisdom. Only a genuine human being can be called a Shaikh, only a human being with wisdom can be called a Shaikh.

It is the qualities that are called the Guru. It is his duties that are called love. It is the spring that flows from his love that is called grace. That state is called the kingdom of God, it is called heaven. The fruition of that heaven, the fruit of that love is the balance called God. When you understand that state, it is called wisdom. When you melt and dissolve and open your heart, the love within it is the flower garden of the kingdom of God. The fragrance that emerges from that garden is the fragrance of God's grace, the fragrance of the kingdom of God. It is the fragrance of heaven. Those beautiful blossoms are God's ornaments in the kingdom of God. That is where your heaven is.

That is heaven.

So that you can understand this, open the path, learn about the scale, and increase its capacity—more and more and more and more—learn while being open. All the aforementioned sections must be made to die. The Shaikh must cut arrogance, karma, maya, *tārahan, singhan, sūran,* lechery, hatred, miserliness, greed, fanaticism, envy, intoxicants, lust, theft, murder, falsehood, "I" and "you," religious prejudice, desire for land, desire for woman, desire for gold, attachments to the ooze of blood ties, mind and desire, the dogs and the monkeys, tens of millions of forms and qualities, and countless similar inner qualities. The Shaikh must cut them out by the roots. You must transcend each one step by step. His cutting them out by the roots is what will make you grow, that is what will increase the limit. As it increases and increases, the scale and its limit will be revealed to you. This limit must be adjusted in proportion to the scale. Then that will be life. His work is to cut out those evils by the roots. The scale is there. He will do things according to the scale. That is how his wisdom will act.

Such a person will be a representative of God. The *ambiyā'* and the lights of God acted in balance according to the command of God. They gave you the explanations and embraced you. You must think of this.

Miracles? Each thing is a miracle. The sun is a miracle, the moon is a miracle, a tree is a miracle, a snake is a miracle, an ant is a miracle, an egg is a miracle, an eagle is a miracle, a vulture is a miracle, a tiger is a miracle. Everything is a miracle. A crane is also a miracle. Every created thing is a miracle. A honeybee makes honey, but what if it stings you? *"Oooh, hoo, hoo, hoo!"* you will say. A snake is very beautiful, but if it bites, you die. A cat is very beautiful, it looks nice, and shows a lot of affection, but if its claws or its teeth touch you, you can get asthma. If a cat hair gets into your stomach, you will get a stomachache. A dog can be very obedient, but there is cancer in its teeth and its saliva. How many germs there are that cause disease.

It is similar for the dog of desire, how many germs it has. We cannot give the responsibility for our lives to the deceptions of this cat that is the mind, to the quality it has of stealing while keeping its own eyes closed, or to the rat that keeps one thing inside and another thing outside while it chews holes in our lives. And this monkey mind. How many kinds of jumping and tricks it has. These things are all within you. How many poisons there are in the fangs of the snake known as evil qualities. It has eight fangs. These are all miracles. Each quality that motivates you is a miracle. Every action that grabs hold of you is a miracle. Each one is revealing itself as a wonder. That is the only miracle. These are a part of the mire of the mind. We must think of them.

The Shaikh's work is to cut them away and to reveal the limit. You must reflect upon this. Think of these things, progress step by step, and learn to see what justice is in proportion to the limit in your life.

We must think of this.

My love you, my children. There may be shaikhs everywhere in the world, there may be grace everywhere in the world, there may be miracles everywhere in the world, there may be gurus everywhere in the world, there may be teachings everywhere in the world, there may be education everywhere in the world, there may be books everywhere in the world, there may be so many similar things everywhere in the world, but to find a genuine human being, a man of genuine wisdom, is difficult.

It is difficult to find a man of wisdom in the world. To know God, you must learn the limits. You must learn and know the limits of your life.

To learn it, you must open your heart, your faith, your determination, your *qalb,* and your life and search. Only if these things are open will that prayer, that wisdom, that ability, those qualities, those actions, what you earn from God, and the duties of God enter into your heart and increase the capacity of the scale. They will make it grow, ounce by ounce.

You will not be open until you open them—you will be locked. It will be like an echo. If you stand between the two mountains of mind and desire, and make a sound, the sound will return to you as an echo. That sound will be greater than the sound you made originally. If you stand like this between the two mountains, the words will not get past them, and those words will return to you as an echo.

If you do not make your heart blossom, if your heart is a rock, if it is a stone, the sound will come back and attempt to harm the one who spoke them. Why? Because of the rock. Your mind is a rock when it is not open. When the Shaikh's words do not enter you, each one of them will appear harmful to you. Why? The place in which you exist is harmful. You have made your worldly attachments into a rock.

Then, all of his words will oppose you. Then all of his words will seem antithetical to you. Then, you will break his words into many pieces, and throw them back at him. You will hurt him with his own words. You will throw his words back at him with many explanations, causing him many kinds of suffering. It will be painful to him. Like this, each of his words, each explanation, each word of wisdom will oppose you, and you will pick them up and use them to do harm. You will take a good meaning into your hand and use it as a harmful weapon against him. As long as you are in that state, his words will not penetrate you.

Therefore, my love you, my children, jeweled lights of my eyes. You must think of each thing I have been telling you. You must look at the scale. We cannot go beyond the scale. We cannot create our own limits in anything we do. It is only if the scale is in the hands of a man of wisdom that the capacity can be increased. When the ounce scale's capacity is increased like that, it will become a pound scale; after that, it will be a hundredweight scale; after that, a ton scale—there are scales for all of them. After that, more and more can be weighed. Then your life can be weighed and put into balance.

It is rare to search for a man of wisdom like this, and to find him. Therefore, if you do find one, this is the way it will be. It will be difficult.

If you want to find God, or wisdom, or if you want to know life, you must melt and dissolve in that place. Your *qalb* must blossom like a flower, and the fragrance must come into the flower, must it not? If it melts and dissolves, liquid will seep from it, water will flow from it, the water of grace will emanate from it. You must establish yourself in a state of wisdom and ability. Then you can live with a balanced scale. Otherwise, the balance will leave your life.

Everything must be in balance.

There is a balance for love, a balance for life, a balance for wisdom, and a balance for everything, a limit. If the balance has been exceeded, the Shaikh will say for each point, "Stop! Stop! Do not place any more onto it! For the state in which you exist, this is all. Do not place any more onto it. It will break." You must think about some of the things the world is doing, that you are now doing too. You must think.

Once, mind and desire went out to steal from the world, they went out intending to steal some things. "Let's go steal some cakes, some *appams*," they said. So they stole three *appams* and went to divide them. When they began to divide them, they could not. There were three *appams*. "You got more! I have more! You have more!" said mind and desire to each other. "You have more! You have more than I do."

Then, they went to ask others how to share them. But no one wanted to get involved. They had wandered throughout the world stealing because of desire for land, desire for woman, desire for gold—mind and desire stole arrogance, karma, and maya. Those are the three things they stole. They stole them and tried to divide them, but no one would tell them how to do it. Finally, they said, "We have to find someone. We can't divide them. We must find someone."

The only one there was a monkey, a monkey who said, "Why are you fighting?"

"No. We have stolen three *appams*. We can't figure out how to divide them. When I divide them, he says I have more. When he divides them, he takes more for himself. We can't do it. We have been looking for someone to tell us how to divide them properly."

"Oh? Really?"

"Will you help us divide them?"

"Yes, I will divide them! Get a scale and bring it here. A scale with two trays. Go get it."

"We will get it." They brought back a scale. They brought back the world. The world is the scale, in this case. That is what the mind brought back.

"All right. Sit down." The monkey broke the three *appams* into pieces and placed them on the trays. There was a little more on one tray. He pinched off a piece and placed it in his mouth. Then there was more on the other tray. He pinched off a piece and put it in his mouth. Then there was more on the other side so he took a little piece from that. Then he did the same on the other side until there was one *appam* left on that side. He took a little piece from the other side. Now there were one and a quarter *appams* on that side, so he took a little of that. Then there was more on the other one. He took a little of that. They watched until all three *appams* were gone and the trays finally came into balance. "Is it correct now?" he asked.

"It is correct, but there are no *appams!*"

"This is how it is done. When things are to be divided, this is the only way to divide them. Any other way, one side or the other will be more, or it will be less. Now it is in balance. This is the world. Everything has been stolen. Stolen goods cannot be divided. This is the world and now it is in balance. Nothing that is stolen will ever be in balance. Birth is the balance and only the earth will remain. All right, go and come back." That is what the monkey told them.

It is like this when trying to find a balance in life: in the end all that is left to show is that you have been born and that you will die in the same place—all that is left is death. From the time you are born, your whole life ends in death. All that is left is the scale. There is nothing left of the things you have held on to for so long. They are gone. They cannot be divided. You came from one opening. You return to it and crawl back into it, the same one. That is the balance. Everything is gone. You come from the earth, you go back to the earth. That is the balance. There is nothing left of what you searched for, what you stole—there is no profit and no loss. You do not see any profit in what you looked for and no good that came from it. There is no good that has resulted from what you searched for, and there is no evil to be seen either. It all stays there. It ends and it is completely swallowed by the karma from which you were born. That is the balance. This was what the monkey mind decided in the end. This is your state.

Like this, everything we search for in this *dunyā*, everything we look for will be divided into shares. If "you" do the dividing, "I" will think you have more. If it is divided the other way, the other will have more. It is like this for all the things the mind of the world brings to you.

In the end, the monkey mind will make this decision. No one else will get involved, nor will anyone else interfere. This is what the monkey mind will do in the end. This is what it does with all the things the dog of desire has searched for and brought back—finally, there will be nothing left. You die in the same opening from which you were born. That is how it ends. You came from the earth, you ate the earth, you grew on the earth, and now return to the earth! It is over. That is the balance.

Heaven? Goodness? Those are not for you. You did not gather those things. That is the balance. These are the things you sought, but these stolen goods cannot be divided. In the end you will be killed and it will be over and that is the balance you will be shown. "All right. Go." The monkey is done.

However, if someone can triumph over this, overcoming this monkey, overcoming the desire in this life, overcoming the hypnotic delusion, overcoming this theft, overcoming this dog of desire, overcoming these qualities, an indivisible share will remain. It will be a share no one can divide. That share is God. That truth, that grace, that explanation, that treasure, that completion is indivisible. It is everywhere. It is not necessary to divide that completion. It is full. It is complete. Everything else will disappear in that manner. The monkey mind will do that. You must think of this.

This is what a Shaikh, a man of wisdom, will tell you. That man of wisdom is known by many names. Similar to the names mentioned previously, that man of wisdom is known by each characteristic, by each quality, by each action, by each type of good conduct, by love, by compassion. As you yourself grow in this manner, you can see it like this in each step, and that man of wisdom will tell you, "This is what is called God. This is what is known as heaven. This is what is called God, and He is like this."

As you climb each step and see these things, you will understand according to your limit. In your current state, you will see him as a human being—in that state, this is what you will see. In the next state, you will see him as a man of wisdom. In the next state, you will see him as the Shaikh. In the next step, you will see him as love, as a flower, as a fragrance. In the next state, you will see him as grace. In the next state, you will see him as a soul. In the next state, you will see him as heaven. In the next state, you will see him as your Lord. In the next state, you will see him as Completion. This is heaven—you will see him as your heaven. This is the path and the way.

Those other things are not miracles. This is the miracle.

What animals, demons, ghosts, and evil spirits do are not miracles. That is not the point. How many miracles one mind and desire perform for you. How many miracles one desire performs. How many miracles one incident of lust performs. How many miracles one craving, one incident of hunger performs. How many miracles are performed to mesmerize you. How many miracles water and air perform. How many miracles one glance performs. How many miracles the energy of a craving performs. How many miracles a blood attachment performs.

How many miracles the bondage to kinship performs. How many miracles one piece of land performs. How many miracles gold performs. How many miracles one possession performs. Everything in your life is a miracle. They are all miracles. Still, when you think of these things, what kind of miracles are they anyway?

Climbing up is the only true miracle.

How many miracles one piece of music performs. How many miracles one taste performs. How many miracles one speech performs. How many miracles a mind performs. How many miracles love performs. They are all miracles. Are there greater miracles than these? What miracles are you looking at? Climbing up is the only true miracle. You must understand this point. You must understand this one thing. You must know these limits, these points. Please think of this.

My love you, my sisters and brothers, my daughters, grandchildren, grandsons, and granddaughters. My love you. This is how you must understand. This is the limit of life. You must endeavor to clearly understand each thing with an open heart. Come with an open heart, an *open heart flower garden*. Then the fragrance will come. Think of this. My love you. May Allāh help you. *Āmīn*. All praise and grace belong to Him. *Āmīn*.

CHAPTER 11

A'ūdhu billāhi minash-shaitānir-rajīm.
I seek refuge in God from the accursed satan.

Bismillāhir-Rahmānir-Rahīm.
In the name of God, the Most Compassionate, the Most Merciful.

PURITY

*Friday, February 20, 1981, 8:35 A.M.
Colombo, Sri Lanka*

Cattle have no discerning wisdom. Even though they live as pure vegetarians—*saivam*—without killing anyone, without hurting anyone, and even though they do so much duty, they do not know right from wrong.

A bull pulls the wagons and the plows, and performs all the necessary work day and night, performing his duty without attending to his own hunger and illness. It is only when he is untied that he can graze on weeds that he finds on his own; after he does all his work, it is only when he is untied that he can graze on weeds he finds by himself for his hunger. All the rest of the time, he does only duty, doing it without hurting anyone. This is what he does.

A cow does all her duty and then gives her blood away as milk. She gives her milk away to other beings. She lives for others. She is unable to care for her own child, because her milk is dedicated to others, is this not so? She does so many things.

And yet, how does she conduct her conjugal life? Once every year or every two years, she conducts her conjugal life for five minutes. Her conjugal life. She raises her child and gives it milk for two years. Some cows wait a year, others for two years, and then they conduct their conjugal life for five minutes. All the rest of her life is dedicated to performing duty to the lives of others, to other beings, and to human beings.

However, in order to eat, cattle have to endure difficulty and search for weeds to put into their stomachs. This is the work cattle have to do, the work cattle and goats have to do. Some birds are also like that. Horses are like that. We can see things like this with our own eyes, can we not?

In spite of being a vegetarian like this, doing so much duty, giving away her blood as milk, and doing all those other things, the cow that is vegetarian does not know right from wrong, nor does she have discerning wisdom.

Cows mate, they take care of their children, they give milk, they graze with awareness, and they return to their homes. They are afraid of death and they feel pain when they are hit.

Nevertheless, they go to the supermarket. Why? They have no discerning wisdom and they will not attain liberation for their souls. They do so much, but in the end they are sent to the supermarket, giving away their flesh, their skin, their meat, and even their bones. Does a cow that does so much duty reach heaven? No. No. What is her ultimate fate? The supermarket.

A human being must think. We say we are *saivam*, although we drank blood before we were born. As we grew we killed so many lives, we consumed so many, many sections. We ate so much. We want liberation but do no duty to achieve it.

If heaven is to be attained, how can it be reached? It cannot be reached like that. We must think of this. We must consider what *saivam* really means. We must understand it through wisdom. Peace, tranquility, serenity, wisdom, forbearance, compassion, and patience must be understood. Without separation or prejudice, without doubt, suspicion, or divisiveness, we must live in unity, as one family, one people—understanding right and wrong, understanding the connection between God and man, understanding the meaning of truth and falsehood, avoiding falsehood, accepting the truth and acting with it, doing good, and dispelling all that is evil.

When the light of the soul is understood, when the light of the soul that is absolute purity is understood, when that peace is attained, when the pure soul in all lives is understood, when absolutely pure wisdom is understood, that is *saivam*.

When the absolutely pure heart manifests, when compassion and love are understood, when the endeavor to merge with the Ultimate Unique Being—only that—is undertaken, when it is understood that all of creation will disappear and perish, when it is understood that all of it has a limit, that is *saivam*.

When we make our qualities into God's qualities and act with God's actions, when we remove from within ourselves all the things that God does not have, when we remove from within ourselves that which is not within God, that is *saivam*.

When we make that which appears within God appear within ourselves, when we act within ourselves with the actions that are within God, when we make the equality within God the equality within ourselves, when we make the peace within God the peace within ourselves, that is *saivam*.

When we make our own qualities into the qualities that are within the Fathomless Bestower of Grace, the compassionate and just Almighty One who is God, when we act with those actions, that is *saivam*.

When we remove everything that is not within Him, when we take in everything that is within Him, when we act accordingly and see it within ourselves, that is *saivam*. That is purity.

To understand through that wisdom, to understand the Treasure that is Wisdom within wisdom, to see oneself and one's Master in that Wisdom and to know them is *saivam*. That is Āndavan, God, Kadavul.

The word *kada-vul* [when it is deconstructed] means to transcend the world, to transcend mind and desire, to transcend scripture and philosophy, to transcend doubt, suspicions, and separations, and to intermingle with the Treasure of peace, the Treasure that is complete, and to establish yourself within it, to dwell within it. That is the situation and the state that is absolute purity. It is the purity known as *saivam*. Until this is understood, everything eats us, especially the things we ourselves nurture.

We must think of this. We must think of this. When we reflect, that purity alone will be *saivam*. Not everything we nurture within ourselves can be called *saivam*. *Saivam* means to exist in a state of not killing or eating others, not causing pain to others. This we must think about.

If we give flowers, fruit, and coconuts, and we perform *pūjas* and give offerings to deities and to *swāmis,* can we become *saivam* through doing these things? No. There is no *saivam* as long as we hold any kind of separation within ourselves.

A beautiful flower gives comfort, fragrance, and perfume to man. Man hurts, picks, thrusts strings through, and destroys that which is beautiful and happy. Man wears it, but the flower's life is lost. Its fragrance is lost. Its happiness is lost. Is it *saivam* to gain happiness from killing another? No. Is it *saivam* to cause harm to another in order to wear it? No. That is not it. No. We must think of all these things. When a flower can live freely dwelling on the tree until its limit arrives, that is its happiness. To live until its limit arrives is its happiness. It possesses fragrance, beauty, qualities, love, and happiness. When we harm the state in which it lives, hurting it in order to obtain the joy of wearing it, that is not *saivam*. That is not *saivam*, and that is not devotion. Think of this.

We must give the flower of our *qalb* to God. That flower is not harmed in the giving. We must give pure and resplendent love to Him. That is His food. It is the *qalb* and the completion within it—that truth—that must be given to the Treasure that transcends the purest of the pure. That truth must be given to the rare and precious Treasure of Light, that Fathomless Bestower of Grace. That is *saivam*. That is what is called *saivam*.

We offer suffering instead of offering that treasure. Some people even sacrifice cows and goats and kill other lives. Should we kill for God? Should we sacrifice other lives? People perform all kinds of tasks, causing suffering and killing because they want to be happy and attain a state of devotion. You must think of this. Human beings must think of this.

Man must become *Manu-Īsan*, Man-God. Then he will understand the meaning of the Supreme Being. He must know this.

What man will do when he does not know! It is dangerous to other lives when man experiences felicity, happiness, or joy. Any happy event that occurs is a danger to other lives. When happiness comes to man, danger comes to so many other living beings. How many murders, how many sins he commits. No matter what kind of happy event it is for man—whether it is a holiday, a holy day, a birthday, a death day, or any day—he is happy, but for other lives it is a danger. Do we really think that a day when everything else is harmed is a happy day for us? This is not it. This is not it.

We must realize that the day all lives are made peaceful, tranquil, and serene is the day we will have peace, tranquility, and serenity. We must know what that day is. The day man lives the way that God who is One lives will be a day of freedom, a day of peace, a day of tranquility. Peace. If he attains that day, he will have peace. That is *saivam*. That is what is called Man-God. You must think of this.

We must understand countless things in this manner. We must realize that if we understand and gain clarity, it will be very good.

What is the benefit in separation and divisiveness, in reciting and studying scriptures and philosophies? What is the benefit in saying we are *saivam*? Can we become *saivam* merely by not eating meat or fish? No.

We are *saivam* when we do not hurt any life, when we do not cause suffering and pain to any life through our thoughts, our actions, our angers, our sins, our ethnic groups, our religions, our scriptures, our philosophies, our colors, our separations, our *purānas,* our histories, our doubts, and our suspicions that cause one man to harm another.

We are *saivam* when we live with peace, tranquility, and serenity, in the way that God lives. He is the Truth that dwells in all lives, He is the Truth that dwells in all living beings, the Reality without which not an atom can move.

We are *saivam* when we understand that God's kingdom, God's love, God's duty, God's service, God's explanations exist atom by atom in all lives, that His blessings of grace are there in those atoms, showing compassion to all lives, bringing them peace through the quality of equality.

On the day a man establishes that state and understands it; on the day he understands the state of not harming any life; on the day he does his duty accordingly and without harming anything at all; on the day he separates from himself the qualities that separate him from unity; on the day he separates from himself the qualities that separate him from peace; on the day he separates from himself the qualities that separate him from equality; on the day he separates from himself the qualities that separate him from God's grace; on the day he separates those differences from himself; on the day he discovers these things and understands them through wisdom, he will become human.

If, after becoming a human being, he searches for the wisdom with which this must be understood, he will know the explanation, the Light, and the Resonance of God, the Supreme Being who is Wisdom within wisdom. When that understanding comes to him, all lives will bow down to him. All lives will bow. All lives will be his life. All duty will be his duty. All peace will be his peace. All sadness will be his sadness. All well-being will be his well-being. This is what he will know. When he is in that state, all lives will bow down to him. When all lives bow to him—that state is *saivam*, absolute purity. That is what can be called God's quality. Man must realize this. *Āmīn*.

CHAPTER 12

A'ūdhu billāhi minash-shaitānir-rajīm.
I seek refuge in God from the accursed satan.
Bismillāhir-Rahmānir-Rahīm.
In the name of God, the Most Compassionate, the Most Merciful.

PEACE
O HUMANKIND, DO YOU WANT PEACE?
DO YOU WANT PEACE OF MIND?
LOOK AT THIS A LITTLE.
LOOK AT THIS AND ACT ACCORDINGLY.

Friday, October 10, 1975, 7:13 P.M.
Philadelphia, USA

Loving children, children who are the jeweled lights of my eyes, children in America, children in Europe, all the children of this world, you must realize that the One who is God does exist. You must realize that His secret is within you and that your secret is within Him, that His peace is within you and that your peace is within Him. You must realize that your food is within Him. You must realize that His food is the food of love, the food that you give Him with love. What you give with love is within Him. It is like this that you must realize the good qualities and actions of grace.

God has created Man with great beauty. He has placed His *dhāt*, His grace, within Man. He has placed His grace there within Man. Man has to place his wisdom, ability, and his qualities within

God. God has placed the qualities of grace within you. He has placed actions of wisdom and authentic, perfect treasures within you. You must give Him His qualities, His wisdom, His glory, and His love. This is the secret of Man.

Man's life is extremely subtle. He is not like other creations. His actions are not like their actions. He is not like other creations. Of the six kinds of lives, the soul of Man is a sun, a ray of light that has come from God. It is a sun for the world; it is called a sun. The soul of Man is a "sun," a ray of light that has come from God. God is Perfect and All-Pervasive. Therefore, you must think a little.

God has said, "I have created Man as the most exalted creation, as My wealth. I made him clear. I gave him seven lights by which to see Me. I gave him seven faculties by which to know Me, to touch Me, to discover Me, and to understand Me: perception, awareness, intellect, assessment, wisdom, discerning wisdom, and the Divine Luminous Wisdom that is Nūr, Light, and completion. These are the levels of wisdom I have given him. If he uses them, he will see Me. He is My secret and I am his secret. He has to know Me through them.

"I will know him through his *qalb*, his heart. I will know him through his breath. I will know him through his gaze. I will know him through his sound. I will know him through his heart. I will know him through his actions, conduct, and qualities." This is what He has said. "That is how I see him. He must see Me through those seven types of faculties. Through them, he must understand My wealth. If he understands My qualities, if he understands My actions, and if he understands My compassion, he will obtain My beauty. Then he will see Me and I will see him. This is the explanation."

This beautiful being is called Man and this is his prayer: to understand the explanation, its resonances, the illumination of wisdom, the light of the soul, the connection to that "sun," and God's plenitude. This is prayer and worship. There is no other mantra. This is not a mantra.

God has said, "We have given this explanation to Man." Like this, He has given His teachings to Man through His incomparable grace and unparalleled compassion. Man is the one who exists in this state; man is the one who has received the strength and the power. This is power. The power of Man is God's power. God's power is the power within those seven kinds of faculties. This is how it exists. However, children, there are certain things of which we must be aware.

You must be aware of this state. It is from this state that the people now in this country and in the world can obtain soul-peace, *ānmā shānti*. You can obtain God's love, His grace, and His wealth. That is the state of peace, *shānti*, the state of mind-peace. You must pray and meditate to reach it.

However, children, jeweled lights of my eyes, there are four sections within you.

You must have proof of who you are. You must have proof of who God is. You must investigate the point in which you are growing, and you must endeavor to think with wisdom about the causes, the effects, and the supports for your body and be aware of them through wisdom.

There are four fundamental things in the form of your body—the mind is another and that makes five. The four are: earth—the section in which you were born, your body; fire—hunger, illness, old age, food, hell. Earth is the creation of maya. Fire is the fire of hell. *Āvi* is the air for the four hundred trillion ten thousand living beings. There are so many kinds of air: the exhalations of the demons; the exhalations of the *rūh;* the exhalations of the angels, the *malā'ikah;* the exhalations of satan; the exhalations of maya; the exhalations of the demonic idols; the exhalations of the senses. Everything you see, everything in creation exists within Man. These are their vapors. Included in these vapors is the pure spirit, the *parisutta āvi*. There are countless kinds of vapors.

God said, "One handful of earth." To create Man, He took one handful of earth. That is the heart. He placed everything into the heart and contained it there. The eighteen thousand universes, maya, satan, the seven hells, and the seven seas: the silver sea, the black sea, the sea of blood, the blue sea, the sea of gold, the sea of maya, the sea of desire. There are seven seas like this.

The eighteen thousand universes exist within the heart. The heart is a city of maya. It is a magic city. It is a city of demonic idols. It is a jungle in which animals that drink blood dwell. It has the nature of a vortex. It is a section that lives in the air. It contains currents of maya-magnet-power. It has the power of the energies of the demonic idols. It contains the power of the *jinns*. It contains the energies of the *malā'ikah*. It contains the energies of satan. It contains the energies of the mantras.

Like this, there are four hundred trillion ten thousand kinds of *shaktis* in that one handful. It is within those energies that this world exists, satan exists, delusion exists, and baby qualities exist. Monkeys, seventy thousand battalions of monkeys are there. The religions are there. The glitters are there. Birth is there.

Arrogance is there. Karma is there. Maya is there. *Tārahan, singhan,* and *sūran*—the connections to birth—are there. Lechery, hatred, miserliness, greed, fanaticism, and envy—these six evils are there. Intoxicants, lust, theft, murder, and falsehood—those five are there. These are the seventeen worlds. In the Tamil language, they are called the seventeen ancient scriptures, the *Purānas*.

These are the worlds of maya. This is where satan dwells, where illusions dwell, and where darkness dwells. This point is the mind.

This is what is called the mind. This is what is called the heart. There are so many things within it. Even God exists within a certain section there. Even God is there. Maya is there. Heaven is there. Hell is there. Innumerable things are there.

However, children, jeweled lights of my eyes, you must think of how much has been formed in the heart, the *qalb*, the mind. It does not simply exist there for nothing.

God sent down the *ambiyā'*, so you can realize who you are. He sent 124,000 *ambiyā'*. Eight *ambiyā'* were made the most clear. Twenty-five *ambiyā'* were made presidents over the rest. Amongst them are Adam, Noah, Jonah, Joseph, Job, Abraham, David, Solomon, Jacob, Ishmael, Moses, Jesus, and Muhammad, may the peace of God be upon them all. Twenty-five *ambiyā'* were selected and made clear. From these, eight *ambiyā'* were selected, and God's explanations were given through them. He revealed the four steps through them: the forces of earth, the forces of fire, the forces of air, and that which is called the scripture of Furqān, Islām, related to sight, smell, sound, and speech. That is called the scripture of Furqān.

He has given these four sections. Hinduism is birth. Hanal is fire. Hinduism is Adam ☮, the creations. The angel Israel ☮ is fire; the angel Michael ☮ is water; the angel Raphael ☮ is air. These are the four *malā'ikah*. These four *malā'ikah* are this body. We must think of this.

The mind is the ether, it is maya. How many stars can be seen in the sky. Like the number of stars that can be seen in the sky, the moon, the sun, the clouds, the colors, the hues, the thunder, the lightning are all there along with rain, sunlight, and heat. This is the mind. The mind, the ether, is constantly changing. Just as these physical things can be seen, just as the colors are seen in the sky, these points are seen in the waves of the mind. That is the mind. That is how we can see it, as the mist in the sky, as the fog on the ocean.

The stars can be seen in the ocean of maya. The moon can be seen. The sun can be seen. Their reflections all can be seen, but the stars are not really in the ocean. You can see the stars when you look down into the ocean, you can see them below you in the ocean. When you look up, you can see them above you. The waves we call the world can be seen in the mind like this. Even *gnānam* is seen in the mind. *(Bawangal laughs when he says this)*

Light is seen, the sun is seen, the moon is seen, and the stars are seen in the mind that is the ocean of illusion. Everything in creation can be seen there. They are like waves. They come like waves. They come like breakers. They come like clouds. They can all be seen in the mind.

Since they are seen in the mind, they are not truth. This is the mind and what is known as maya. The elements look at the illusions and enjoy them. Nevertheless, they are illusions. They are the magic and the glitters of maya. They do not belong to human beings.

The wisdom of Man is similar to the sun; the moon and the stars disappear when the sun comes up. Seeing the light, seeing the stars, seeing the sparkling things—these are all the glitters of the mind. When the sun comes up, the moon and the stars and all the things that glitter in the darkness come to nothing. The waves, the mists, and the clouds might still be moving, but nothing that was once visible in the darkness can be seen in the sunlight.

It is similar to this when wisdom comes to the mind that is the ocean of illusion. Similar to the way in which those things disappear with the sunrise, when the sun of wisdom comes to you and when it rises, all the sights you have seen with your eyes will disappear. The lights, the glitters, the stars, and the moons will all disappear. Everything that once appeared in that sky will disappear.

What will be seen? The waves of the elements will attempt to approach you. They are like the clouds and the rain—the colors, the races, the ethnic groups, the religions. They will attempt to block you. That is what will move in front of you and attempt to pull you. These are the blood ties, the blood connections. They will attempt to block you. In that state, they will not stop for even a moment. They will be in a state of constant motion every second.

There are four seasons, four times. In the ocean, the water flows from the eight compass points in four ways. It flows from the east to the west. At another time, it will flow from the west to the east. It will flow from the south to the north. Then it will flow from the north to the south and so forth. It will flow like this in eight directions. In one day, the water will flow in eight distinct directions, creating a current as it flows.

Similarly, in the ocean of maya that is the mind, the waves will move in eight distinct directions. When it flows in one section, another section will have peace. When it flows in that other section, the previous section will have peace. When it comes from another section, the opposite section will have peace. When it approaches as a swell from over there, the peace will be over here. Like this, when one side of the ocean moves, the other side will have no waves. When it moves to the other side, the previous side will have no waves.

Similarly, when the karma of our birth—Adam—moves to another section, when the mesmerism of sexual desire comes to someone, when that pleasure comes to him, he will have no other section. That is his target. There will be nothing else. That is all he has—that section alone. He will have no other waves, only those.

Everything else will have peace. As soon as that is finished, as soon as he turns around, another wave will come to the west. It will come from the east to the west.

When that is over his strength will be gone. His nerves will be weak. He will be tired. After those two minutes or five minutes are over, he will be tired. He might be too tired to swim, and he will have peace in that section. There will be no waves in that section.

Then when the waves move over here, there will be fire. The fire has started. Hunger has come. He is on fire. Now he is on the next quest and he has to find something for it. When the next phase comes, the previous section has peace.

Then, it comes to the north. He needs air. Old age has arrived. It is difficult to breathe. What does he need at that time? He has to draw in the air. The five elements must be given air, they need it. When they move past that, there is peace. When it runs from the south to the north, this side has peace.

The mind runs like this in four distinct ways. When it runs, the other side has peace. This section applies only to the mind. It runs in eight separate directions. You must understand this.

Yet no matter what you understand, only God's Commandments and God's words will bring you peace. So that is why this is a school for you. We must understand this school, this university. Your Father's book is a treasury book that is within each one of you. It is a book of nature, a book of knowledge.

It is a dictionary. You need wisdom in order to understand the definitions in it. You must use your wisdom and look into your dictionary. Everything has been placed there. All the explanations are there. All of God's creation has been placed into it.

Because His entire treasury is within it, it contains many millions of languages. Millions and millions and millions and millions of languages are there: the language of the ants; the language of the birds; the language of the fish; the language of the elephants; the language of the horses; the language of the rats; the language of the cats; the language of the fairies. How many there are in addition to the language of Man!

Since there are so many languages within it, you need human wisdom in order to read that dictionary. You must be someone who knows those languages. If you look at the dictionary in that manner, the definitions will bring you peace. You can pick it up and gain control. This is how it is.

Children, jeweled lights of my eyes, you must think of this a little now. This is why God sent down the prophets to bring the Commandments. We have come here to look at our dictionary, to look at God's story.

Children, jeweled lights of my eyes, you must think. There is a lot to think about regarding these four sections. Amongst them, one thing you must understand is who you are. Another thing you must understand: What is it that is known as meditation? Another thing you must understand: Who is God? To whom is the meditation directed? For whom is the peace? Who are you? These are the things you must understand.

How long is your *estimate* [life span]? What is Man? What is God? What is life? What is peace? You must understand what they are. Children, you must understand. You must understand with wisdom.

I have seen that you have been looking for peace on the continents of America, Africa, Asia, and Europe. But peace needs to come through the command of God. You must comprehend what kind of peace you need to know.

You are trying to create peace now. You have recited many millions of mantras, many millions of mantras in many millions of languages, in many millions of ways. Yet, you have not accepted even the prophets who have come by God's command. You do not have the wisdom to learn with understanding the explanations of truth that they have brought.

God's Commandments and truth are not a business. They are not a mantra. They are not a trick. A Commandment from God is a thing that issues forth from compassion and love. It is a thing that is understood through God's actions, qualities, conduct, and His treasury, the *qalb*.

His love, His "sun" is the wisdom that resplends from the soul. It is Light. There are three thousand blessings within it. Each blessed quality is a quality of God. Each of His compassionate qualities has three thousand heads and six thousand hands. Each quality is like that. The three thousand qualities are heavenly beings, messengers, and guardians who bring you peace, who safeguard you, who protect Man, the "sun," and the qualities. God has created three thousand angels, *malā'ikah,* like this. He has created them as a divine secret.

If you have wisdom and faith in God, if you accept the truth of the prophets, if you have a connection to One God, One Lord, and the word Allāhu according to Commandment, you will be protected. Those qualities will protect you. You must have the qualities that meditate upon Him. You must have the qualities that trust in Him. You must have the qualities that love Him. At the very least, you must try to develop this state.

If you want to read that dictionary in those languages, you must have the wisdom of grace to understand it.

To become Man, the "sun" of God, *insān kāmil,* you must have a Guru who is *kāmil,* a saint. You must have a saint, a *walī*. It is through him that you must obtain this. You must endeavor to study that wisdom through the qualities of the Qutbiyyah.

It is not a business. It is not a mantra. It is not a mantra-meditation. To act with God's qualities is meditation. To think of Him is meditation. To love Him is meditation. To trust Him is meditation. To act with His actions is meditation. To conduct yourself with His conduct is meditation. For His vision to come into you is meditation. To speak His words is meditation. To smell His fragrance is meditation. To hear and delight in His sounds is meditation. To hear the resonances of His *Qalb* and to resonate with it is meditation. To conduct yourself with His conduct and to reveal it thus is meditation. You must act with this wisdom and with these qualities.

Children, jeweled lights of my eyes, you have tried to create peace, yet you have forgotten God's Commandments. You have forgotten your own actions. You have forgotten that your food, your breath, and your words come from Him. You have forgotten the state that protects you. You have forgotten the state in which He gives you food.

However, children, jeweled lights of my eyes, God has created many seeds from one seed. This is not something the "I" can do. You can own a farm. You can own America. You can own Europe. You can own the continent of Asia. You can own the continent of Africa. You can rule all the eight compass points. You can do all of that. However, God creates many fruits from one seed. He creates many seeds from one seed. The one seed is in His hand. He has shown you how to multiply it. He has shown you how to make it grow. He has revealed how to turn one into a thousand, ten thousand, a hundred thousand. But you cannot satisfy your stomach with it. It is only straw.

The germination point of a seed is a small point and it is in His hand. That is what is in His hand. That is in His hand. He has shown you how to multiply one into ten thousand. He has given you a hundred million. However, that is for your elements, for your five elements, for your maya-mind, for your body's dog of desire, for the monkey of the mind, for the donkey, for the horse and the bull, for the lion, for the tiger and the bear, for maya and for satan, for hell and for hell-fire. That is how those things exist. However, there is one point that is in His hand. He has given to everything else in that manner, but to Man, He has given only one point. That point is His *rahmah,* His compassionate grace. That is the seed.

When Solomon ☮, son of David ☮, went to feed that one fish, he could not do it. The food was piled as high as many, many worlds, but he could not feed even one fish. One fish. Only that one point satisfied it.

In God's hand there is one *rahmah* to purify your hearts, to satisfy your hunger, to put an end to your tiredness, to give you strength, to give vision to your eyes, to give you courage and strength, to give you ability, to give you wisdom, to give you love, to give you His qualities. That is the food. When it comes and falls into your mouth, that is what fills your stomach. It satisfies your hunger and puts an end to your tiredness. You must think about this. Children, jeweled lights of my eyes, this is the state that God demonstrated to Solomon ☮, the son of David ☮.

Similarly, simply because you live on the European and American continents, you think, "We rule the world and we will feed the people." What God revealed by making many seeds come forth from one seed, and what you make and endeavor to defend is just straw. It is not something that will satisfy the stomach. He gives that too, but it is for the goats, the cattle, the asses, the horses. He does give. He makes one into a hundred thousand. Who is it for? Dogs, foxes, demons, ghosts, asses, and horses.

However, for a human being, for the "sun" of God with faith in God, the food is His love, His intention, His qualities, and His actions. The food is faith, determination, praying to his Father, and thinking of Him. It is His love. This *īmān,* absolute faith in God, is the grace. This food will satisfy his hunger. For one who has become a human being, this is his food.

This will grant him wisdom. This will grant him the grace of God. This will grant him the wealth. This will grant him limitless bliss. This will grant him peace. This will grant him happiness. This will grant him the light that safeguards him from the evils of satan. This will grant him the light that dispels all darkness. This will reveal to him the extent of God's qualities, His wealth of grace, happiness, bliss, and well-being. The kingdom of God exists wherever he exists. The kingdom of God exists wherever he lives. The kingdom of God exists wherever he goes. Heaven exists everywhere he exists. Heaven exists wherever someone in that state dwells.

You must think of this, children. You have studied science, books, psychology, and many things. That is very good. It is definitely good. But you must look at the dictionary. The dictionary is within you. This is the peace you must obtain. You are trying to obtain peace. This is the meaning of peace. For a human being, this is peace. Peace will not come for animals. It will never come. Man will reach peace only if he reaches this state.

Children, jeweled lights of my eyes. You have been thinking you have now discovered how to live in peace, since 1945. You have been trying to discover a place in which to attain peace of mind. You have discovered how to feed the world. In this state, according to your discoveries, you have discovered mantras, tricks, and various meditations while forgetting God's Commandments, the words of the *ambiyā',* divine justice, the justice of the rulers, the people's justice, and conscience. You have lost these kinds of justice.

We have lost them. We lost them and began to attempt to achieve well-being. What is that well-being? *Sarihay, kiriyay, yōgam,* and *gnānam*—many kinds of *gnānam*: four hundred trillion ten thousand mantras; many *shaktis;* magic; witchcraft; demonic meditation; ghost-meditation; psychic power meditation; yogic meditation; sixty-four kinds of yogic meditation; sixty-four kinds of scientific meditation; sixty-four kinds of sexual meditation; sixty-four kinds of artistic meditation, and similar types of meditation suitable to the waves of the mind. You have made these meditations foremost.

As a result, you have started to use marijuana, intoxicants, LSD, opium, and millions of other things that mesmerize your sense of judgment. You have begun to use them in order to try to make your minds peaceful. Who are you? For that there are many mantras. *Om! Ahm! Eehm! Sum! Soom! Bim! Come, let's go! Ahh! Eee! Mmm! Aheehmm!* There are many millions of *aheehmm* mantras. You have handed over your money and your minds and tried to find peace. You have tried to chant these mantras and perform these meditations.

What is the peace you have discovered from all that you have learned and nurtured since 1944? You have forgotten God. You have not only forgotten religion, you have also forgotten the truth of the religions. Granted, you left religion behind. However, there is a section inside: God's qualities, justice, and integrity. Because justice is there, that section is not a business. Try to think of this. Think of the wisdom of this. Try to realize its truth. At the very least, you should try to understand the truth of the *ambiyā'* and the truth of God.

You left your religions, you left your churches, you left your temples and mosques, and similar places, and began to meditate in your minds upon satan's mantras and energies, the sun, the moon, and the stars, the demonic idols, and the evil spirits that drink blood. Truth, good conduct, good thoughts, and good qualities are gone.

We have lost even our animal wisdom. When a snake goes to sleep, it circles around three times, and then lies down. That is the language with which it meditates upon God. "My God," it says. A dog circles around three times before it sleeps. "O God, I am in Your protection." A cow circles three times in the same way. A horse lies down in the same manner. The birds too do this three times. A rooster flaps its wings, crows three times, shakes its head, and lies down. All the animals meditate upon God before they lie down.

People meditate on satan before they sleep. They meditate on satan, they meditate on maya, they meditate on the demons, they meditate on their desires, they meditate on the monkey, and they meditate on asses, horses, cattle, and goats before night falls while they attempt to attain peace. Much of this has grown since 1944. You have tried to attain peace through those things.

Through doing this, your state has changed, races and religions have changed, the scriptures have changed, kingdoms have changed, and ordinary people have changed. The time has come—even the bodies of ordinary people are being enslaved. It is a time of destruction. Why? You have forgotten the truth. You have forgotten human justice. You have lost your conscience.

As a result, you have established a friendship with satan. What has happened as a result of that? Poverty has come. You meditate, *Ah! Ee! Ah! Ee! Mm!* in order to become a business owner. In order to heal an illness, you say, *Ah! Ee! Mm! Om! Ahm! Hmmm!* You cannot heal illness through that. You try to become a business owner, but there is no gasoline here. Harvests have decreased. Rain and tidal waves are coming. Earthquakes are coming. Destruction will come from hurricanes. The possessions you gathered will be obliterated. With poverty, business will decrease and everything will cost more. Rich men will become poor and the poor will have to beg for alms. Murders will occur because of what you worship. More intoxicants will need to be consumed. Many sicknesses will arise. Modesty, sincerity, respect for others, fear of wrongdoing, and good conduct will fly away.

In every country, murders and sins will become commonplace occurrences. One person will attack another. Prices of goods will rise ten to one hundred times. Everyone's strength will decrease. High blood pressure, sexually transmitted diseases, diabetes, head and tooth diseases, eye diseases, heart diseases, and similar illnesses will increase. If someone afflicted with these conditions performs the meditations previously described, how can he find peace? What kind of peace would that be? The diseases would simply get worse.

As a result of the meditations you have been performing since 1944, by paying anywhere from two hundred and fifty dollars to one thousand dollars to one hundred thousand dollars for secret, personal mantras such as: *Ahh! Eee! Ing! Om! Mmm! Ahm! Mmm! Go! Mmm!* and because you have completely forgotten God in your search for peace, what is happening today in the world is destruction. Even the seasons have changed. The rains have changed. The winds have changed. The snows have changed. Your harvests have changed and decreased, they have all decreased. You must think. Try to think about all of these things. Try to think of your scientific knowledge. You can study it all. But no matter what you study, you must know who it is that will give you peace.

All the animals live in peace. All the birds live in peace. All the geese migrate and live according to the seasons. They do this knowing the seasons. However, man does not know the seasons.

Man does not know his treasury. Man has not opened his dictionary and looked at it. Man does not understand who Man is. He has changed. As a result, although he is trying to make his mind peaceful, his appetite is not satisfied. That is not how to make the mind peaceful, is it? It is like trying to extinguish fire with fire. How can this be done? This is the work of a fool. Only a fool would try to extinguish fire with fire. How can fire be extinguished with fire? The flames will only burn higher.

This is what you are doing in trying to control the mind. The mind is maya, a monkey. If you use the mind to meditate on the mind, it will kill you. It will destroy you. Not only that, it will destroy the whole world.

Therefore, what you are doing is trying to build a shore for the ocean with more water. You are trying to build a shore with water from the lake when the ocean is rising up. When the ocean and the lake merge, the town will be destroyed. You cannot control water with water. You are trying to create peace in satan's section through satan.

You must worship in truth. You must meditate in truth. You have to make the mind peaceful by making God's qualities, God's actions, love, and compassion come into being within yourself. You need faith in Him. You need certitude in Him. You must place your determination in His Commandments. You have to learn the wisdom for that. That alone will stop it.

Ahh! Eee! Inngg! You meditate for forty-five minutes. This is not meditation. This is going to kill you. This is going to destroy the world. You are increasing the majority, recruiting others, one after the other, after the other, after the other.

Instead, believe in the words that Jesus ☺ spoke. Look inside those words. Look inside the words Moses ☺ spoke. Look inside the words Jacob ☺ spoke. Look inside the words Muhammad ☺

spoke. Look inside the words Abraham ☻ spoke. Look inside the words Job ☻ spoke.

How much suffering came to Job ☻ through satan. Was satan able to make him peaceful? It was God who made him peaceful. It was God who protected him. That is the certitude needed. Abraham ☻ was thrown into a pit of fire. Who else could have helped him?

The angel Michael ☻ and the angel Gabriel ☻ came to ask Abraham ☻, "What help can we give you?" The angel Raphael ☻ also came to ask him, "What help can I give you?" The angel Israel ☻ came to ask, "What help can I give you?"

"I am not looking for your help. I need only the help of the One who put me into the fire. I do not need your help." That is the certitude Abraham ☻ had. God spoke of it: "Have you not seen the certitude and the faith of My Abraham? How he asked only for My help and My strength?" That is what He said about all the *ambiyā'*.

However, you are looking for satan's help and maya's help. What is your concept of peace, what are you requesting? "I want to make love…to one, two, three or more lovers! I want to have sex! I want to make my body strong! If there is an illness, let us tell it to leave, because I want sex, I want to embrace someone and do this and that. I want to make love!"

Tū, tū, tū, tū! This is embarrassing. If you are a human being, you must use human wisdom. As a result, the time for the destruction of the world is here. At least from now on, increase your faith in God. To believe in God is meditation. To think of God is meditation. To place your intention upon God is meditation. To place your intention upon God and to establish Him in your heart is meditation. To know the way and then to learn wisdom is meditation.

If you do not act according to this point, it is a sign of destruction. Now each society is recruiting members for their businesses. Each society is recruiting members for business. "Meditation. You can have peace," they say.

Who actually gets peace? You can never have peace in that way. That is showing you destruction. That is not it. That which is known as the mind is maya—it has waves. They tell you to meditate for forty-five minutes or one hour, but if you can stay in that state of authentic peace for even one second, you will reach God. If you can just *be* for one second, you will reach God. If you can control the senses and control the mind for one second, you can reach God.

You will never get it otherwise. You will have peace only if faith in God, God's qualities, and the thought of God exist in your intentions. You will be destroyed if you perform this useless worship that satan performs, the worship that a monkey performs, the worship that a dog performs, the worship that a cat performs, the worship that a rat performs, the worship that an elephant performs, the worship that the animals perform.

Children, therefore, you must think a little. You must reflect. Prayer to God is good thoughts. Prayer to God is good conduct. Prayer to God is His qualities. Prayer to God is His actions. Prayer to God is to think of Him, our Father, and to know Him. Prayer to God is to obtain His beauty. Prayer to God is to see with His sight. Prayer to God is to obtain His wisdom. Our prayer is to understand explanations like these.

Therefore, children, jeweled lights of my eyes, the time of destruction is drawing near. Do not recruit others for the day of destruction. Do not recruit others for the sake of two hundred dollars or two hundred and fifty dollars. Do not look to this business. Destruction will come from it.

In this world, it is rare to find one out of ten million people who meditates on God. One is rare. You are increasing the majority. The majority for hell will increase. Barely one in ten million will come for truth. According to what the Bible says, according to what the Qur'ān says, according to what Jesus ☺ says, at the end of days, at the time of destruction, the people will accept satan and worship satan in the end. The people will change and become satan's children and perform satan's prayers and satan's worship, and long for hell, maya, iblīs, and delusion at the time of destruction, in the end.

That is what will bring famine, poverty, hardship, terrible, terrible diseases, new diseases, suffering, difficulty, battles, murder between husbands and wives, child murderers, alcohol, intoxicants, and animal qualities. Satan's qualities will come. As a result, they will accept satan. They will not accept human beings or the truth. The Bible, the Qur'ān, Jesus ☺, Abraham ☺, Moses ☺, and so many others have described this. That time has come.

Today, there are very few human beings. There are people, but they have changed. The animals have not changed. People have become animals. Their thoughts have changed into animals. Their worship has changed into animals. All of these actions have come into being like this. Therefore, this time is the time of destruction.

It has been foretold that the forces of the time of destruction will come into being through mantras, magic, demons, maya, and satan. The energies, the *shaktis* that will destroy the world will come about through them. Many difficulties will arise because of them. Destruction will come, cyclones will come, tsunamis will come, destructive winds will come, earthquakes will come, and fires will come. The harvests will decrease, eyesight will decrease, wisdom will decrease, the life spans of the people will decrease, and they will be subject to extreme suffering.

God has said, "O My servants, please escape from this. All who truly accept Me, please escape. Atom bombs, wars, weapons, poison, poisonous creatures, volcanoes, and other such destructive things will occur. O My servants, O you who accept Me and the words of My *ambiyā'*, do not get entangled in the net of satan. Do not pray to satan. Do not listen to the words of satan. Do not pray to satan. Do not recite satan's mantras. Do not keep satan in your hearts. You must live as God's children.

"There is very little time. The time is near. There will be very few human beings; human beings will be extremely rare. Those who accept Me will be very few. It will be rare to find one in ten million. In the time of destruction, I will protect those who accept Me. I will protect them. As for all the rest—whatever they nurture will destroy them. I will make them tremble through those very things. Each one of them will be destroyed by the destructive things he himself has sought. Hardship will come from these things." God has said this to the *ambiyā'*. He has explained this to them.

Therefore, jeweled lights of my eyes, those times are very close now. America has changed even in these last ten or fifteen years. Everyone does mantras, everyone does business, everyone says, "Om! Am! Go on! Gone! Om! Aheeeing! Omnmmm! Amnmmm! It is all *mmmmm*." It is all business. These are not even mantras, they have no meaning, they have no use, they have no explanation. Therefore, please think a little. Think and at least attain a good state from now on.

At least one out of ten million of you must try to escape. It is very difficult. At least one out of ten million children must learn wisdom, search for truth, and endeavor to worship God who is our Father. Then the storms that would otherwise have come will be lessened.

In America today, there are universities being created for mantras; there are universities being created for demon worship; there are universities being created for dog worship; there are universities being created for cat worship; there are universities being created for all kinds of destruction.

However, my precious children, at this time there are two hundred million people in America, and if even only twenty of you in America can come forward, the difficulties can be averted. You can avoid the destruction. The destruction can be stopped if at the very least twenty of you can endeavor to live as human beings. You must come forward to accept God. If you do, it will be good.

These words are my words as well. I have told you what the *ambiyā'* have said. They have also said those words. Whether you have heard them or not, it is our work, and I have told you accordingly. The destruction is very close. Each person is feeding the fire. They are feeding the fire of maya, the fire of satan, saying they are seeking peace. But they themselves are the firewood for hell. They are seeking peace in this state. How will it end? They will be burned. They will be destroyed.

Therefore, please think of this. If even only twenty people out of the two hundred million people in America would come forward to pray to God, it would be good. To do that is very rare, very difficult. But if you do reach a good state, it will be a mountain that faces the danger, a huge mountain. If even one child reaches it, it will be a great mountain standing against evil. Not a mount like Mount Sinai, but an enormous mountain. That mountain will block it. If twenty children could be like twenty mountains, the dangers that are approaching would be blocked.

Therefore, genuinely accept the section of God. Endeavor to go on the true path. We must try to escape from destruction.

Please try to enter this state. You cannot create peace when there is increasing famine. Gas prices have risen by a dollar; minor things now cost two dollars—eggs that were forty-five cents now cost a dollar, and soon they will cost two dollars. Everything you need to buy will increase ten times in price.

Then [the people who cannot afford to purchase food] are going to annihilate all the rich people. Why? Because *you* are going to reach peace! *"Ahh. Eee. Mmm."* You are wasting forty-five minutes. You say, *"Ah. Eeing.* We are creating peace. *Ooom. Aam. Om."* In the end, it will sound similar to the howling of foxes. *"Ooooooo."*

As a result, this is the time of destruction. Search for peace from God. Endeavor to understand who you are. Ask God. When He Himself gives you peace, when those qualities come to you, peace will come to you. Those intentions are peace. You do not need to spend forty-five minutes on it; it takes just a second. If you can have that intention for two minutes, it will be enough. Say, "My Father," close your eyes, and do this for two minutes.

If you think of Him in that way, it will be enough time. You can reach peace if you can think of Him for four minutes a day.

These gurus are just running a cash business. In a newspaper article that I saw, an Indian *swāmi* who came to America said, "In America, you have the money. The American people have a lot of money. We should have a few brains. If we put our brains into it a little, we can live very well. They will give us all their money." A *swāmi* said that. I also saw his book. This brother saw it too.

They caught that guru in India with six hundred thousand dollars. They also confiscated one hundred seventy-five thousand British pounds, and a number of traveler's checks. That is why he said, "The Americans have the money. If we have a few brains, the money can come to us. The Indians have to use their brains. If we use one drop of our brains, we will get their money."

What he said was very true. *(Bawangal laughs)*

If we look, we can see it. Here in America there is *yōgam, kāgam, pūgam,* and *āham*—yoga, crows, flowers, and rebirth—and when we look around we can see it. It does not exist in India. It will not spread there. Why? It will not spread there because they know it is false. But here in America, they call you fools. That is why that guru said, "If we use even a little portion of our brains—they have money. We just need a few brains, and if we use them a little, the money will come to us. Then we can easily lead our lives."

When we look around here, we can see it. What he said is correct. Therefore, try to think a little. Children, you must look for truth and prayer to God in order to prevent destruction. You must look for His path. That is the truth. That is the wisdom through which you must understand this. That is the intention you must have. That is what you must do. You are trying to move forward by holding on to a tiger's tail. When it gets hungry, it will eat you. What can be done then?

Therefore, children, please try a little. Look for truth. Do not continue to look at this world, look at yourselves. Try to correct yourselves. You have certain things—you have the dictionary. God's dictionary is within you, but you need wisdom in order to understand it. It is written in many languages. You must understand it through those languages and escape. At least a few children must escape. If you can escape, it will be very good.

Children, jeweled lights of my eyes, think about it. That is what will end the famine, not the other. That is what will end your poverty, not the other. Those things cannot create peace, they are trying to destroy peace. Their actions are going to create difficulties.

However, it is a good business. Many people are engaged in it. If you can collect five hundred students, you will get a teacher title.

Ayee. Ing. Mmm. If one of your pupils collects five hundred disciples of his own, he also gets a teacher title; if one of his disciples collects five hundred more disciples, he gets a teacher title as well, and this goes on and on. Each disciple has to pay two hundred and fifty dollars. That is how the guru gets seven hundred fifty thousand dollars and you get a teacher title. This is the way of the world. This is what some of the yogis and *yoga-rishis* do here. So please do not do any of this. Please search for the truth.

All right, try to do this, children, *anbu*. Please understand your wisdom, your ability, your faith, God's beauty, His qualities, and the inner meanings of what the *ambiyā'* have said. Please try to understand, and look deep into yourselves, just a little. Try to understand. That will be very good. Then we can escape.

Anbu, vanakkam—my love, my prayers.

[Bawangal's instructions for this talk and the next one were, "Send them everywhere in the world, to all the societies, to everyone. Print thousands and thousands and thousands and thousands of copies and send them everywhere."]

CHAPTER 13

A'ūdhu billāhi minash-shaitānir-rajīm.
I seek refuge in God from the accursed satan.

Bismillāhir-Rahmānir-Rahīm.
In the name of God, the Most Compassionate, the Most Merciful.

TWO WORDS

Saturday, October 11, 1975, 4:15 A.M.
Philadelphia, USA

Children, jeweled lights of my eyes, there is something we should reflect upon regarding this world. Children, jeweled lights of my eyes, this world is huge and extensive—it is the mind that is the world in the life of every human being. This mind is the world. This mind exists as an enormous world, and this body is a secret. It is difficult for a human being to overcome and to transcend this secret body and this secret mind. Thus, you, we, and everyone must reflect. This mind and this secret body are always subject to accidents. Anything we see can cause an accident. There can be an accident anywhere we go. An accident can arise anywhere the eye looks and the body turns. It can come from any direction.

The mind is a thing that flies around in the skies, and wanders there. The mind has many millions of qualities. The mind has many millions of shadows. The mind has many millions of shapes. The mind has many millions of colors. The mind has many millions of kinds of darkness. The mind is filled with many millions of vapors and winds. The mind contains many millions of diseases. The mind contains many, many millions of qualities, conditions, and tricks. The mind has many millions of monkey shapes.

The mind has 1,008 kinds of snake-like qualities. The mind has the qualities of demons. The mind has the qualities of maya. The mind has the qualities of ghosts. The mind has the qualities of *malā'ikah*, angels. The mind has the quality of darkness. The mind has the quality of birds, the quality of flying around. The mind has the quality of shadows.

The mind is connected to the ether. The mind has a connection that causes it to fly and wander throughout the ether. The mind has a connection to many millions of rebirths. The mind has a connection to earth. The mind has a connection to air. The mind has a connection to fire. The mind has a connection to water. The mind is connected to so many rebirths. The mind has millions of dog-like connections. The mind is connected to desire. The mind is connected to cravings. Similarly, the mind has countless connections to blood ties. The mind is connected to the sex act. The mind is connected to delusion. The mind is connected to turmoil. The mind is connected to differences. The mind is connected to arrogance. The mind is connected to ignorance. The mind is connected to karma. The mind is connected to maya. The mind is connected to impurity. The mind has so many connections like this.

When the mind, the embryo, and these connections take form, the qualities of the mother and father, the qualities of the earth, the qualities of the thoughts of the mother and father, the qualities of their blood connections, the connections of their arrogance, the connections of water, fire, and food, and many other such connections become karmic connections.

The connections that are transmitted from both the mother

and the father to the fetus are many. The grievous sins do not touch the original zygote, but the tens of millions of types of karma that join together in the blood, the bodily fluids, and the flesh—these qualities, the connections of the mind that come from both parents that are happiness, sorrow, sadness, turmoil, torpor, darkness, fighting, and quarreling—are many. These connections are embryonic connections, and belong to the mind. The mind takes form in the embryo. The connections of the mind exist in this state, and through them, the mind attains countless states. Many propensities exist within the mind.

Even as it was formed, correct actions and incorrect actions, right and wrong, hell and heaven, truth and falsehood, darkness and light, good and evil, purity and impurity, love and unhappiness, love and anger, happiness and unhappiness, all these qualities filled the mind.

This mind that contains all these energies is a baby. It is a baby mind, a monkey mind, a dark mind, an ether mind, an elemental mind. Since it is filled with these things, it has many *shaktis*. No one can make it peaceful. Therefore, we must think a little of how we can stop something that no one can make peaceful.

The world possesses such a mind and attempts to search for peace. But this can never be done.

A baby takes form for ten lunar months. For three days, he is imprisoned in the entrance to the womb. Afterwards, for nine months, he is imprisoned in that dark room while he takes form. After the ninth month passes, he emerges from there in the tenth month, into freedom. As soon as he becomes free and comes to the outside, his parents and his relatives carry him, wash him, clean him, and keep him in the jail of their laps. They hold him in their laps without letting him go here or there. Later, he is imprisoned in the cradle and in the laps of his caretakers. After that, for one or two years he is in the jail of his crib, the hands of his caretakers, and the prison of his nurse.

After he leaves that, he enters school jail. He has to study in each grade and with each step the imprisonment increases. When he leaves that and goes beyond, he enters the jail of higher education. When he leaves that jail, he enters job jail. After that, there is marriage jail. After that, there is wife jail. After that, there is children jail. After that, there is old age jail. After that, there is illness jail. After that, there is the jail of diseases. There are many jails of good, evil, unhappiness, and money that will come into being. In the meantime, his entire life is a jail. After that comes the jail of his death. After death, no one knows whether he will attain the jail of good deeds or evil deeds. He continuously exists in the jail mind that is life, in the unhappiness and the sorrow of this state. He lives in jail continuously. Not for one day, not for one second does he escape from this jail and attain freedom from it. He is in a perpetual state of fear in this jail. For the sake of the body, for the sake of money, he holds on to the very things that can cause accidents.

For the sake of the body, for the sex act, for money, and for happiness, we try to meditate. But we do this without ever escaping from our jails. It is not possible for someone in such jails to attain peace, is it? We must think about this.

Man's ordinary life is a jail. He has been in jail since the time he emerged from the darkness until now. Some attempt to be happy in those jails. Some attempt to find happiness in money. This is how they attempt to reach peace. Some get married and attempt to find peace. Some take drugs and attempt to find peace. Some drink whiskey, beer, and brandy and attempt to find peace, trying to make their minds peaceful. Some meditate and attempt to find peace. Some do yoga and attempt to find peace. Some study all kinds of *gnānam,* saying, "*Namo, namo,*" this and that; they recite mantras, do *pūjas,* and attempt to find peace. Some spend money and do many things like this in their attempt to find peace.

However, we must think: What will peace come from? What is the thing through which peace can come? Man must find a way to escape from jail. That alone is how he can find peace in his life.

The world has now discovered new ways to find peace of mind. The world has discovered many new kinds of meditations, performed in many ways through money and business since the end of World War II. The world has told us that this kind of meditation is the way to discover peace of mind. The world has discovered how to do this in many ways, with many kinds of meditations: a new way.

Having forgotten the states of God's Commandments, conscience, justice, integrity, patience, serenity, kindness, and duty, humankind has now begun to discover new kinds of meditation, new kinds of peace.

However, they are talking about peace from inside the jail.

Peace can never be attained in this way, children. If you want to reach peace, you must think a little. If you want peace, you must leave the prison and be free. You must think of this a little: if you want peace, what is it that will create peace for you? What is peace? One who is going to make the mind peaceful must be free and out of jail. His whole life is filled with accidents and jail: his eyesight, his thoughts, the sounds he makes, his ears, and so forth, are the things that imprison him, the jails that control him. Religion-jail, ethnic group-jail, family-jail, blood tie-jail, money-jail, desire-jail, love-jail, the jail of the body that is his cage, and all such things are jails. Only when he is freed from these jails, can he obtain peace, peace of mind.

The mind is made up of such things. When a person who has all these things locks his house, bolts the door, climbs a tree, lifts his legs above his head, closes his eyes, sits cross-legged, holds his breath, closes his mouth, and closes his eyes, it does not matter how many exercises he completes; no matter what he does, he will still be a prisoner. It is very difficult for a prisoner in jail to find peace. Therefore, you must think a little.

How will the world reach peace? If you think and reflect a little, there are extremely simple ways to attain peace. We must think of what they are. We must free ourselves of whatever we have used to construct this prison.

That is, there could be Someone who has created you. Something has been nurturing you. There is One Truth. We must understand through this Truth. If we understand through this Truth, we can be free and leave the jail, leave those connections. Only then will there be peace. It is easy.

Man saw it once and now he desires to see it again. What did he see in the beginning? He saw it once and now he desires to see it again. What did he see as he was coming here? What does he want to see again? We must think a little. We must deeply think about this mind, these eyes, this desire, this nose, these ears. We must think more deeply about the passageway through which he came in the beginning, and what he wants to see again. Thinking about this may bring peace to the mind.

He saw it once and now he desires to see it again. What did he see before? What is he going to see now? If we think a little of the passageway through which he came before, the place through which he was born, the place in which he was imprisoned, the prison cell of the dark room, and how he came out, we might understand a little more about this jail.

If we understand this, we will see peace. Why did he enter that passageway? From what did he take form, from which sections did he take form? Earth, fire, water, air, and ether—how did they get inside? What connection does he have to arrogance, karma, and maya? What happened to those eight sections? They were used to build the prison. The mind is the cause of it. This is what we must think about a little.

The thing that went inside was imprisoned for ten months and then it emerged, did it not? What is it that was in prison for all that time? That is what goes back inside. Why does the mind go back into it? What is the reason for its going back? He must think of this a little with wisdom—with perception, awareness, intellect, assessment, wisdom, and discerning wisdom. He must try to untangle it and look at it a little with discerning wisdom.

If he does untangle this and see it, he will see the path that creates peace. He will see a path, a way. He will see the way to create peace. When he sees the way, he will say, "Oh, this is that path. How is peace going to come? Through this path." He will say that when he finds the path to peace. What will peace be like? One who has seen it will say, "Oh, this is the path of peace. This is the path to peace." That is what he will say, as his understanding develops. When he understands like this, he will begin to ask, "What is it that will bring peace to this mind which performs so many millions of kinds of actions?"

What does he need to make the mind peaceful? Two words. He does not have to do this all day. He must think of it, know it, and understand it. The way to accomplish this is by understanding what he has to place in front of this baby, this monkey who has everything and who plays with everything. What must you place in front of him? What must you show to him? You must give this baby a new thing, an entirely new thing. You must give the baby something he has never seen before.

The baby picks up everything he sees and plays with it; he asks for everything he sees in the market. It must be given to him so he can have it and play with it. When he sees another thing, he will ask for that. When he sees something else, he will ask for that. He will ask for whatever he sees in the market. If you bring the baby with you to the market, when he sees something, he will always ask for it.

You carry this baby all the time, you continually carry this monkey in your arms, you hold on to the dog constantly as you proceed. The monkey is one thing, the baby is one thing, and the dog is one thing. You are carrying those three things with you everywhere to help you.

These three things will come with us wherever we go. Therefore, one of these three things is a baby. The dog known as desire will always want things that smell disgusting: dried fish, anything that stinks, and feces. It will keep sniffing out these things and drag you along with it. It will keep on dragging you; it is a big dog, an Alsatian dog. That dog will make a *"wooo"* sound. *"Wooo!"* It will drag you towards those sections because it is stronger than you. So then, you will follow behind it.

Next is the baby. He cries for everything he sees in the market, "*Ah!* Give me this, give me that, give me this, give me that, buy me this, buy me that!" As soon as you buy him something, he will play with it for a while, but the moment he sees another thing, he will ask for it. When he sees another thing, he will ask for that. When he sees another thing, he will ask for that. Thus, the pile of toys will have to grow. He has no peace whatsoever. That baby cries all the time.

While he cries, there is also the monkey, the monkey mind. The baby is with you and the monkey that is actually seventy thousand monkeys is also with you. When it sees a tree it jumps, when it sees a fruit it jumps, when it sees a leaf it jumps, when it sees a branch it jumps. It jumps when it sees trees, jungles, and any other scenes. It jumps at everything it sees like this. It takes various and gigantic forms, it jumps, and it hops. Since it is like this, it will be easy to talk about peace if you carry these three with you, hoping to reach peace.

However, you will only be talking.

When you close the door and chant, *Ah-ing! Oh-ing! Om! Am!* or whatever else you might say, the baby, the monkey, and the dog will not leave you. Whether you close the door and say it, whether you close your eyes and say it, whether you stand on your head and say it, whether you keep your feet above your head and say it, whether you twist your entire body and say it, whether you say it from inside a cave, or whether you say it while you remain hidden in the darkness, those three will dwell in all these places. This is where the monkey will jump, the child will cry, and the dog will tug on you.

Therefore, children, jeweled lights within my eyes, you must think in this world. If you keep these three things with you, how are you going to meditate? *Ay-ing, ah-ing!* is simply useless work. It is business-work. It is a new meditation technique. You have found a new form of peace. Since 1944 you have found many, many new worship techniques, new meditation techniques, new peace techniques—but this is not peace.

Understand these three sections. The dog that says, "I want this! I want that!" must be put aside, hit, and tied up. Get a rope and tie it next to the kitchen. Get a good stake, a strong chain, give it a good blow, and tie up the dog. You should not walk with it. You must simply give it what it needs at the proper time.

The child will cry all the time. The monkey must be caught and tied to a tree, tied to the tree known as faith. A human being must tie the dog next to the kitchen, next to what is necessary for it. It must be tied, over to one side. It is a dog of desire.

Patience. The dog must be made subordinate to patience. You must say, "Wait a little. I will give it to you," and tie it next to, "I want this, I want that." Tie it facing what it wants.

Catch the monkey. It must be tied to the tree known as faith. You need faith. Tie it to that.

Next, catch the baby, and buy him a good thing. You must buy a good thing for the baby you hold in your arms. That is what you must find. There is no market in the world he has not seen. There is no market the mind has not seen. There is nothing the mind has not seen. It has looked at everything, wanted everything, played with everything, taken hold of everything, thrown down everything, picking it up, throwing it down, crying, picking it up, throwing it down, crying, laughing, crying, and picking it up.

Thus, this child known as the mind that has a relationship to ether and to the earth, this child that is connected to them, flies in the sky and wanders all over the earth, playing there. Therefore, you must give it a thing it has not seen. If you want peace, you must look for that thing.

The thing the mind has not seen is truth. The thing the mind has not seen is wisdom. The thing the mind has not seen is God. The thing the mind has not seen is light. The thing the mind has not seen is bliss, light, plenitude. The thing the mind has not seen is the wealth of bliss. That wealth is very beautiful. It is very light. It is very powerful. It is very blissful. It simply cannot be described.

This is the thing that desire, mind, and the monkey mind—these three—have not seen. You must think of this thing. Think. If you want peace, if you want peace of mind, if you want to be freed from the jail, if you want to get away from the dog of desire, if you want to drive away the monkey mind, if you want to attain peace, peace of mind, and serenity, there is an easy way.

You have to lock the state of compassionate love into your heart. You have to lock the seat of God's justice into your heart. You have to lock the qualities of God into your heart. You have to lock the actions of God into your heart and think about them. You have to think God's thoughts in your heart. Those thoughts will give you peace. Those intentions will give you peace. Those sights will give you peace. That state is a valuable palace that can grant you peace of mind. It is a valuable treasure. It is a peaceful treasure. It can grant you peace and tranquility.

In this world, in the world of visions, in the world of memories, in the world of dreams, in the world of wisdom, in the world of the soul, in the world of *gnānam,* in the world of God, our Father, in that world of plenitude, in the world of sheer Light, it will give you peace. It will grant you peace in all these worlds.

However, instead of doing that, you have wasted years upon years, spending forty-five minutes, an hour, four hours, five hours every day discovering new techniques, saying, "We are going to attain peace." Give up these techniques if you want peace, and control your mind for ten minutes, for twenty minutes, or even five minutes. Think about this. Think about this. Do this. Focus. Do this with faith, certitude, and determination, with the determination of *īmān,* and with wisdom.

Having thought about this with your wisdom, say these two words in your heart, as you look at your heart. Sit, and think this thought for ten minutes: "Nothing, *lā ilāha,* there is nothing other than You; *illAllāh,* only You are God. Nothing—there is no God other than You. *IllAllāh,* only You are God. Only You are God. There is no God other than You. You alone are God. There is nothing other than You."

Say this in your heart. Sit in one place just for a little while, for twenty minutes or ten minutes, for twenty minutes or at least five minutes. It is all right to say it while standing, but do not say it while walking, stay in one place. Look at that heart and melt it. Say it morning and night or at the very least for five minutes before you eat. Stop, look at your heart and melt it, look at your chest; the more you do it, the more you will see bliss there.

You will see light there. You will see a heavenly world there. You will see a great palace there. You will see a great blissful house there. You will see a great light there. You will see many *houris*, many heavenly maidens there. You will see a great flower garden there. You will see a great fruit orchard there.

You will see a great river there. You will see a great river of milk there. You will see a great river of honey there. You will see a great river of ambrosia. You will see those who have imbibed His bliss intoxicated there. You will see great and blissful seven-storied palaces. You will see mountains upon mountains of gold and silver, and golden ornaments piled high. You will see the eight-storied palace of the heavenly world. You will see the house in which you are going to live. You will be able to see the bliss that you have gathered.

You will see heavenly *houris* coming to invite you. You will see heavenly maidens. You will see messengers coming to invite you. You will see *malā'ikah* coming to invite you. You will see the section where Judgment takes place. You will see the beginning of creation. You will see its disappearance. You will see many living beings there.

You will experience so much bliss. It will become greater and greater as you continue to say it. Increasing and increasing and increasing and increasing and increasing and increasing! You will see the things that fly there. You will see the things that go there.

You will go there and see that light. You will enter it and see what is within it. You will see how to open the seven heavens and go further. You will see how to transcend the seven worlds. You will see how to transcend maya and all its pleasures and go within. Wonder upon wonder will appear as you continue to go within. You will see wonder upon wonder in your heart.

You will experience blissful sweet honey that touches your lips without your having to eat it. You will experience the taste that comes to your mouth, of fruit that you do not have to pick. You will see fruit that smiles as it comes towards you, and squeezes its juice into your mouth without your having to touch it. Any food you might want will come to your lips before you can even think about it.

You will see them serving you before you can think of it. You will be lifted and carried wherever you need to go before you can think of it. You will be there and see *'ālamul-arwāh*, the world of pure souls, and all of everything.

You will see the eight heavens there; you will see the seven hells; you will see all the wonders that are occurring there. You will perceive the sounds and the secrets of God. You will hear the bliss of God. You will hear the resonances of God. You will see the lights there. You can see the wonders there.

Similarly, as you witness that bliss and as the Source of these words becomes established in your heart, that house will be opened like this. As soon as that house is opened, the mind will reach peace in the bliss you experience there.

When the baby that is the mind sees that bliss, when he watches and watches the bliss, when he sees it, he will say, "*Ah, ah, ah,* what bliss! What bliss! What bliss! What bliss or peace is greater than this?" Then the baby will immediately fall asleep. The mind will immediately become still and fall asleep. The mind will want to experience this bliss every day. Every day the mind will look at it and say, "*Ah, ah, ah, ah,* that is good, that is good, that is good."

From then on, you will go on increasing and increasing and increasing and increasing and increasing and increasing the time—ten minutes, twenty minutes, twenty-five minutes, thirty minutes, thirty-five minutes, forty minutes; as you experience bliss upon bliss, you will continue to say these words. As you continue to think and think this thought and to say these words, this is what will bring you peace.

This will take you to the end of the path. You will be shown the secrets of the three worlds. You will be shown bliss and it will make you understand. This state is bliss. If you attain this state, it will bring peace to the mind. Children, jeweled lights of my eyes, establish this state. This is meditation. This is the way to make the mind peaceful, this is the way to make the mind tranquil, this is the way to make the mind happy.

This way existed in the past and it exists now. However, we have forsaken it. You have subjected yourself to new techniques. That path appeared when Adam ☪ appeared, and it has continued to be the same until today. But man has forsaken that path. As he has discovered more and more world, he has let go of truth. He has forsaken truth, that is the situation. He has forsaken it and made himself vulnerable to distress.

This is the way now, as it was then. If he once again holds on to that which he has forsaken, he will have peace of mind and tranquility. This will give him everything.

It will bring him wealth. It will bring him money. It will cure the 4,448 diseases of the nerves. It will remove the eighty-four kinds of diseases caused by air. It will cure the diseases of karma. It will cure the diseases of maya. It will cure the diseases of arrogance. It will cure the twenty-one diseases of the eyes caused by cataracts. It will improve the vision of the eyes and make the eyes brighter. It will cure the eighteen kinds of sinus diseases. It will cure the eighteen types of rectal diseases, bleeding hemorrhoids, prolapsed hemorrhoids, and all the diseases associated with the rectum. It will cure all the urinary diseases, including sugar in the urine. It will cure headaches, dizziness, and depression. It will cure the ninety-six obsessions. It will cure oozing diseases of the skin; it will cure eczema. It will cure diseases of the flesh. It will cure diseases of the bodily fluids. It will cure diseases of the bone marrow. It will cure all diseases like this. It will cure the diseases of the nerves, the diseases of the bones, the genetic diseases, the karmic diseases, exhaustion, fatigue, asthma, bronchitis, tuberculosis, and cancer. It will cure all the diseases like this.

It will cure diseases and make man's life long. It will make him look sixteen years old again. It will make him beautiful. It will bring beauty to his face. It will create blood within the bones. It will change his blood into the blood of a young child. His eyes will become like the eyes of a young child. His skin will become like the skin of a young child. His bones will be like the bones of a young child, so flexible.

It will create in him the beautiful qualities of a young child. It will reveal the blood attachments that a young child has. It will reveal cells like those of a young child. It will reveal the bliss that young children have. When you continue to perform this meditation in this way, this state will reveal fresh qualities, fresh beauty, fresh light, fresh color, qualities, and beauty.

Therefore, you will receive everything you want like this, whatever you need. You will get cash, you will get money, and you will get peace. This is something that is capable of giving in every situation. It will remove diseases, illnesses, poverty, difficulties, dangers, and accidents. It will remove all these things. This is the state, the primal state, the everlasting state. We human beings have forsaken this. Therefore, if it is brought into being once again, there will be peace. That is peace.

Therefore, say it for five minutes, ten minutes, twenty minutes: "*Lā ilāha,* other than You there is no God. *IllAllāhu,* You are Allāh."

If you think of this in your heart with faith, certitude, and determination, whether you close your eyes or whether you open your eyes, if you look at your heart when you do this, you can achieve whatever you intend and find peace within it. When the peace comes, the mind will fall asleep at once. The more it sees, the longer it will sleep.

As you look into your heart like that, heaven, the heavenly world, and the angels, the *malā'ikah,* will be there in your thoughts. Whatever you intend will be there, everything you look at with that faith will be there, so many things. As you continue and continue, they will open and be visible. The mind will fall instantly asleep. Desire will be instantly disabled. As soon as the monkey sees the light, it will feel exhausted. The monkey will be exhausted. Desire will be mesmerized. The mind will forget itself. The mind will find bliss in the light.

This state is meditation. Do you want peace? Then say this. This is the way to peace of mind. Tranquility? This is tranquility. The heavenly world? This is the heavenly world. Life? This is life. Bliss? This is bliss. Freedom? This is freedom. If you want these things, you must do this, children.

You need this very much. Of all the things that you do in the world—do this. Every child must do this. This is peace. God said this then, and even now, this is what God says. This is good in every way. We are suffering because we have forsaken it. Do not forsake it. Say it, at least from now on, and peace will come from it. *Āmīn. Āmīn. Āmīn.*

Take what I said yesterday and today, put it into a book, and give it to everyone in the world. If you want peace, come, do this.

Part Three
DESTRUCTION

CHAPTER 14

A'ūdhu billāhi minash-shaitānir-rajīm.
I seek refuge in God from the accursed satan.
Bismillāhir-Rahmānir-Rahīm.
In the name of God, the Most Compassionate, the Most Merciful.

WHATEVER COMES

*Monday, June 25, 1979, 9:00 A.M.
Philadelphia, USA*

Whatever goes, let it go.
Whatever comes, let it come.
May everything happen as God wills.
Whatever goes, let it go.
Whatever comes, let it come.
It is God's will, there is nothing other than His *tawakkul*, nothing other than trust in Allāh.

Whatever goes, let it go.
Whatever comes, let it come.
Whatever goes, let it go.
Whatever comes, let it come.
May everything always happen as God wills.

Whatever goes, let it go.
Whatever comes, let it come.

May everything always happen as God wills.
Whatever goes, let it go.
Whatever comes, let it come.
May everything always happen as God wills.

Let man regard everything he sees as a miracle.
Let the Letters of Truth [in the Qur'ān]
be destroyed in the *dunyā*.
Let man regard everything he sees as a miracle.
Let the Letters of Truth be destroyed in the *dunyā*
and be forgotten by him.
Whatever goes, let it go.
Whatever comes, let it come.
May everything always happen as God wills.

He is within Himself,
in the Grace within the grace,
in the Meaning within the meaning,
in the *Qalb* within the *qalb*—
let Him be clearly evident there.

May the divine grace of the Creator always overflow,
be clearly evident in the *qalb*, and create bliss there.
As the Love within the love,
as the Grace within the grace,
as the Meaning within the meaning,
as the Wisdom within the wisdom—
may Allāh be clearly evident.

Whatever goes, let it go.
Whatever comes, let it come.

Whatever goes, let it go.
Whatever comes, let it come.
May it all be His doing, may it all take place in His grace.

As the Light within the eye,
as the Beauty within the *qalb*,
as the Resonance within wisdom—
may He exist within my intention and be clearly evident there.
Whatever goes, let it go.
Whatever comes, let it come.
May everything happen as God wills.

The *rahmah* of His *qudrah*,
the compassionate grace of His power,
exists in this world wherever He exists.
Existing as He exists within Himself,
as the Grace within the grace,
as the Resonance within the *qalb*,
as all the things we see that are contained within Him,
as the Love that is the Master
of all embryos and forms—
may that protective One God exist there.

Whatever goes, let it go.
Whatever comes, let it come.
Let it all happen through His action.
So what if something comes?
So what if something goes?
So what if something comes?
So what if something goes?
What sadness does that create for me here?

The One who created me,
the One who rules within me,
the One who dwells within my *qalb*, is
the One who knows my intention.
In the presence of my Creator,
in the presence of my Creator,
why is my *qalb* afraid?
Why is my *qalb* afraid?
Why is my intention intimidated?
Why is my body suffering?
Whatever goes, let it go.
Whatever comes, let it come.
May everything happen as God wills.

Allāh is One.
He belongs to everyone.
Allāh is One.
He belongs to everyone.
His grace will always exist in the open space of the soul.
The One clearly evident in all *qalbs*—
He is the One who gives what is fair
to all who are good and to all who are horrible.
He is the One who gives
the Judgment and the Questions perfectly.
He is the One who knows the *qalb*.
He is the Creator who understands.
He is the One
who rules in this *dunyā* and in *ākhirah* from there.
When He rules us from there,
when He rules us from there,
what fear can we have?

What fear?
Whatever goes, let it go.
Whatever comes, let it come.
May everything happen as God wills.

Know this, O *qalb*.
Say what has to be said without forgetting your Creator.
Listen to what has to be heard.
Everything will happen as your Creator wills.
In the presence of the Creator
who has compassion for and who protects
all embryos and all forms,
why are you afraid?
Why are you afraid, O mind, O *qalb*?
Just open your heart and look at God.

Whatever goes, let it go.
Whatever comes, let it come.
May everything happen as God wills.
He exists in the embryo.
He is intermingled in form.
In birth, there is His help.
In death, there is His mercy.
In death and in life,
in *maut* and *hayāh*,
He is the only King.
He is the One who has relinquished selfishness.
He is the Almighty One who rules alone.

He is the Beloved of all living beings.
He is the Master

who shows compassion to all living beings.
He alone has created them.
He alone will protect them.
He alone will judge them.
He alone will forever rule over them.
He alone will rule, dwelling in all universes.
Therefore, why are you afraid, O my mind?

Do not be mesmerized by anything.
Listen to God.
Serve Him.
Do His duty.
Stand before Him and bow to Him.
When you live in His *tawakkul*,
trusting Him day and night,
why are you afraid, O mind?
What mistake can you make?
Why are you afraid, O mind,
What mistake can you make?
What suffering can come to you?
What suffering can come?

Realize this and act accordingly.
Open your heart and go on the path.
Realize this and act accordingly.
Open your heart and go on the path.
Join together in worthy *'ibādah* and worship.
Then you will live forever in this land and in heaven.
Whatever goes, let it go.
Whatever comes, let it come.
May everything everywhere happen as God wills.

He is the Jeweled Light within my eyes,
the One who knows my intention.
He is the Jeweled Light within my eyes,
the One who knows my intention.
He is the One who opens the *qalb* and looks inside,
the Great One who is our Creator.
He is the Creator.
He is the Protector.
He is the One who will give us sustenance.
He is the One who will take us to the shore.
He is the One who knows the three times.
He is the One who lives in all times.
He is known as the Solitary One and
the One who exists forever.
He is the Almighty One who rules alone.
He is the Almighty One who rules alone.
In His presence, why, O mind, do you suffer?

Whatever comes, do not be mesmerized.
Do not be intimidated by anything.
Whatever comes, do not be mesmerized, O mind.
Do not be intimidated by anything, O mind.
Believe in Allāh, the One.
Always praise the Truth that is His grace,
the Truth that is His grace.
Unite with good people.
Endeavor to do only good in that land.
In that land, O mind, endeavor to do only good.
Whatever comes, let it come.
Whatever goes, let it go.
May everything happen as God wills.

Oy, mind, always live with faith.
Always live with faith in God.
Put good words in my mouth and say them always.
Tie up the world with love and rule it.
Tie up the world with love and rule it.
Then, through your wisdom,
you will receive the blissful house of the heart's grace,
the blissful house of Allāh's grace.

You too must try to never let go of it.
Try to never let go of it.
Join with the grace that will always be your companion.
O mind, join with the grace that will always be your companion,
the grace that will always be your companion.
Any suffering that might come will fly away.
Any suffering that might come will fly away, fly away.
Oy, mind. *Oy,* mind.
Whatever comes, let it come.
Whatever goes, let it go.
May everything happen through God's grace.

There is Something that shines as gold above the five.
There is Something that shines as gold above the five.
It will shine as Light within your wisdom.
It will live as the Wealthy One within *īmān*.
It will see the absolute completion within your heart.
It will see the absolute completion within your heart.
Therefore, what will you ever lack, O mind?
In the presence of Allāh,
why are you afraid?
In the presence of Allāh,

why are you afraid in this life?
Why are you afraid in this life?
Oy, mind.
Whatever comes, let it come.
Whatever goes, let it go.
May everything happen
through the grace of God, the only One.
May everything happen
through the grace of God, the only One.

There is a treasure that is clearly evident as one among the six.
There is a treasure that is clearly evident as one among the six.
It is the wisdom that stands in the open space
of your heart as the Qutb.
It is a treasure of *gnānam* that brings peace.
It is a treasure of *gnānam* that brings peace.
It is the grace that shows us serenity.
It is the grace that shows us serenity.
It is the great grace that shows us serenity.

Believe in this in your thoughts and in your dreams.
Believe in this in your thoughts and in your dreams.
Make this *niyyah,* this intention, in your life.
Make it your *niyyah,* and live forever.
Make it your *niyyah,* and live forever.
See it before your eyes.
Say it, so you understand it in your intention.
Say it, so you understand it in your intention.
Say it, so you understand it in your intention.
See it, as the light within your eyes.
See it, as the light within your eyes.

Its source will appear to you everywhere.
Its source will appear to you everywhere.
You will see limitless grace.
The understanding of who lives in your heart will appear.
The understanding of who lives in your heart will appear.
See it, as Love within love.
The beauty of the Blissful Form
that is the Bestower of that Grace will appear.
The beauty of the Blissful Form
that is the Bestower of that Grace will appear.

Whatever comes, O mind, let it come.
Whatever comes, let it come.
Whatever goes, let it go.
May everything happen as God wills.
May everything happen through His divine will.
Why are you afraid, O mind?
Why are you afraid?

See with the two times six.
Recite the *illAllāhu* that ascends and descends there.
See with the two times six.
Raise and lower the two.
Push the *lā* that was in the back to the forefront.
Push the *lā* that was in the back to the forefront.
Lower the eternal *illAllāhu* and take it in.
Lower the eternal *illAllāhu* and take it in.
Then the uncontrollable fire of hunger will be quenched.
Then the uncontrollable fire of hunger will be quenched.
Then all the karma
of the universes will be overcome and burned.

Then all the karma
of the universes will be overcome and destroyed.
The "I" will be driven out.
The One who is our Master will come,
He will be resplendent and the grace will explain.
The One who is our Master will come, He will be resplendent,
the grace will explain, and the Nūr will resonate.
The Nūr will resonate and
then you will understand that subtlety.
Then you will understand that subtlety.
O mind, you will understand.
You will understand, O mind, you will understand.

Therefore,
whatever comes, let it come.
Whatever comes, let it come.
Whatever goes, let it go.
Let everything happen through God's grace.
Why are you afraid, O mind, why are you afraid?
Melt the heart and look within.
Endeavor to filter again and again
all the meditation you do.
Look intensely into your heart,
and afterwards, look again and again
at the meditation you do.
Then keep what is valuable in it.
Filter and filter it.
Filter and filter it.
Endeavor to separate the profit and the loss.
Take all that is good.
Take all that is good.

Leave this land, go beyond, and join with the Good Treasure.
Leave this land, go beyond, and join with the Good Treasure.
Discard and throw away everything that is not valuable.
Discard and throw away everything that is not valuable—
those will be the things you leave behind.

Lā ilāha will describe the things you left behind.
IllAllāhu is the treasure that exists before you,
it is the treasure that exists before you.
It is the treasure formed by the One Who Has Lost Himself,
the grace that explains one thing to the entire world.
It is the Meaning that is clearly evident in all living beings.
It is the Grace that shows compassion to and
blesses all living beings.
It is the Meaning that is clearly evident
in the weeds and the grasses.
That Treasure is the God of Grace.

Allāhu, who clearly exists as that Wonder and who reveals it,
Allāhu is the Treasure that is clearly evident
as the Mysterious Grace.
O mind, you will understand that Treasure.
O mind, you will understand that Treasure.
O mind, you will understand.

Whatever comes, let it come.
Whatever goes, let it go.
May everything happen as God wills.
May everything happen through His grace.
May He be the Abundance in all things.
May He be the Abundance in all things.

He is the Master who knows good and evil.
He is the Master who knows good and evil.

He is the Master
for our country, for the container that is the body,
for our country, for this container that is the body, and
for our search.
He is the Original One who feeds and protects us.
He is the Father who gave us life in the beginning, in *ādi*.

He exists as the meaning of Mother and Father,
the One Resonance known as Allāhu.
That Explanation must always resonate in our hearts.
That Explanation must always be clearly evident in our hearts.

The meaning of that Explanation
will not be understood through words.
Merge with the meaning and
say it continuously with a melting *qalb*,
say the meaning that is intermingled with the Meaning.
That wisdom will carefully grant the grace.
See it, know it, be clear about it,
understand it, and recite that clear meaning.
See it, be clear about it, recite it, and
understand the meaning.
O mind, O my mind.
O my mind, O my mind,
whatever comes, let it come.
Whatever goes, let it go.
May everything happen through God's will and His grace.

It is His treasure alone.
It is His doing only.
It is not our doing, O mind.
It is His doing only.
It is not our doing, O mind.

Believe this, believe this, always believe this.
Believe that there is nothing other than your Master.
Believe that there is nothing other than your Master.
Other than our Beloved Lord,
there is nothing in our container or anywhere else.
There is nothing other than your Master.

Believe in that Grace.
Believe in that Rare Treasure.
Believe in that Grace.
Believe in that Rare Treasure.

Believe in Him.
Believe in that Original Supreme Being.
Believe in that Supreme Being.
Believe in that One.
Believe in that One.

He is the Mother and Father
who exist as Life intermingled with life.
He is your Father.
He is the One who bestows the Judgment.
He is the One who grants the everlasting state.
He is the One who bestows the Judgment.
He is the One who grants the everlasting state.

He is the One who bestows life.
He is the One who stands to the right and to the left of us.
He is the One intermingled in our life.
He is our Only Relationship.
What other God is there?
He is our Only Relationship.
He is our Only Relationship.
What other God is there?

O mind, believe in Him.
Believe in Him.
Whatever comes, let it come.
Whatever goes, let it go.
May everything happen through His grace.
May everything happen through His grace.
Believe only in God, O mind.
Believe only in God, O mind.
Always believe only in God, O mind.
Āmīn.

A'ūdhu billāhi minash-shaitānir-rajīm.
I seek refuge in God from the accursed satan.
Bismillāhir-Rahmānir-Rahīm.
In the name of God, the Most Compassionate, the Most Merciful.

KALI YUGA

Monday, May 6, 1985, 9:23 A.M.
Philadelphia, USA

This world has been in existence for approximately two hundred million years, four *yugas,* each *yuga* spanning fifty million years. This is the last *yuga,* the kali yuga, and it is drawing to a close. We are nearing the end of these last fifty million years. The nature of these two hundred million years has been such that in God's creation there has been truth as well as falsehood, good as well as evil, faith and trust in God and devotion to God as well as mantras, magic, *siddhis,* and miracles. Although there were *shaktis* and *siddhis,* the faith in God possessed by some people predominated.

No matter how much they accomplished through mantras, tricks, and magic, everything remained in God's control. The negative and the positive exist in nature because this control exists. There are two kinds of air: polluted air and clean air. Both kinds of air, good air and bad air, exist. As a result of the good energies in the body, in the trees, and in the flowers, the bad air is purified, taken in, and released as good air that is healthy. Man has been given peace and health in many, many ways through the natural wholesomeness in each of the things he eats, drinks, and wears. They block the illnesses that might otherwise affect him. They block the illnesses and diseases that might otherwise have to affect him. No matter how much he has altered things, he has not been able to break that which is natural. He has not been able to break nature despite the many wars and battles he has fought in the last two hundred million years, despite the miracles and his lusts.

Although God, the Lord, has come, and the *avatār*-souls have come, man does not know this. Nature has not changed. Since nature is part of the power of God, it has destroyed the polluted section. Man has not transcended that power; he still exists subordinate to the power of God. It is only because of God's support that man has naturally escaped the illnesses, diseases, and evils. God has supported the nature of the sky, the earth, and the underworld and prevented all that is artificial from harming man.

One thing results in another. When a good thing is split open, a harmful thing will be within it. That is the polluted air. If it is extracted and placed into the earth, the earth will consume it. The earth will consume it and give back a good thing. Certain trees draw in the polluted air, consume it, purify it, rejecting the bad thing and giving back the good thing.

Man's heart and lungs are like that. They take it all in and make it clear, letting the good blood go through, and discarding the bad blood. They keep clearing the rest, clearing the rest, clearing the rest, and some of it is excreted from other sections, as feces is from food. Some of what is placed inside is kept while the rest is excreted.

Every section operated in that manner at that time. Although there may have been many divisions, man was subordinate to the Power known as God, and God was still there. Although man performed so many miracles, he lived subordinate to the Power known as God. No matter how many countries he ruled, or how many countries he captured, or how many battles he fought, he remained subordinate to Something. Like this, that which was natural protected him. All the major events that approached him were pushed back. Then, little by little, during the last few thousand years—one or two thousand years—changes began to take place.

As a result, God sent the *ambiyā'* one after another, one after another, one after another. He sent His representatives and man rejected them. He rejected them and trampled upon them as well. As a result, he fought wars and battles. In these last one hundred years, man has begun to alter the beauty of man. He is prepared to alter the beauty of man in order to alter himself. Instead of trusting the Power known as God, he has come to a state in which he is utilizing the energies he considers to be himself, and he has begun to declare, "I can rule anything, I can do anything!" Man has begun to change.

Many kinds of research have come into being. In the last hundred years of this research, destruction has risen to the top and nature has stepped aside. The bad air has risen up. The harmful things cannot be filtered where they should be filtered. Nature has been blocked. The bad air has begun to fly throughout the skies.

In those times—one thousand, two thousand, three thousand years ago—if a man died, he was buried in the earth in a beautiful way.

There are so many diseases within man. He has so many qualities. When what has been taken from the earth is buried in the earth, his qualities, the odor, the worms, the insects, the diseases are not allowed to rise up. The earth eats the diseases he has and turns them into fertilizer. It consumes the odors, the illnesses, and the qualities. It controls them and makes use of them, keeping the good essence, making it useful; it gives back that good essence. It destroys the harmful and gives back the good as fertilizer. The earth creates that state for all things. The earth is the primary transformer of all things. It transforms things, destroying the harmful and returning it as good. The earth is the primary foundation for this. Earth transforms everything and gives back the good section. When something is placed into it, the earth takes the harmful and gives back the good. Whether it is within man or any other thing, it takes what is polluted, changes and controls it, and returns the good section. The earth is the mother that can transform every section.

Air, when it has a disgusting smell, will touch everyone's nose. If you place that air underground and contain it without allowing it to rise up, the earth will destroy that smell. Foul smells can come from water and foul smells can come from air. It can all be transformed by earth and be given back as a benefit, naturally. The earth gives back the good naturally. Everything else spreads the pollution. Everything else takes the disease and spreads it. The air does that and the water does that.

Currently, they cast man into fire and burn him. They put men and animals into fire. There are diseases in each one of them, many kinds of diseases, many kinds of qualities, many kinds of microorganisms. Some microorganisms live in heat. Some microorganisms live in fire. Some microorganisms live in the cold.

Those microorganisms live in many, many ways in bone marrow, in blood, and in the bones. There are diseases and microorganisms that live in various ways. There are 4,448 illnesses of the nerves, the bones, the skin, the muscles, and blood. There are so many kinds of illnesses. They think those things will be burned if they put a man into fire.

If a man dies, and lies on the road, the odor will be carried by the air to the leaves, the branches, and the weeds. The odor is taken in by them as food. The water does similar things. The water carries it here and there, and it comes back mixed with human drinking water. The disease returns in that manner. Those elements do not clear away what is bad. The same section returns and comes to someone else as a communicable disease. This occurs in water, fire, and air.

They think that those things will be cleared up if they put a man into fire. No. If you pour oil into a frying pan, the oil will rise up and coat the lid. When something is being fried and heated, and when the lid is held above it, the oil will rise up. The fat will rise up. The oil, the oily essence, will be on it. The odor will be there, the smell of the herbs will be there, the smell of the curry will be there, the smell of the vegetables will be there. The smell will rise up.

Similarly, when a man is being burned, the qualities, the microorganisms, and the fat within him all rise up. They rise up with the fire. As they burn, they rise up as oil. They leave him as a fatty essence. The qualities also go with it. The microorganisms also go with it. Traveling in the sky, they settle there, and return to the ground. Some of it falls onto the leaves, the water, the branches, and the food supply. The rest travels in the sky and falls with the rain, the clouds, the mist, and once again intermingles with food. The diseases, the qualities, the actions that were burned in the fire go back again into man. The disease has not gone. It has not been destroyed in the manner the earth destroys it in nature. It has not been destroyed hygienically in the way the earth destroys. The disease returns, and as it lives inside man, it mutates and new kinds of diseases are created.

Man has done research, but he does not understand. He does not understand what he has done—he has not performed that kind of research. The disease mutates and becomes another disease and another disease. Beyond his research, the substance that comes from his actions returns many times over. This is what the people have done in the last hundred years. They have begun to burn each other, because it is easy. So many things come from the clouds because of what is within them. When something is buried in the earth, if it is gently placed in the earth, the earth will purify it, transform it, and give back what is good. It will transform it.

In this same way, the only things man has discovered through his research are the medicines, the explosive devices, the atoms, the atomic energies, the destructive energies, the microorganisms, the energies in the air, and the poisons. Man has discovered how to destroy with poison, how to kill other men, how to take over other countries, how to kill other lives. He has discovered only the destructive energies that alter nature. As he utilizes them in the sky and on the earth, he breaks apart the processes in the sky, the processess in the rain, the processes in the air, the health-promoting processes. He agitates and breaks apart the sections in the sky and the sections in the earth. The good section collapses.

If a loud sound hits an icy mountain, the ice on the mountain crumbles. All good things are similarly delicate. The harmful things are strong. Good things are broken as a result of the disturbances created by all the research. Harmful things are strengthened there. The harmful things create the polluted air and that is the reason for all the diseases. All these things, the harmful qualities, the harmful states, the harmful actions, the harmful energies, the harmful sections have come to block the power of God.

Before this, the state of God existed, His power. Now, instead of relying upon that, people say, "I will do it." They have come to a place where there is no God. When they come to a place where they say there is no God, and perform their research—all that research will destroy what is natural.

The negative and the positive, the true and the false, the good and the evil, what has been discarded by God and the good have been revealed in each thing. The outer hull is discarded from rice and what is inside is eaten. For some fruit, the inside is eaten while the skin is discarded. For other fruit, some of what is inside is discarded while the rest is eaten. Some of what is inside certain fruits has to be discarded. Some of what is inside a jackfruit must be discarded. In this way, one part of what is inside must be discarded while the other part is eaten. Like this, the natural is in the artificial. Nature contains both the negative and the positive.

As we look at each thing, we see that there is a part that should be discarded, and a good part. The harmful part is discarded. It is the harmful part of life. The natural part is what protects man, makes him healthy, and brings goodness.

Similarly, this has been created and placed in every quality and action in man's life. Through wisdom he has to examine what he has to do, what he has to discard, and what he has to leave alone.

Yet man has discovered only, "What I do is correct!" Everyone thinks that what he himself does is correct. He has discarded what is correct and has taken up the negative. He has embraced the negative and forgotten the positive, he has discarded the part that will do good, and adopted the harmful part known as the "I." He has abandoned the section that is God. He embraces "I." He thinks, "I can do it." Everyone says, "I! I!" What results from that research is the murder of his health. Only the diseases that will kill him will manifest.

Those natural processes that have been altered and those substances that have been released into the sky and onto the ground are creating countless diseases, poverty, difficulty, suffering, affliction, earthquakes, and hurricanes. Many kinds of microorganisms, many kinds of fevers, many kinds of illnesses have entered the food supply. The many varieties of chemicals in the food are changing the blood and cancers are coming through that blood. Altered qualities are the consequence of that food, and the qualities of man are being altered to those of animals that merely look like people. Men are doing the work of animals and they are trying to make animals do the work of men.

Men are trying to do women's work. Women are trying to do men's work. Men are trying to become women and women are trying to become men. God made one man and one woman. The man is still a man and the woman is still a woman but their qualities have changed. Nature has been altered.

Man's food, his research, and his qualities are the cause of this altered state. We have forgotten God and the truth. We have forgotten the connection between the sky and the earth. Many good things and many bad things have been created through scientific research, through the many sounds, clouds, thunderbolts, smoke, harsh medicines, atoms, atomic research, research into the earth, and research into the sky.

As a result, the harmful things circulating in the skies come down in many ways, as dust, as odors, as various substances, bringing many kinds of illnesses, many kinds of heart diseases, many kinds of diabetes, many kinds of heart attacks, many kinds of bone diseases in which the bones dissolve. None of those diseases existed in the past. They have all appeared in the last hundred years, most prominently in the past fifty years. As this research has progressed and progressed, so have the diseases. Human health has declined, what is natural has declined, what is natural is being destroyed. Their artificial things are now spreading.

As a result, their qualities have changed in many places. There is fighting in many places, hatred in many places. One person is angry with another. One person is fighting with another. One person is making war on another. One person is fighting another for land, fighting for women, fighting for possessions. This is how the section of destruction is destroying.

Animals live peacefully in a jungle, but where there is man there is no peace. There is no peace anywhere man lives. Wherever man lives there is destruction, destruction through diseases and illnesses, and many, many kinds of death. Animals and the creatures in the oceans that live in places where men do not live have peace. There is difficulty everywhere man does his research. There is no peace in those places. Man has begun to live a life in which there is no peace in the heart of man. He has a great disease. The *qalb* of no man has peace anywhere man lives. There is no peace in his life. Man has begun to say, "I will live a life without peace or tranquility." Everything he inaugurates results in destruction. The diseases that come from that inauguration are the same.

Just as the earth exists as the mother, takes what is harmful, sanitizes it, and gives back the essences that are good, if man can do research in a similar way, existing in the state of God doing that research, doing it with wisdom, with certitude, with good qualities, both the world and he will have peace.

If he can do that research with faith in God, he will be able to bring peace to other lives. Man has forgotten this state of destroying what is harmful and utilizing what is good to bring forth a benefit. Man has destroyed this state.

Good cannot be achieved through what is harmful: no matter how good the intention, it will end in harm. It will end badly. Harmful things are coming to the forefront. Good is silent and minding its own business. The harmful things are coming to the forefront. Those are the first tools man grasps in his hands. He himself uses them for harm. As a result, the world is very quickly approaching destruction in this state. Everyone is prey to a cruel fire, each person is prey to the cruel fire he himself has ignited. Everyone is connected to the disease he himself has developed.

Man lives between the earth and the sky, between *maut*—death—and the one span stomach. He has *maut* and he has the one span stomach. When hunger comes, the Ten Commandments fly away. When *maut* comes, he has to run, leaving behind the *dunyā* and everything in it. If there is no rain between the sky and the earth, he will not be able to live. Without the earth, he cannot do anything at all. Amidst all this he says, "I am trying to rule this kingdom." He cannot control the one span stomach, he cannot stop the *maut* that is coming, and yet he says, "I will take over this world." He is trying to make war and do research. He is doing that at this particular time. In this state of the time of destruction for man, man is being destroyed, the world is shrinking, and terrible diseases are spreading. This is how it is approaching.

As a result, when we focus on the future that is approaching man, we see that these last hundred years have gone by very fast. The time is going by very fast.

In these last one hundred years, we have not been able to answer the questions children ask. A three-year-old will ask questions about secrets an eighty-year-old man does not know. A two-year-old child will begin to speak about such things. A two or three-year-old child will examine questions of life even an old man will not comprehend. Furthermore, we have no answers for what they tell us, no answers for their questions. These circumstances have now arrived, and they are drawing closer. At present, we cannot say if someone whose life span should be a hundred years will live for twenty or thirty years. Diseases are coming from the ground, from the water, from food, from chemicals.

They make our food grow bigger by using chemicals. Yet, when we look inside the food, there are various diseases. When you cut them open, various diseases will be inside them. They will be outwardly large, but hollow within. When we slice potatoes, they look large, but there is not much inside, they are different inside. There is nothing inside the swelling. They make the animals swell, but the energies in them are insufficient. Although man himself has swelled, his energy is also deficient. He has no strength. The people have grown larger, but they do not have the strength of focused minds. They do not have it, they have illnesses instead.

It is in this way that man has made the world ill and he has made humanity ill. He has made his mind ill, he has made the world ill, and he has made his life ill.

When we look around at everything, it all points to a destruction that is very close. Whether it is hot or whether it rains, there has been a change in nature. Everything has been altered. Even the teeth that are growing in man have been changed. His eyesight is changing. When we look at his body, every section has changed. When we look at each child, there is change.

In life too, there are changes upon changes. The wars are like this. Everything is like this. The battles are like this. The ethnic groups are like this. The separations are like this. Everyone is doing whatever he sees others doing. He emulates others. If another person does it, he will do it. If someone else does it, another person will do it. Without discernment, they will do whatever others are doing.

However, if you give peaceful advice to someone to stop him from fighting, he will not do what it takes to have peace. There is no peace. He does not want peace and neither does the other person. "Either you will perish or I will perish. Let's do it. You will fight to the end and I will fight to the end." That is what they examine.

When a bull runs into another bull, it will move aside on its own as soon as it understands it will lose. They are animals. If a rooster loses, it will run away, and the other rooster will also run away. All the animals are like this. But man! If two men are fighting and one man loses to another, he will not leave it alone. He will follow and follow him, again and again, attempting to kill him. People do what the other animals will not do. Holding on to arrogance, one man will attack another. This is the state that has now arisen through his qualities. This is because he has altered nature, the nature that God has created.

They have changed in their faith, they have lost even the concept of God, and through energies, miracles, elemental forces, science, and research, they have begun to say, "I am doing it!" Consequently, the destruction has now come through these energies and this research. There are new and unknown diseases, new and unknown types of earthquakes. There are extreme dangers and disasters that we will have to experience. In our food, in our drink, and in our lives, there will be new and unknown diseases, new and unknown difficulties. We must reflect upon and look into this a little.

After we reflect upon this and look into it, we must understand what kinds of diseases exist within us. We must try to find the path to peace and tranquility. We must see what kinds of food we need to eat for serenity and peace. We must lead our lives in peace. We need peace. We need a peace in our lives.

Without peace, we will not get peace.

We and our neighbors must exist in peace. There are so many things in our *qalbs* for which we need peace. How many thoughts there are that need peace. How many faculties there are that need peace. How many nerves there are. If one hurts, the others will feel the pain. If one tooth hurts, the adjacent teeth will hurt, and the whole mouth will be in pain. If a headache strikes one side of the head, the other side will also be struck. If pain comes to one nerve, it also goes to others. This is how we feel.

Thus, we and our neighbors are one. Humankind are children of one mother. The God in whom we trust is One. If one person feels pain, the others will also have to feel the hurt. Our bodies should feel whatever they feel. This is how we must think of our brothers and sisters, as we embrace them with peace and tranquility. We must have certitude and determination that there is a God, and that He is natural. Through that nature, we must lead our lives naturally. Then we will be well. We must realize each condition that exists on the ground and in the sky in which we exist. We must give up the harmful things.

Each thought we fail to form within ourselves through careful reflection will return to us as a disease. Everything we do without understanding will attack us with destruction. We must think of all this. We must think, and look at the depth and the breadth of our lives. We must look at the depth and the breadth of each situation, and we must look at our capacity and our state before we do anything.

So many changes have taken place in the last hundred years, and there are more to come. This century is ending—it is now 1985. There are fifteen years until the year two thousand. Many unheard of things will happen. There will come a time when a husband will eat his wife, a wife will eat her husband, and a child will eat his father. Why? Because our minds, our states themselves are creating famine. The rains and all that is natural are going to change. Our qualities will come to fill the earth—our jealousy, our treachery, our vindictiveness. Only the vindictiveness exists here now, the natural state does not.

All the things that God has given us naturally have decreased. What we have given to the earth, all the destruction we have caused to the earth—our qualities—will destroy us as famines, diseases, battles, and wars.

Nevertheless, we can live as good children, become engaged in going on the path to God, and search for good qualities. If we want to change destruction, we must turn towards the good path, towards the path to God, towards good qualities. We must begin to turn towards and live in the section God has described. Then it will be good. *Āmīn.*

This is the way in which we can reinstate nature. We must stop the artificial qualities, the harmful qualities within ourselves, and reinstate nature and God's section. There is still a way to stop these things. Just as the earth consumes the harmful things, when the good qualities come, they will consume these things, discard the harmful part, and give back the good part. Let's see.

May God help us.

CHAPTER 16

A'ūdhu billāhi minash-shaitānir-rajīm.
I seek refuge in God from the accursed satan.
Bismillāhir-Rahmānir-Rahīm.
In the name of God, the Most Compassionate, the Most Merciful.

TAMPERING WITH NATURE

Monday, October 17, 1983, 7:50 A.M.
Philadelphia, USA

A'ūdhu billāhi minash-shaitānir-rajīm. Bismillāhir-Rahmānir-Rahīm. I seek refuge in God from the accursed satan. In the name of God, the Most Compassionate, the Most Merciful. Children, the assemblies of mankind are doing many kinds of research with many qualities and many kinds of wisdom. They are doing research and exploring various procedures, both good and bad.

There are vast differences between God's creation, His protection, and His state of guardianship, and man's creation, man's protection, and man's state of guardianship.

God creates from one and makes that one increase to become a thousand. His protection is proportionate to the increase, and that section exists as an entirely discrete section. In *'ālamul-arwāh* itself, God established a discrete, ideal paradigm for the method of creation, protection, and the growth of those creations. It is a secret, His secret.

For every seed God created in *'ālamul-arwāh*, He made a substance for that section—the same portion, the same essence that joins with the egg in the chicken. The original substances intermingle naturally as two sections, two "chemicals." The substances emerge from the consciousness of the two beings, from their awareness. God created the snakes, the ants, and the many millions of species and creations in ʿālamul-arwāh itself, in this manner. They have come into being naturally, from that creation.

When they mate two by two, two by two by two, their consciousness—their awareness—creates an essence. When the two sections of the sperm and the ovum merge, their consciousness creates that point. When two beings embrace, when they hold each other like that, they each possess a specific consciousness. When they roll together, when they grab hold of each other, when they embrace, there is a consciousness present in that section and sixty-four kinds of essences that combine with that structure are manifested. Sixty-four kinds of arts and sciences are manifested. That is for the portion that is the body. Their essence is within. This is how the respective qualities and actions inherent in each species are naturally imprinted. It is the same even for the snakes.

Creation is not being created every day. It occurred at the time God joined everything together in pairs in ʿālamul-arwāh. Those seeds live on in these bodies. It is from those seeds that He has made them proliferate. The body is brought into being when the two sections come together, and then the soul is created—that section is created. That is what occurs when two beings come together, an ass with an ass, a horse with a horse, a bull with a cow. They are brought into being in this manner.

When man alters that process, this consciousness is not there, and various other energies are created. If he takes someone's semen and gives it to another, if he takes something and gives it to someone else, the qualities are altered, and the actions that can modify that section are altered. Although what he makes could turn out to resemble a horse, although the mule could resemble a horse, its section and its consciousness will not come to the horse section. Half of its qualities could be that of a horse, but the other half of its qualities would be that of an ass. That section will be there and it will possess that inherent nature—the difference will be revealed in the sounds it makes. Thus, their research has not been able to turn an ass into a horse.

Similarly, the many kinds of consciousness produced by that embrace do exist. They have been fashioned by God.

When a mother bird lays an egg, the mother or the father and mother guard it. Why do they guard it? Certain kinds of heat producing mechanisms exist in their bodies, certain natural energies exist there. There are certain currents in the body of a chicken. There is a magnetism within it. When the magnetic energy flows from the chicken, when the amount of heat reaches its limit and comes to its ideal state, the magnetism will be there, and chemicals will be produced by the rays of heat. This is the section of the body.

As a result, the chicks develop, and are protected through the section of the mother. As soon as they hatch, she shows them how to peck on their own, and trains them to do this and that. She shows them the ideal way to catch worms, to catch insects, to catch other things, and to dig. She trains them. In nature, she trains them with so many of her own ideals. When danger comes, she trains them in ways to escape from it and how to save themselves. She calls to her children, and shows them the ideal way to huddle under her wings. She teaches them how to run, hide, and conceal themselves from danger. She even teaches her children how to protect their children, she shows how a mother can stand fast to confront and fight an eagle or a vulture, should they come near. She shows the children. This is what occurs in nature.

This was all created naturally, long ago. It comes from the seed, and that section exists within each body. It comes from the embrace. When the creations come together in pairs and embrace each other, all those traits, those sections, the magnetism, those energies, and those chemicals come together to intermingle as the sperm and the ovum. Those things are made into a mixture and they intermingle. The mixture is made during the performance of that art. The mixture is made when they come together as pairs and intermingle. The mixture is made when two beings come together and unite as one, when they roll here and they roll there. It occurs in nature like that. It is then that the essence is created in that manner.

However, instead of that, man has discovered a different way.

Creation is not a new thing. It existed in *ālamul-arwāh* itself. The section of two by two still exists. After the form is made, God is watching when it is given a *rūh*—a soul. That is His *qudrah*. After two beings make a form and the ideal structure comes into it, the soul descends automatically, after approximately three months. After the two rays develop and those rays are properly formed, the point that makes birth possible—the life—comes into it. There is a limit for it, a time for it. The limit defines the time—how many minutes, how many hours, how many days. That section comes into being at that time. Two beings come together appropriately and life comes into being.

It grows as a seed grows in the earth—it splits open and emerges at the right time. Two beings come together. The seed has two parts created from the essence of the earth. Similarly, these sections are created from the essence of the body: two bodies come together, do these things, and this is what emerges. This is God's *qudrah*, His *rahmah*. The parts, the bones, the sperm and the ovum, the nerves, the sinews, the blood vessels, the muscles, the flesh, the minor nerves and the vital nerves are all created when one being unites with another.

Those seeds existed even then in *'ālamul-arwāh*, and they exist in the body now. They come into being from within it. So many chicks and so many eggs that people can eat come from one egg that a chicken lays. How many come from it, how many perish, and how many survive.

People have discovered how to make eggs in chickens without a father. They give it certain "chemicals," certain feed, certain kinds of food. They have discovered this now. However, the energy, the point that forms the embryo in the yolk is diminished. The essence is missing. The husband's embrace is missing. Because the husband's embrace was not there, because the two beings did not come together in an embrace, that *shakti* is diminished. The energy of creation is missing.

That chick will exist in a dull state.

It does not possess that essence, that section. Why? The "chemicals" will be there—they are put into the mother, and they put certain sections into its feed. They have discovered these chemicals. They can make eggs. But the primary point will not be within it. It will not possess the energy to reproduce.

Then what will it do? It will grow by consuming chemicals but it will simply perish, existing without the ability to make anything new or to proliferate. The ability to produce something comes from the couple's union. The ability to produce something new and to proliferate can occur only if the union occurs in the manner that God created in the beginning. Without it, none of the creatures man has discovered how to make can make anything new. They can only be cooked and eaten at that time. They will perish. That is all that can be done. That is what they have discovered. Those creatures will simply perish. That is the end. Man makes them and they end, he makes them and they end. This is the only way it can occur. Growth does not come from them.

There is another thing. When two beings naturally get together, what is formed will grow, and many, many sections will come into being within that form. The original is within it—its creation. Like the things that are brought forth from the earth, this must be accomplished two by two, a male and a female, a male and a female, a male and a female. God has made this section in birds and in everything else. He has created this section between two beings. The ideal structure comes through it. It is brought into being as a natural consequence. It comes into being and grows.

Man must think of this with wisdom.

There is a difference between the ideal structure of God's creation and the ideal structure of what man creates through research. Nothing man creates can approach the ideal structure God has created. It will not come to that. "I have created this!" says man, but everything man makes will end in the destruction that is his ideal. The wisdom, the ability, the qualities in man's creations will not possess God's ideal structure. They will not come into it. They will not come into it. This is a section of destruction.

If an electric current is passed through a man, he can become the current. If he is gradually, gradually, gradually, gradually acclimated to the current, a magnetic power can be established in his body. He can be trained, little by little by little, until he can make light. This can be done. However, if at that time, its opposite—such as water or any other section you make—touches him, it will destroy him.

What is accomplished through doing that? Only the destruction of another. The current will burn him, and he will be a robot. You will have made a robot. He will just be a robot.

Nevertheless, that will not happen through his own ideal structure. Man's research does not possess that awareness, that magnetism, or that section. His research does not take place the way God created, the act of two beings coming together. Now look at this. If you take sperm from a man and an ovum from a woman, you can implant them into a woman and make a child. When the two substances go into her, the chemicals will go too, and the form could come to exist within her. But the two sections have not come together. The awareness, the magnetism, the consciousness, the aspect of the embrace, the visual connection, the thought will not be there.

There is a section for each one of those things, but those things will not exist in that zygote. Those are the things that train it. It is trained by those "chemicals." The sixty-four sexual games train it. The currents and the essences, the thoughts, the magnetism—that science—enter the zygote through them. Those are the energies God created in the body.

Strength comes to an individual through a certain thought. Those forces come to an individual through another thought. Power comes to an individual through yet another thought. He can exert a lot of force through a certain kind of thought. He can be drained of that essence. He can embrace in a certain way. All those energies are there. There is a point, a purpose, for each one of them. All these points enter into the zygote through those things. This state does not develop if you just extract these things and insert them into a woman—this state does not come.

When a living being takes form naturally and emerges in the future, when he is born, he will have that consciousness, those forces, that section, that state, that stopping point, that visual connection, that thought. He will possess the section that is brought into being at each of those moments.

When semen is extracted from the male and then injected into a female, although it has a power, that state will not be there, it will not exist. Doing that will be similar to the way in which chicken eggs are made. The child will turn out like a robot. If you raise a chicken without a mother, it will not hatch chicks. It will lay eggs, but that ability to hatch chicks will not be there. It will lay eggs but nothing will proliferate from them. It will not be able to proliferate. It cannot assume that pure consciousness. It will simply continue to eat until it perishes.

Similarly, if the consciousness, the *shaktis*, the energies, do not embrace when the mother and father unite, the result will be like a chicken. It will be just a robot, doing only what it is programmed to do. Its own structural ideal will be diminished. It will speak just as a robot is programmed to speak. For that person, the structural ideal will be diminished. That section will be diminished. The ability to proliferate, that section, that structural ideal will be diminished in him. He will have only one section that carries on. He will not have anything else. He will not have the consciousness that distinguishes and examines. He will only carry on in one section. He will not understand the other section. It will be closed off. This section is made up of these forces.

The nature in which you make him is the nature he will display.

He will not act on the right side. If you tell him to kill, he will kill. Only one section is open and revealed to him. The other section is not open and revealed. Why? That state and that essence have not combined. No matter how much men produce, they have not learned how to train their creations. This has not come into their creations.

The manner in which the chickens embrace—the embrace of the mother and father—every point that exists as the semen enters the mother and has its own energy, its own awareness, its own consciousness, its own forces, its own happiness. The moment the man forgets himself, a great *shakti* is brought into being within him. *Tārahan, singhan,* and *sūran* are like three great animal qualities that are brought into being within him. They are like lions. The maya, the hypnotic delusion, is there. As he attempts to perform the act at that time, he takes many forms as he finishes. That is *sūran,* the hypnotic delusion. None of these actions exist when you extract the semen.

It is the same whether you take semen from a bull and insert it into a cow, or you take it from a cow and put it into a bull. No matter what you extract or you make, no matter what you extract them from, those states will be diminished.

There is a difference between what God creates and what man creates. You can do the research—there is a difference! The difference is in their wisdom, qualities, actions, and all their behavior. There is a difference in that consciousness. What will occur through them? Only evil will predominate. The good will not prevail.

Although you can grow things without a father inside the section of a mother, various other dispositions and states will develop in that body as you continue to discover things like this. It will not reach the other sections. Why? Because its consciousness will be limited to that. Thus, you will not be able to raise it as a human being. You can alter one section, but that section of its brain will not be open or display appropriate human inquiry. Its wisdom will not be open or display that inquiry. It will exist in a different, different way.

God is not like that.

He has bestowed two components to His creation in order to create that section. He has made things come into being the moment the two components come together and unite. Whether it is a chicken, a cow, a calf, a snake, a worm, a fly, a beetle, or a honeybee, He has placed the appropriate section between the two components as the method of bringing them into being. It exists in the body. The essence is there and it is created when the two beings come together.

You think, "God is coming to create all these things." No. He created and put them in place long ago. He put them in place long ago. That is what awakens when two beings make the form. When two beings come together, that is what awakens, awakens, awakens, awakens. However, if there are bad energies between the two components, if they are opposite to nature, it will not take form, it will not be done. The chemicals will consume it. Differences in the original chemicals will occur, and there will be a difference between this structure and that ideal structure.

Now some people have no children. Some give birth to a child, but it perishes. Some have children that die in the womb. Some have children that are deformed. What is the reason? Why does this happen? The couple did come together, so why do these things occur? These things can happen.

When a bull and a cow mate, it is correct for the manner in which they were formed. However, if a cow, an ass, and a horse all mate, that section will be damaged. If a cow and a horse mate, another section will be damaged. There will be no such thing. Even if various chemicals are used and the research is done, the issue will be damaged. The chemicals will cause it to wither. If someone takes alcohol, intoxicants, drugs, or LSD, they will cause that section to wither. Ganja, marijuana, and opium will kill the sperm cells and the ovum.

There are other chemicals people take and other activities that create problems with conception. If they engage in activities opposite to nature that block the menstruation that should occur regularly, the place from which the flow emerges is damaged. Its strength is destroyed. When its strength, those tissues, and that section in which that system exists are damaged, the menstrual flow will begin to be continuous. It will come all the time. There will be no strength, none at all.

When those kinds of situations exist, even if the conception of a child does take place, it will be too heavy, and cannot be supported. The womb will not be able to hold the embryo. It will not be able to keep it. When the embryo grows to be one ounce, two ounces, four ounces—or in the case of some that grow to be close to five ounces, a pound, sixteen ounces, thirty or thirty-two ounces—the womb will not be able to hold it anymore and it will break. It will be unable to hold it, unable to bear more. Then the pain will come, the contractions will begin, and it will go. That is how it will go.

In unnatural ways, people alter the nature of how they should live, what they should do correctly with what, how they should be, and what they should live with. They alter what they should do. It will be like this when they alter nature as they go these many ways, as they go on their journey. Some live with satan and demons, with mantras and *tantras* and evil spirits. Demons will do things like this. They are trying to create evil spirits in human beings. Evil spirits can come from bad qualities. The alterations will come through these things, and they will cause destruction.

They can lose a child because of the chemicals. Or else they can lose a child as a result of their own actions. Or else, amidst these doings, certain microorganisms can come into being, through the food they consume and other things. These microorganisms can consume this essence. That is nature. Or else a chill can occur there, it can become very cold, and the embryo can die from that cold. Or else the tissues can begin to grow, because of those actions. Tissues, tumors can form there, the pain will come, and the pregnancy will terminate.

Some people will use scientific means to prevent conception, so that children will not come, saying, "We will just conduct our conjugal life without children." Some do this as soon as they come of age and that can also be a cause of infertility. Certain difficulties can arise through doing these things. Menstrual difficulties, this and that, can arise. There are many explanations like this. That is why these issues arise.

People say, "This is God. Why did it happen this way? Why did it happen that way?" God made two beings suitable for each other when they unite. One will be appropriate for another. He made them appropriately. This and this will come together. That and that will come together. That and that will come together. If opposing sections come together, difficulties can arise. There are many, many issues in this. We are not speaking about them, we are speaking only about the research.

If people are looked upon as robots when man is doing the research, this is how it will end. The chicken we develop in this manner will turn out in that way. They give them chemicals. If we give animals chemicals when we raise them, and as we continue to do each thing like this, these chemicals will then also be ingested by people. They will come to the people.

Now the animals are given these chemicals. Pigs are given these chemicals to make them fat and very huge. Chickens are given these chemicals to make them fat. They grow very big. They get very big in a short amount of time.

They do not develop naturally. The chemicals make them swell. *Tuk, tuk, tuk,* they are quickly made large. This is business. Science is a business, just a business. It is common practice now to make them big, *tuk, tuk, tuk,* and finish. They do not grow naturally.

They grow this way because of the chemicals and the feed.

When man eats things that develop in this manner, he too will grow from those chemicals. He will get very big. When you look at a ten-year-old child, he will seem to be sixteen or eighteen. When you look at a seven-year-old child, he will seem to be as large as a child of twelve or thirteen. When you look at him, a ten-year-old boy will take a woman, before he even learns about the wisdom, the qualities, and the actions of doing so. He will be like a grown man. A young girl will be like a grown woman, all because of those chemicals.

Those chemicals make him grow. They make his body bigger in the same way they make a chicken bigger. They make the person grow, they make him larger. He lives on chemicals. Great, great diseases are created when he grows on chemicals. Cancer, heart attacks, obesity, pulmonary obstructions, angina, and so many illnesses are created. As time goes on and on and on, as he grows and grows and grows, and as he continues to eat and eat and eat those chemicals, his body will change. The state of his body and his consciousness are altered.

Why is this so? His body is being developed with chemicals just as the bodies of the animals were developed. Why? They exist in his tissues. His tissues will grow just as those animals grew. Their essence merges with him and creates those conditions in him. Similarly, in their research—in the way they are making things bigger now, in the way they are making people grow larger, the brain does not mature accordingly. They still have the brains of small children, that essence. He seems like a grown man. We see a grown man, but in reality, he has the consciousness and the brain of a baby. He seems like a grown person, but the brain of a small child exists there. The reason for this is that the chemicals that make the person bigger have altered him.

Even if all his education grows large, his consciousness and his ideal structure will speak from that immature place. Although that science displays him as if he is mature, he will not have the control and he will play like a young child. Nature will bring it to a conclusion like that. It will end in the games of a small child. Just as the chemicals make his body bigger, they will make his brain and his consciousness seem greater. They will make him seem older, but what will his qualities reveal? A small child. They will only make those other things grow bigger. His state, his qualities, and the way he leads his life will be like a small child's. He will be like the original small child.

That is the situation into which it will be brought, that is what will be displayed. All the other things are mature, but the original will still be small. He will not grow in that state. *Tuk*, and it belongs to death. It is opposite to nature like that. It is in this way that there are differences between man's discoveries and what man creates and God's creations. There are differences in each one.

People can replace their parts in this way. A man can have his parts replaced. Another man's parts can be put into him. Look at this: you can take an old car to a mechanic and have the parts replaced. A good mechanic can use parts from another car, or he can use new parts to make the repair.

Even though we can do it like this through science, and this part might work for a while, the other organs will break down one after another. Why? This part is opposite to that one. Something will break down. If one thing does not break down, another will. After replacing that, another one will break down. The natural one is missing. They replace that one and another one will break down. Then another one will break down in the same way. After that, another will break down. Then it will have to stay in the garage.

Similarly, in science we should not think, "We have replaced these organs." Although that organ might work, another one will go. When that works, it will hit and destroy another nerve, or blood vessel. When that works, something else will come into the body. Something will come to the heart. It will affect so many sections like this. As one is repaired, another one is broken. When that is repaired, something else will be broken. When that is repaired, it will come to another. When that is repaired, it will come to another.

Thus, it is like repairing an old car. We should not think we have triumphed. We should not think that merely by replacing one part with another we have cleared up everything through what we have learned.

This is just mechanics and it is not correct.

Science does things like that. We cannot remake someone and make him live for a long time. We will only create another condition. If we do that, another condition will come into being. If we do that, another condition will come into being. If we do that, another condition will come into being. If we do that, yet another condition will come into being. This is how it is and how it will be.

However, if God does it, if God is the One doing it, it is fully reconditioned. God can change anything in anyone immediately. He can replace the organ in that person. God is the One who has the parts, and who can check everything immediately. If there is something that needs to be replaced, He has the company and He has the battery. The moment He thinks of it, He can transform it and it will be reconditioned. Then everything will work properly.

There is a huge difference between His research and ours.

Everything He does ends clearly. One thing after another breaks down in everything we replace—one by one, one by one by one. This continues to occur. Thus, we cannot do it successfully.

When we begin to think of our research, we will realize that we only know how to grow one section, and that what we develop in that manner will simply perish. We will develop it and it will perish. We cannot bring something else into being from what we develop.

We cannot create nature.

Nature has been made by God. Each organ has been created by Him one by one, in each being. He has made the tree within the seed. If a seed is correctly placed with a connection to the earth, the tree will exist within the seed: the branches will exist within it, the flowers will exist within it, the fruit will exist within it, and the leaves will exist within it. The budding fruit, the ripe fruit, the taste, and the color will all exist within it, and a seed will also come from it again. They are inherent within it. God has created it.

The seed of every flower exists like this in *'ālamul-arwāh*.

When two things are intermingled artificially in that section, this is not created. We cannot create something out of nothing. Although we make something, it will not bring forth a benefit. It will not bring a benefit later. It might be visible, but it cannot move. It will be of no benefit. This is what our creations are like.

God is the Researcher, the Learned One, the Mechanic, the Father, the Teacher who teaches. Because He is like that, we need His help. We need His help for all our research. Our wisdom must study through Him, through that research. We can study truth and nature if He is the One teaching us. Then we will study truth, nature, and growth inside Him. That is what this is.

God will not create anything that grows quickly, quickly and is quickly, quickly cut down. He creates everything naturally, in a way that it can be cultivated, in a way that it can be developed later, and in a way that it can bestow a benefit even before that. He displays the state of the way that can bestow a benefit later—grow, and bestow a benefit. This is the state He displays.

Everything we do is instantly, instantly brought into being. All we do is hurry. We use a chemical to make things come into being quickly. We are doing research to create human beings quickly, but it will very quickly end in man's destruction.

These chemicals, this growth, this awareness, this section is the cause of the wars. Why? It is because of these chemicals and what is in man's food that man blocks his wisdom, his awareness, and his true states.

He is like a robot.

What does he do? He does as he is told. "Hit! Kill! Catch him! Cut him! Kill him!" What comes into being through this for every man? Only an evil section. Why? He has not discovered what it is that a human being needs. He has not discovered how a human being needs to grow. He has not discovered how human beings can have unity, peace, tranquility, and freedom. Instead of finding peace in his life, he grows in that other section, becomes large, and instantly discovers destruction.

He discovers wars, battles, alcoholic beverages, intoxicants, drugs, LSD, ganja, marijuana, and opium. Through them, his wisdom, abilities, qualities, and goodness all leave. As soon as he takes these chemicals, he becomes completely insane. The ideal structure that is human leaves, and an intoxicated confusion descends upon him.

When they send him into battle and to places where discord and problems exist, they send him with intoxicants. There, alcohol is his food. He consumes those substances without knowing himself. He does not know how it adulterates his blood; he does not know anything other than the killing. He just sees the killing. He sees the killing as a joy. The reason for this is that he has no wisdom, awareness, ambition, brain, compassion, or mercy. He has only one point like a robot. As soon as a man is given these chemicals, alcoholic beverages, and intoxicants, he becomes a robot. When man is like a robot, these are the things he will do.

A human being possesses that ideal structure. He possesses compassion.

But these substances alter those qualities. Wisdom, ability, patience, *sabūr, shukūr,* thoughts of mercy and generosity, love, and good thoughts like them are altered and robot thoughts are inculcated: "Do this! Go! Kill! Win!" And that is what he will do. As soon as he takes these chemicals and drugs in that state, he will commit murder. This is what man is creating. As soon as these substances are given to him, the sight of blood makes him jubilant. Torture and killing delight him. These chemicals and that research have altered man in this manner.

Thus, destruction is created through them. The entire country is given over to destruction through poverty, famine, and the catastrophic diseases caused by the millions and millions of poisonous chemicals and toxic microorganisms. This is the research man is performing today, research like this. Although he can discover what is in an embryo, if that which we call nature does not intermingle with it, everything that is created artificially will be like this. It will be like this.

What we grow through chemicals, extract, and keep, when we preserve the semen for such a long time, and when we insert it back into a body, what will grow from it? It will grow like that. What is natural will not grow. This growth is like growing a chicken. The perception, the awareness, the essence we spoke of previously, those qualities, and those forces are not formed within it. This is what it is like even for cattle.

What man has discovered is only one section. He has not discovered the other section. God has discovered both sections. Man has discovered only the section of destruction. God has discovered the good section. Thus, this is a destructive section, a section that is wrong.

God is the right section.

Thus, all of God's creations can move and bestow a benefit. They can bestow the benefit in the correct manner. None of the sections man has blocked, and none of the ways in which he has accomplished things will bring a proper benefit. In the section of his mind and his desire in the world, he thinks these are benefits. He thinks everything acceptable to his intellect is valuable. He thinks they are beneficial and he continues to consume those things.

It will do no good, and end only in destruction.

It will last only for that moment. He destroys himself and he destroys others. Convinced that his research is good, he goes forward, he touches it, and destroys himself. If he touches it, he perishes. If he touches it in the wrong manner, it will destroy him. His research can destroy him and it can destroy others as well. We think it is useful, but it will ultimately end in destruction like this.

There is a Truth beyond it, and that Truth exists as God. That is what bestows goodness. It bestows goodness now and forever. If we comprehend this and follow it, this destruction will stop. Then we can understand the methods of cultivating goodness and the methods of avoiding evil in our education, our wisdom, our qualities, our actions, and our behavior. We must endeavor to understand them.

This is the reason we must have a faith, and believe in a God. This is the reason we must endeavor to study and to know this wisdom and this truth through that faith. We must be aware of each section within ourselves, understanding each section and knowing which section goes with which.

God has naturally placed into a male and a female the section of uniting, coming together, and then separating. He has placed this section between two beings. He created them that way. He has formed in the body the processes that reveal the benefit, the destruction, and the goodness that come from that.

Those processes can exist as a perception, they can exist as an awareness, they can exist as an intellect, they can exist as an assessment, they can exist as an intention, they can exist as a thought. The distinctions must be made through at least one of those processes. We must analyze, make the distinction, and acquire the good section.

If we take the good section as we endeavor to do the research, as we discern and see with wisdom—that will be atomic research.

If we comprehend this within ourselves and discover the atom known as the soul, if we comprehend this within ourselves and discover the atom that is the Soul within the soul, if we discover the perfection and the Power that exist within the soul, if we discover the state that exists in that Power, it will be the perfection that is the Mystery known as God. If we discover it, that Mystery will be the truth, the kingdom of God, liberation. If we discover that liberation, it will be the house for our life. That is heaven.

When we see it, bliss will be there. Bliss will exist in our lives, well-being will be there, peace will be there, tranquility will be there, and all lives will be there. The borders of heaven begin where we see all lives as our own. That is peace and tranquility. That is serenity. That is God's kingdom in our lives, the kingdom of absolute purity. That is the kingdom of the liberation of the soul, those qualities.

If we find it here, act accordingly in our lives, and comprehend it, if we see the kingdom that belongs to our Father, there will be peace, a great peace. We must investigate this section within ourselves through this discovery.

Whether it is scientific wisdom or true wisdom, we must analyze it within ourselves. Whether it is lack of wisdom, scientific wisdom, or true wisdom, all wisdom must be investigated within ourselves. When we discover the research of our Father and understand it within ourselves, we will have peace. We will know what to cultivate and what to cut away. Then there will be peace. We must reflect upon this.

We must investigate this, and we must also investigate that. There is lack of wisdom, false wisdom, scientific wisdom, wisdom, and the true wisdom that is truth, wisdom, and resplendence. This is what we must discover. We must discover and comprehend all these things within ourselves. When we do discover them, climb the steps, and see what exists there, this state will come. If we comprehend this state in our lives, there will be peace and tranquility.

Everyone will belong to one ancestry, one family, one life. Differences will not exist. God has no differences, the living beings have no differences, and there will be no differences in our lives. Everyone will exist inside that Power as one family.

The *hayawān* will exist in another section.

The section of *insān*—the section known as humankind—will exist as one family. This is the exalted section. This is God's family, His family, the family that belongs to truth, the one family. We must endeavor to reflect upon this.

Therefore, we must discover these parts. These are the important parts in life. If we discover them and are clear about them, it will be easy to be reconditioned. We then can live without that disease. We must endeavor to think about it.

My love you.

We need the wisdom and the education, all of it—and we can do it all. A doctor can do all those things. However, he needs God.

If there are parts that need to be replaced, God has to come to replace them. We need Him. He will replace the part in such a way that it strengthens the adjacent organ. He will do it so the adjacent parts do not break. God is the current that will instruct it to be strong. He will instruct it to strengthen the adjacent organs.

We must tell Him, plead with Him, and then install these parts. That is faith in God. The doctor's primary point is this: if something has to be replaced, first God must make the other organs strong, so they do not break down. That is God, the Power. The doctor must first ask God, receive His power, transmit it, and then do the replacement. Then it will be easy.

If the doctor does the replacement without God, all the parts will break. If he replaces one thing, another condition will arise, if he replaces the other thing, yet another condition will arise. The patient will not be able to survive for long. He will not be able to live the way he thinks he will. We must reflect upon this. My love you.

This is the difference between the creations of man and the creations of God. This is the difference in their research; this is the difference between the way God creates and the way man creates. These are the differences between this state and God's state. There is much, much more, we have just spoken about a little of it.

No matter where you are, you must get water from a reservoir if you want to supply it to others. Then it will be good. The reservoir supplies the town with water. Then it will be good. Similarly, in any matter, man must take everything from God. He must take it from Him and then use that supply for himself and for others. Then it will be good. If you do not obtain it from God, you cannot supply the world. Whether you are a doctor or a businessman or anyone else, that section must be taken from Him before it can be supplied to others.

If it is not taken from God, what man supplies *(Bawangal laughs)* will be like having only one bucketful of water for a single time—he will not be able to give it at another time. If man thinks he is giving it, he will not be able to give it. He will run out of water for himself too.

It must be taken from God. Any good a man wants to do must be taken from God.

No matter what he does, he must also endeavor to give it to others and to share it. Then it will be good. He needs to do that. If he wants to save others in his life, supply them, and help them, he must get it from God, only Him. The Point is there, the Point where it can be obtained, the Point that gives, the Point that gives inexhaustibly. My love you. *Anbu.* Be happy. *As-salāmu 'alaikum.*

CHAPTER 17

A'ūdhu billāhi minash-shaitānir-rajīm.
I seek refuge in God from the accursed satan.
Bismillāhir-Rahmānir-Rahīm.
In the name of God, the Most Compassionate, the Most Merciful.

THE LIMIT

*Thursday, March 4, 1982, 6 A.M.
Colombo, Sri Lanka*

Bismillāhir-Rahmānir-Rahīm. In the name of God, the Most Compassionate, the Most Merciful.

Children, some of you have come to ask questions about the destruction of the world, asking when it will occur, what it is going to be like, how the destruction will come about, and so forth. It is certainly an important question in the world, and the people of the world have been continually asking it. Here we will speak briefly about world destruction.

The One who created the world—the One who must protect it and nourish it, the One who gives the Judgment, the One who gives the Verdict—is a unique Essential Principle. It is Something that does exist and that we must think about.

The reason everything created will be destroyed is that everything has a limit. We must understand that there will be a time and an hour when that will occur. This time has been set aside. The Essential Principle who knows this time is called God.

That Essential Principle is called God, Allāh, Yahweh, Kadavul, Āndavan, Adonai. There are many names given to It, although It is One.

Since the time of the creation of the world until the very end, the world has considered knowing the limit an important thing. This exists in another section. My precious children, God knows the day and the time that exist in this section. This time exists entirely on its own. The time and the hour do exist.

However, during the one-week limit of his life, man has begun to destroy the world. Man has begun to destroy the world. Man's mind and his thoughts have begun to destroy it. Men in the past had faith in God—determination, certitude, and *īmān*—and they gave it the name "prayer." They prayed as many groups, in so many ways. They exhibited compassion, love, peacefulness, tranquility, equality, and mercy towards the living beings in the world.

With those qualities, they gave peace to the world, to themselves, and to other lives in the world. Everyone had peace and tranquility. Due to the state and the thoughts of those who were unfailing in justice on the path of integrity, God has been watching and checking the time, the destruction, and the state belonging to destruction.

As long as the good state still exists, He will make the world prosperous and beautiful. He will make the world wealthy, He will make the world heaven, He will make the world into the world of God. This has been given to each heart, to each *qalb*. That heaven exists in every *qalb*. That peace, that justice, and that integrity are there. We must be aware of this.

How will destruction come? What is causing destruction? Man himself is destroying the world and its people through the inherent nature of his mind and through his actions. This destruction has no relationship or connection to God. These types of destruction are not related to or connected to God.

This destruction comes from the state of man's own mind. He is destroying the world and he is also being destroyed. He is being destroyed every day.

We must understand that the world exists by itself, but man himself is being destroyed every day. He is destroying himself; he is demonstrating destruction every day. Man is destroying himself through his research, through his actions, through his pride, through his need for fame, through his self-business, through his impatience, through his haste, through his jealousy, through his egotism, through the separation of "I" and "you," through religious differences, through the separations of "my religion" and "your religion," through the divisions of "mine" and "yours," through languages, through scriptures, through philosophies, and many, many similar pursuits.

Man himself is creating the destruction and he himself is being destroyed. We have to be more aware of this state of destruction.

There are only a few people in the world who trust in God. Those who believe and who act upon that belief are a minority. There are very few who act according to the belief that God is the Responsible One, that He is the One who must protect them from The Destruction, that He is also the One who will bring The Destruction. They are very few.

Those who believe in a God like this will act placing everything in the world into His responsibility.

Man has lost that truth, justice, integrity, and conscience, the very conscience that gives him the explanation from within himself. Mankind has lost and forgotten that state. They are the full majority. Some, taking one side, explicitly say there is no God. They are the group without God. They have guns, spears, science, research, and they rule the world in this state, seizing other countries, making jungles into cities, making cities into jungles.

They murder the wise, elevate the ignorant, make the learned out to be fools and make the fools out to be learned. They make chaste women out to be prostitutes, making women with good conduct out to be prostitutes, making women without good conduct out to be exalted. These dictators act like this with four hundred trillion ten thousand kinds of evil, arrogant qualities, and break apart faith in God, destroying those who pray, laying waste to their fields and to their successes, demolishing all the goodness in the country.

They are taking over the world, burning the houses of good and honest people, laying waste to their crops, annihilating their peace, destroying the wealth of their countries, destroying the wealth of the people, creating poverty, illness, disease, destroying all the days of their lives, and making them slaves to the dictators. They are enslaving and dominating them. They take their bodies, their lives, their liberty, and they make them their slaves. They call it freedom and endeavor to rule the world. All their efforts to rule destroy the world, liberty, man's life, peace, tranquility, justice, and integrity. They rule the world by turning men into animals. In those circumstances, justice, truth, and man's liberty are being destroyed. We can see this destruction. It is destruction. When God's justice and His actions are being attacked, it is destruction.

Then there are those in another section. They have forgotten God and lost all His qualities. Their humanity has changed and they have become like satans, demons, ghosts, evil spirits, animals, dogs, foxes, cats, and rats. They have manufactured many animal forms suitable to their minds. They have crept into so many of those animal qualities, those demon qualities, and those blood-sucking vampire qualities.

They have dispelled the light, and brought darkness to honesty and wisdom. They have brought darkness to the light of human lives, the light of their souls, the light of liberty, the light of peace, the light of wisdom, destroying all the good thoughts that are the lights of God's power. They block the light and create darkness. They have begun to worship the gods of darkness; they have begun to worship the glitters of the darkness, and they have surrendered themselves to it. They have surrendered to satan, and they roam the world, taking over, engaging in the sexual diversions of the world, endeavoring to obtain the treasures of the world, all the things of the world.

They destroy God, truth, justice, integrity, peace, tranquility, and conscience. They annihilate the honesty of a real life. They worship satan in the darkness. Their worship is the worship of darkness. They make satan a great being, building enormous, completely dark temples and churches that contain no light whatsoever. Many sit naked in that darkness, without garments or clothes. Some of them wear clothing and jewels, others do not. They sit in the darkness and worship in large groups, praying to gods of darkness, satan, demons, and ghosts. This is another group. This is how satan worship has come into being.

Under those conditions, the entire life of man will be dark. His world will be dark; his mind will be dark; his life will be dark; his wisdom will be dark; his justice will be dark; his integrity will be dark; and his qualities will be dark. They will worship countless millions and millions of darknesses like these in their lives. Each of those qualities will make their lives dark.

They will live in the darkness of that world and begin to destroy the light, to dispel the light, to destroy God, all light, all truth, all justice, all honesty, and create destruction. They have come to take over the dark world. The very existence of that darkness, they, and their thoughts and actions are destroying the world. Yet, they themselves will also be destroyed. Mesmerized in the darkness, they will veil their lives in darkness and be destroyed along with the world. People in this state will be the majority.

The groups that deny the existence of God and the groups that worship satan will join together to a certain extent. Their actions will destroy the world, and they themselves will perish through those very actions. They will harm other lives, they will torment them, and they themselves will perish in the same manner. This is how they will be destroyed.

God is not the cause, and this is not how He dispenses justice.

The crops a man sows can either nurture him or kill him. If he plants poisonous seeds, they will kill him. If he plants seeds of goodness, they will bring him goodness. Similarly, if a man does good, he will obtain a good result. If he does evil, he will obtain evil. Is that God? No. It is the result of his own cruelty. It is the crop he himself planted. This destruction originates from man; this destruction seeks destruction.

In addition to them, there are still other families. They say they have faith in God, faith in the scriptures, and faith in the doctrines. What do they really believe? They take the scriptures and doctrines, carry them in their armpits, and speak of them with their mouths. They carry the books on their heads and in their armpits and recite the name of God as they approach us. Countless gurus, countless *shaikhs,* countless *swāmis,* countless *munivars,* and countless experts in scripture exist. As they live like this, they make themselves into gods. They say everything that comes into their mouths, everything.

Yet they do not know surrender to that One Essential Principle, that One Truth, that One God. They do not know themselves. They do not accept surrender to God and they do not surrender to God. The point is not to destroy land, woman, and gold. The point is to destroy desire for land, desire for woman, and desire for gold. They have not overcome the sections of arrogance, karma, and maya. They have not cut away the six evils—lechery, hatred, miserliness, greed, fanaticism, and envy. They use the evil weapons of intoxicants, lust, theft, murder, and falsehood to smash whatever is in their way.

They take on the qualities of "I," "you," divisiveness, separations, pride, jealousy, envy, vengeance, hypnotic delusion, the sixty-four sexual games, and the sixty-four arts and sciences. They take on the qualities of all the animals in the world, the qualities of all the demons, the qualities and actions of the malignant spirits, the qualities of the snake, the qualities of the rat, the qualities of the elephant, the qualities of the peacock and the crow, the eagle, and the vulture. They take on the qualities of scorpions, worms, and insects, the qualities of birds of all kinds, the qualities of the two-legged birds and fowls and the four-legged animals.

They take on the qualities of the creations in the oceans and the creations in the lands, the creations in the jungles and the creations in the cities. They take on the countless qualities of the creations in the ether, the demonic creations, the dark creations, and the qualities of dogs, cats, foxes, rats, and countless other beings.

They speak with lust, desire, attachment, gold, riches, titles, praise, honors, great miracles, and supernatural powers, and they perform tricks. They cover up that which can be known by their own conscience and wisdom. They cover up their faults. They cover up what they themselves could otherwise know, and they speak for the sake of the world and for self-business. They speak for the sake of their stomachs and their own glory, keeping one thing inside while speaking of other things outside, all the while trying to obtain honors, great names, and praise from the world. There are countless millions who have lost the benefit of justice, truth, and conscience, and who act in this manner. Their actions are those of the great majority.

They have lost justice, God, truth, conscience, compassion, love, and peace. They have divided everything into separate sections, saying, "I am different, you are different; my religion, your religion; my God, your God; my color, your color; black, white, yellow, purple. I am a Hindu. I am a fire worshiper. I am a Christian. I am a Muslim." They speak in so many different ways. They have forgotten unity and that One. They have lost justice and peace. They have forgotten truth and good conduct. They have lost their conscience. They are trying to work at destroying peace.

The world is being destroyed because of those actions, because they have forgotten God and turned themselves into god, because they act without the state of good conduct, without wisdom, without virtue, without those good qualities. That state will destroy the world and that state will destroy them as well.

Such a person will be subject to death and rebirth. He will die and be subject to taking many millions of karmic rebirths. He will become food for hell and the fire. Those who have joined him and placed him in his position will also be subject to that destruction. Those who follow him and support him will be subject to that destruction; they will perish in the world. Their destruction originates from their connection to him. That destruction has been continually occurring. It has been occurring in this world.

Those in another section act using religion and scripture. They have lost justice, integrity, unity, honesty, and conscience. They have separated themselves from those things and lost them. They have lost God. They are opportunists, and they will profit from anything that occurs, from anything that earns them money, anything that gives them a house, anything that brings them a jungle, anything that brings them property, anything that bestows freedom, praise, and flattery upon them. They will act in any manner that brings them whatever they wish to appropriate.

"This is what the religions, the ethnic groups, and the scriptures tell us," they say as they perform these deeds. They act without justice as they promote these things. They display separation, saying, "My scripture, your scripture." They lose integrity and truth, they discard and throw away unity. They take whatever they need for their lives, whatever they need for the world, and make it their own. They do this and act in this state. They create divisiveness in the world, they display the "I," and they divide by saying, "My scripture, your scripture," reducing peace to a pulp.

They lose human peace, tranquility, justice, conscience, unity, compassion, and love. They promote injustice, and divide by keeping one thing on the inside and another on the outside. They veil what their conscience understands. They deceive others for their livelihood. They begin to call themselves glorious, great, and honorable people. That is how they destroy. These are some of the reasons the world is destroying itself.

However, by invalidating others, destroying them, and burning them, they invalidate themselves, destroy themselves, and burn themselves in fire. They invalidate themselves, destroy themselves, and burn in the fire of their own qualities, in the fire of sin. Every second, they are dried to a crisp in hell. They are dried to a crisp in sin, they shrivel up, and die. They destroy themselves every second, every day, every week, every month, every year. They are the instruments of the destruction of the world, and they experience the destruction as well. This too is destruction.

Another group runs the world by acting with the sixty-four arts and sciences, performing magic in the sky, performing magic with mantras, and performing magic with maya. They improvise and act in an expedient way. They have abandoned all modesty, reserve, respect for others, and fear of wrongdoing. They have abandoned good conduct and justice. They have abandoned their integrity. They have forgotten God. They have abandoned compassion. They have forsaken love. They have abandoned their serenity. They have abandoned conscience.

Those people have turned into animals. They have changed their garments and clothes, and turned into the actors of the world. They wander about, thinking that their lives are the world. "The world is our life, our heaven," they think as they continue to act. As they act in the world mimicking destructive animals, this act deceives other human beings and alters the section that is human. These are the destructive animals that destroy themselves day after day—the destruction of the world is caused by them. They themselves create it, they themselves are destroyed by it, they themselves are burned by it, they themselves are dispersed and driven away. They use colors, hues, languages, religions, and ethnic groups in their acts.

There are just a few, a minority of a minority, who act as described earlier, giving God the responsibility. They are very few. They alone believe in God, in God's kingdom, in That Day, in Judgment, and in Destruction. There are very few who live giving God the responsibility. They are very rare. Those who look forward to That Day, to God's Day, are few.

Destruction is not approaching because of those few or because of God.

There is a Day. That Day is the Last Day. Before That Day, all the destruction is caused by man. He creates destruction every day. He creates battles between nations, battles between villages, battles between religions, battles between ethnic groups, scientific battles, weapon battles, gun battles, rocket battles, color battles, language battles, divisive battles, battles to take over the world, to take over other countries, battles of hatred. They start wars in this manner. They do research and develop scientific weapons. Although they might have faith in the name of God, they also have pride and the "I," and they have begun to destroy the world.

Using the excuse of color, hues, and languages, they have begun to destroy the world. Although they speak of God with their mouths, although they speak of justice with their mouths, although they speak of peace with their mouths, they each want to rule the world. Although they say those things with their mouths, their aim is to become the rulers of the kingdom of God. They say that they are the ones who feed and protect the people, the ones who create and destroy. This is how they perform their research. They say, "I, I am the one who can create and destroy," and then they develop their weapons, armaments, battles, and wars accordingly. Those people will construct a state that can generate destruction. They do this in millions of ways.

With poisons, toxic gases, and countless similar things, they are destroying the world, the people, the creations, the reptiles, the birds, and the animals. They destroy lives, crops, good qualities, and good actions through certain acts. They destroy peace; they destroy tranquility; they destroy justice; they destroy conscience; they destroy the state of regarding other lives as their own life; and they destroy the wisdom that is aware of the suffering of others as their own suffering. They destroy the awareness that the hunger of others is like their own, and also all the qualities and actions that could bring peace. They will finally destroy the peace and tranquility in the life of man with their cruelty. After they destroy, they will use this destruction as their justification; they attempt to rule the world through destruction.

They establish themselves by destroying the people, the world, and all living creations. They try to rule the world with this kind of destruction. They say, "This is how destruction will rule the world," and they display destruction to destruction. Like this, they utilize destruction and make all mankind, all living beings, and all creations experience destruction as they continue to devastate everything. This is their progress. That is what they have discovered.

These divisions and destructions have increased in the last hundred, two hundred, three hundred years. These causes of destruction began two or three hundred years ago. It is through them that a destruction in which man cannot find any peace has appeared within him. The destruction in which man cannot find any peace or tranquility has appeared in each person's own life and it is destroying everyone.

In the last hundred years, faster and more intense types of destruction have arisen. Destruction has progressed. Injustice has progressed. Divisiveness has progressed. All kinds of differences have progressed. Justice, peace, tranquility, integrity, God, good qualities, all kinds of justice have been dispelled, and injustice has begun to rule the world. That injustice is now destroying the world, the living beings in it, and peace. This is destruction. This is destruction.

God does not destroy. God has reserved a Day for The End. Man is the only one who is destroying. He is the one who is destroying himself, and relentlessly heading towards destruction. In the last hundred years, he has looked only at destruction. We can see this destruction everywhere. He has poisoned everything with his gadgets and fumes. He has poisoned the waters with his research. He has poisoned the food with his battles.

He will die from his own chemicals. Good qualities will die. He will burn in the poison of his own thoughts. The brain of a man of wisdom will take in chemical food. Poisons such as marijuana and opium, drugs such as LSD, and alcohol—alcohol mixed in his food and in his drink—will become part of his body, and as a consequence, his brain will change and his qualities will change.

Education itself will change because of this state. If, as he studies science and performs many kinds of research, he takes drugs, LSD, and marijuana, and goes to study in school, he will be intoxicated, act there with sexual arts and games, and his natural wisdom and natural qualities and conduct will change. Man's natural actions will change. The connection to God, being the true son of God, will change. The course of justice will change.

The course of his prayers will change; his faith, certitude, and determination will change; his peace, unity, and tranquility will change. He will take in book knowledge, marijuana knowledge, LSD knowledge, drug knowledge, and knowledge of alcoholic drinks. He will use these things. Many millions of colors, hues, and lights of maya will exist in his mind; he will be *rounding* and *rounding* in hypnotic delusions. His mind will see many colors and come to this state. He will rule the world with these countless thoughts.

At first, he will see evil as evil, but because the world says it is good, he will begin to do evil things. When he begins to put all the evil things inside himself, and go on the path of evil, his intellect will work with evil wisdom. Evil actions will begin to emerge from him. He will see them, do them, and experience them. He will be changed through them, through his education, through his research, through his intoxication, and through his actions. He will lose his original humanity, his original wisdom, his original education, his original qualities, and the original peace that is God's peace. He will lose all justice.

Without justice, the people will change because those evil pursuits will be mixed with their food and their drink and their actions. That state will change the people. They will begin to say,

"There is no God." They will say, "These things are all natural. Marijuana is completely natural. These chemicals have always existed. Poison has always existed. Darkness has always existed. Hell has always existed. The fragrance in the flowers has always existed," although flowers without fragrance have appeared now.

There are the two sections of right and wrong. In any subject, there are two things, one and two. Male and female, black and white, light and darkness, good and evil, truth and falsehood, right and wrong, taste and tastelessness, sweet and sour exist in pairs like this in everything. They are natural. Both will be displayed. Yet, only goodness will always actually be natural. Goodness is natural. Evil is its opposite. God is good. His qualities are good, His actions are good, His justice is good, His peace is good, His unity is good, His compassion is good, His actions are all completely good. All of satan's qualities are always bad. All poisonous qualities are evil. Dark qualities are definitely evil. Light qualities are definitely good. Both are definitely natural.

Thus, man has forgotten that good is natural, and he has begun to accept evil energies and thoughts as natural. His education has been like this: "This is natural too," they say. "Destruction is natural too. Life is natural too. The soul is natural too. The five elements are natural too. God is natural too. Satan is natural too—he came so long ago. Earth is natural too. Water is natural too."

However, a man can drink water, but if he eats earth, he will die. He can drink water, but if he eats earth, he will die. That is natural too. Food is natural too, but there are natural poisons in it as well. Thus, having changed man's natural section, having changed the good side, they utilize the bad side. In education, in actions, in food, in behavior, everything on the bad side has been made out to be natural—intoxicants, alcoholic beverages, dance, LSD, marijuana.

There are men and women. A woman is a natural thing in life. She has to give birth to children, raise them, and give them milk. She has so many strengths. A man is natural too. Men and women are natural. The two have to join together and live in the world. Male energy and female energy—the two energies must join together. Metal and electricity must join together. When the electricity comes into the wire, something can be accomplished. But if only electricity is there, you cannot touch it. You will die. The current and the wire must come together. A man and a woman must come together. Each action must be accomplished conclusively. Then that action will result in goodness. It is natural.

Now if a man and a man join together, how can they accomplish anything? They can accomplish only destruction. If a woman and a woman join together, what can they accomplish? They can accomplish only destruction. Is this natural? It is, but only insofar as destruction is natural. These are two natural things for destruction. People perish through doing these things. They destroy themselves through these things. That is how people are destroying themselves. This is the cause of destruction. It is like this that the educated, those who study books, those who study research are changing and changing.

A person of wisdom will be on the side of God. That is natural too. If the world would live studying this state, other lives could live and attain peace. He would be peaceful, his peace would be peaceful, truth would be peaceful, equality would be peaceful, and he would find peace on God's side.

When the other side is being learned, he will see destruction in his life: the destruction of the world, the destruction of the people, and the destruction of the creations. This destruction has come in every age, and it is continuing to occur. Earthquakes, volcanic eruptions, and the sins man commits through his karma will incinerate him. Earthquakes come as a consequence of his actions. The earth rises and erupts because of sin. Hurricanes will come: they come because of the sins he commits. Volcanic explosions will occur: the atrocities he commits bring them into being. He is doing this. Extreme heat and intense amounts of sunlight will come: man is doing this. These things are occurring because of the cruelties man is inflicting upon others. These things are spinning and rolling towards us. The destruction is approaching because of man's atrocities.

Indeed, he has to think of each thought in his mind. What he thinks of will hurt only himself. It will harm his own body. Everything he does injures his own body, and he is the one who has to suffer. The pain of the desire he indulges will harm his own body. Illnesses, diseases, thoughts, actions, depression, grief, pain, money, cash, and his life all hurt him inside, do they not? Does this hurt anyone else? Does it depress anyone else? Each person is destroying himself. In whom is this destruction being created? The sadness is in himself. That is the sadness.

He is the nurturer of destruction, he is the destruction, and the suffering is for him. Is this being done by God? No.

It is like this in the world. Each person is creating his own destruction and weeping. His education, his arrogance, his karma, his life, his self-business, his anger, and every single thing he cultivates does this. Everyone reaps what he cultivates. This is the cultivation of the soul. This is what will protect or destroy him. Good protects him. Evil destroys him—evil destroys everyone. In every sphere, section by section, the things that a person nurtures, the crop that he cultivates is either right or wrong.

In the last one hundred years, man has made great progress in the destruction section. He has not progressed in the natural section of wisdom. He has not progressed in truth or human wisdom. He has progressed in night-wisdom and in animal-wisdom. He does the work of an animal. He does the work of a monkey. He does the work of a tiger. He does the work of a tiger and gets a title for it. He does monkey work and gets a title for it. He does snake work and gets a title for it. He does fish work and gets a title for it. He does elephant work and he gets a title for it. He does horse work and gets a title for it. He does crow work and gets a title for it. He does eagle work, flying work, and gets a title for it. He does rat work and gets a title for it. He does buffalo work and gets a title for it. He does cow work and gets a title for it. It is like this that he does the work of beetles, snakes, honeybees, ants, worms, insects of all kinds, fish, and crabs, and says, "I deserve a great title." That is what he does.

If human beings did human work, the title for that would be God. Instead, they jump, turn somersaults, drink, and get titles for those things. They do not engage in God's work or the work that truth does. They do not go to that job. Man does not go to the job that creates truth. He does not do good unless he can get a title for it. He does not do the work that unity does, the work that compassion does, the work that justice does, the work that integrity does, the work that conscience does. He does not have peace or tranquility because he does not do these things.

If he did do this work he would get a title from God: *The Good Person, The Person with a Good Name, The Most Exalted in the Land, The One Who Belongs to Everyone, The One Needed by Every Heart, The Compassionate One, The Peaceful One, The Just One, The One with a Conscience, The One Who Is a Companion to the Soul.* Man does not come forward to get this title. He has changed.

If he did come forward, he would have a title that would never end or perish. It would never diminish.

But man has changed, and he gets animal titles. He has

changed and subordinated himself to these titles. This is what he studies. The praise, titles, honors, applause, and adulation are very great if man does the work of an animal. This is how he will become eminent. These kinds of destruction have changed man. If a man learns good conduct and obtains its title, he will live. If he obtains the title "naked as an animal," and if he peels off all his clothes and exposes everything, destruction will come from it. Are both correct?

We arrived naked like this when we were born. But the moment we became aware of proper conduct, we covered ourselves with clothing. When the sense of shame came, we covered ourselves. When we are born, we are born as is. When we are born, we are natural too. When wisdom comes, we must sometimes use what is artificial: when we die, they wrap us in a cloth; they do not take us away as is. Even though we arrive naturally the doctor or someone else covers us with a cloth after we have been born.

Similarly, as soon as the wisdom that nurtures nature, the awareness, and the proper conduct come to us, we will have to wear the clothing of the freedom of the soul when we are with God. We must find garments of light, God, and truth and wear them, as we proceed with modesty, respect for others, fear of wrongdoing, and proper conduct. Conscience, justice, integrity, unity, peace, compassion, love, knowing that the hunger of others is our own hunger, knowing that all sadness is our own sadness, knowing that all lives are our own life—those are the garments we must wear. We must wear that clothing. We must have the body known as compassion, and if we clothe it with justice, we will get the title to go to Him. That will be the title He grants us. We must think of this.

If instead of thinking about this, we say, "Evil is natural," what will occur?

Good is natural too. Man must understand both. If he becomes human, he will understand both. Man destroys himself with evil. He perishes from what he cultivates. We have seen this destruction in the last hundred years. Destruction has been occurring continuously. Destruction is his progress, and thus it will end. His progress is world destruction, thus it will end. He is revealing the destruction of the world. His progress towards destruction will reveal the destruction of the world and finish it off.

God does not need to end it. He is watching That Day. That is a different Day.

The world is being destroyed every second of every day. Man is destroying other men: he is destroying their hearts, he is destroying their bodies. He is hurting everyone and everything. Human beings are suffering from hunger, suffering from diseases, suffering from education, suffering from religion, suffering from ethnic groups, suffering from colors, suffering from languages, suffering in houses and in jungles. Man is perishing. He is suffering and perishing.

My love you, children. Only for destruction does man say both are natural. He has his education, his studies, his books, his research, his sciences. Man is a falsely wise person, an unwise person, a scientifically wise person, and a truly wise person. Man is all four. He is a great book. He should read his own book, should he not? Both wrong and right are natural, as are justice and injustice, good and bad, good qualities and bad qualities, the light of the soul and the light of the demons, the glitters. Both aspects exist within him. Man and animal, man and demon, man and the elements, wisdom and ignorance are all within him. He has two minds, two qualities, and two bodies.

There is wrong on one side—where mind speaks. There is right on the other side—where Allāh speaks, where true wisdom speaks. Both exist in every man; they exist in every plant and in every animal. Good and evil are both there.

What should we investigate? We must investigate ourselves. The explanation is within us. Do we need to go to a doctor for this? Do we need to go to this and to that? Right and wrong are things we must understand within ourselves.

Both people are there. The bad person and the good person are both there.

One will say good things, the other will say bad things. One will act with equality and the other will act with separation. One will accept God and the other will accept falsehood. One will be just and the other will be unjust. One will speak good words and the other will speak bad words. One will have good intentions and the other will have bad intentions. One will have *sabūr*, the other will have jealousy and anger. One will create karma with proper conduct, the other will create karma without proper conduct. One will have *shukūr*, the other will create the section of doubt. Both are within man. They are in every weed. Both exist. Both are indeed man: he who does the work of wisdom is a human being; he who does the work of animals or demons is either an animal or a demon. Both are within him.

You must study wisdom. If you study truth, conscience, justice, and good qualities, you will understand. Man is the book.

If you take marijuana, will it make you healthy? If you take LSD and opium, if you do drugs and go to the bar, drink, and stumble about on the street, will the bar solve your problems? Many doctors treat grief and certain drugs treat depression. Do they remove your suffering? The perception, the awareness, the intelligence, and the wisdom are within you. The medicine to heal your qualities is within you. You must change to one of those two sides. It is all within you. Try to do this and see.

You will never be able to find peace for your life if you live in destruction and attempt to find peace in destruction. You must not look for peace in destruction. You must dwell within goodness. You must leave destruction and change to goodness. If you leave the destruction and emerge from it on the good side, wisdom will begin to speak within you. Then the truth can drive out the evil. Otherwise, destruction will follow you. As long as you exist within destruction, it will continue to destroy you. This is the world now. It is destroying everyone: every country, every house, every mind, every cage, every heart, and every creation in that way.

Have you not seen this yourselves, children? You have been asking, "When is the destruction of the world? Is the destruction coming? Is the destruction coming?" The destruction is already destroying everything. This is not just the Destruction that will occur in one day, this is constant destruction occurring for many days. Understand this.

We cannot imagine that destruction will come on some other day, that we can go live on a mountaintop and save everyone. No. It is happening now. This is destruction. Destruction is what is destroying man. The wars, the research, the battles, the fights in every house, the fights in the jungles, a son fighting with his mother, a mother fighting with her son, the husband fighting with his wife—fighting, fighting, fighting. The real battle is between good and evil. The other is merely destruction.

If you come to the good side, if you come to the other side, if you leave the destruction side, the world will not be destroyed. Then it will not be destroyed. Justice does not destroy. Injustice destroys. As long as you remain within injustice there will be destruction, the destruction of the world.

Actually, the world will remain—you are the only ones who will be destroyed.

If you stay inside the truth, the world will not be destroyed and you will not be destroyed. If you are not destroyed, the world will not be destroyed. If you change and take that form, there will be no destruction.

As long as you are in the other form, all you will see is destruction. Every man will see destruction in every life. This, child, is destruction. Please understand. If you hold destruction in your hands and go to live on a mountaintop, the destruction will be there too. Even if you go to live in the ocean, that will be destruction, you will be taking it with you.

If you make a time bomb, if you set the time on the bomb you are carrying, where are you going to hide? The time has been set. The hour, the minute, and the second for the explosion have been set. If you set the time and tie the bomb to yourself, can you run from it? Where will you hide? "I am going to save myself from this destruction," you say. It is a time bomb that you have made and tied to yourself. You can only escape if you untie it and throw it away. You have attached the time bomb to yourself, saying, "I am going to hide and save myself from destruction," but you will never get away from it. *"Boom!"* you will explode.

You tie yourself to evil like this, and say, "I am going to escape from destruction. I am going to live on a mountaintop." The gurus and the *shaikhs* say, "Disciples! Run this way!" No. No. You are taking the time bomb with you. You cannot escape from it. Please think of this. If you take it with you, there will be no escape anywhere. Destruction will be coming with you. That is destruction. Please think of this.

My love you, children. Destruction has appeared primarily in the last hundred years. The world is being destroyed. Man must turn away from destruction. From that place of destruction, he must change into the form of compassion, into God's form, into the form of justice. If he can abandon the evil, and see peace, his own destruction and the destruction of the world will cease. If his own destruction ceases, the world will not be destroyed.

As long as God's justice remains within man, he will be the son. As long as God's conscience remains within him, there will be peace and tranquility. As long as God's compassion remains within him, all lives will bow before him. When faith in God and compassion and His qualities live within us, destruction will not exist within us, will it? Then there will be no destruction in the world. If none of us keep destruction in our hearts, the world will not be destroyed.

If we have destruction, this is what will occur in the world. We ourselves are the world. Each one of us holds the world within ourselves. When we are destroyed, the world is destroyed. Please think of this. Each child must untie the destruction within himself.

Take the truth that is within you, unite with it, and act. In God's qualities, the destruction will cease on its own. It will do nothing to you. If there is no destruction within you, it cannot attack you. If you have destruction, it will attack you—the bomb will be tied to you as you move. Please think of this.

This is what we have been doing in the last century. There will be no justice if each person loses justice, conscience, and integrity because of the research that has been done. There will be no justice if he keeps one thing inside and another thing outside and acts only for the sake of appearances; if he looks at the majority as he does his duty; if he looks at self-business and does duty; if he looks for importance and big titles and does duty; if he looks for money and titles and does duty; if he loses all honesty and morality in that way; if he looks for position, pride, money, cash, property, and personal well-being.

This is not what God does. This is destruction. The world is like this. The titles and praise are there. The majority will put the world into the fire. The titles of the majority are fire for the world, the fire of destruction. For justice, the titles are waste matter, they are destruction. Titles destroy justice. They are darkness for man's life, the fire that burns life.

If a man thinks of these things and changes, his own destruction and the destruction of the world will cease. Be aware of this and do what is good. You will not be destroyed if goodness is within you. You will not be destroyed if God is within you.

If the truth is there, God is there. You will not be destroyed if God is there. If you are not destroyed, the world within you will not be destroyed—the world you rule will not be destroyed. Each one of you, please endeavor to think of this.

If you do not think of this, you will be wondering, "When will the world be destroyed? When will that time come?" The world will change One Day, but you are discovering destruction every second as you move forward. We must think of this. Please think of this. May God give you the good section. May God remove the section of destruction from you. May He give you the good section, the just section, the natural section that is truth, and remove the natural section of evil from us. Then we will not experience destruction.

May God grant us this help.

Āmīn. Āmīn.

A'ūdhu billāhi minash-shaitānir-rajīm.
I seek refuge in God from the accursed satan.
Bismillāhir-Rahmānir-Rahīm.
In the name of God, the Most Compassionate, the Most Merciful.

THE WAR
DESTRUCTION WILL OCCUR LIKE THIS
*Wednesday, July 7, 1982, 9:30 A.M.
Colombo, Sri Lanka*

QUESTION
Will the war between Damascus [Syria] and Israel come to America, or will it stay there?

M. R. BAWA MUHAIYADDEEN
Not only America, but the entire West will join in. Between thirteen hundred thirty-eight and thirteen hundred forty years ago, the *ashāb* asked Rasūlullāh ☮ about this. His disciples asked about this at approximately when Rasūlullāh ☮ was about to change over, when he was about to disappear. It was then that they asked him about many essential things such as, "How long will Islām last? Will it be corrupted?"

He said, "No, for fourteen hundred years after the appearance of Islām, nothing will corrupt Islām, but after those fourteen hundred years, only Allāh will know the state of Islām. Only God will know it. Only God will know the state of Islām after that."

Another disciple asked him another question. "*Yā* Rasūlullāh, I had a dream."

"What was the dream?" he asked

The disciple replied, "In the dream I saw a colossal tree and a seed; a great light emerged from the seed, from the center of the seed. That light became a colossal tree that grew from the beginning to the kingdom of God, from *awwal* to *ākhirah*. Leaves, flowers, buds, unripe fruit, and ripe fruit were on the tree that grew from *awwal* to *ākhirah*. The taste of the fruit on that tree could be described neither by birds nor by human beings. Even celestial beings came to the tree to taste these fruits. Beings from *ākhirah*, from *dunyā*, from the jungles, and from the cities—all beings came for the fragrance of those flowers. They gathered around the light and came to eat the fruit.

"Everyone who ate the fruit was transformed into light. Everyone changed from form into light and became beautiful. As the tree grew, the entire world obtained peace. Everyone changed and turned into light. The fragrance, the light, and the beauty were in the fruit. Then suddenly the tree fell and even its roots were torn out. The length of that downed tree stretched from *dunyā* to *'ālamul-arwāh*—from this world to the world of pure souls. Some of the branches extended even into *'ālamul-arwāh*. The birds and all beings were very sad," the disciple said. "That is the dream I had."

Rasūlullāh ☮ replied, "These are the difficulties the world will experience afterwards—the suffering, the torment, the pain, the sorrow, and the sadness of living beings. This is what will come to all who depended on the tree, to all who believed in the tree," he said. "Is that what you saw? That is how it will be. That tree is me. I am that tree. I am that, and the time has come for me to change. I too will have to change."

Everyone began to cry.

Other disciples then asked about certain other things. They said, "O Rasūlullāh, after you go, where can we meet you again?"

"You can meet me at the foot of the *mīzān trās* where your good and evil will be weighed. The meaning of *mīzān trās* is justice, the scale that weighs good and evil. When you look at and weigh the right and the wrong in your *qalb*, you can see me at the weighing place. This meaning applies when you keep the good: you must take it into your *qalb*. The place in which good and evil are weighed, *mīzān trās*, means that wisdom. You can see me at that place of wisdom."

They asked more questions and he answered them. One of those questions was, "When will the world be destroyed?"

He said, "The world? For fourteen hundred years after me, Islām will not waver, no matter what is happening. It will exist in a state of peace and tranquility. After that, only Allāh will know, and the destruction of the world will begin. At that time, animals will do the work that man should do and man will do the work the animals should do. Animals will have the qualities of human beings and human beings will act with the qualities of the animals. Animals will have the peace that should be man's and men will begin killing each other like animals. At that time, the jungles will become cities and the cities will become jungles. They will turn the cities into jungles and the jungles into cities. They will make natural things artificial and artificial things natural.

"At that time, they will make faith in God false, saying that He is a lie. They will declare that falsehood is god. They will change seas into lands and lands into seas. They will cut into and dig through the lands and make them into seas; then they will make the seas into lands. They will destroy truth and peace; they will take up evil, jealousy, and vengeance, and establish those things within themselves.

"Religions, ethnic groups, and separations will prevail, however the inner meanings of the religions will be destroyed. The outer meanings will be displayed and shown to be false. They will preach this. They will worship satan in places God used to be worshiped. They will make animals live where people used to live. They will try to raise snakes in their homes. They will give houses in which human beings live to snakes and give houses in which snakes live to humans. They will lovingly raise animals, snakes, and other poisonous beings in their homes, but they will destroy the love of human life.

"They will attempt to control the sky and the sun. They will try to control it. They will attempt to make a new sky, a new sun, a new moon, new stars, new air, new rain, artificial sunlight, and heat. They will attempt to create these things, destroy nature, and make everything artificial. There will be no peace in any house, no peace or tranquility in any family. There will be only fighting and murder.

"At that time the nature of flowers and fruit will change. The flowers, the trees, and the bushes will all lose their nature and become artificial. Their seasons will be changed. A tree that normally produces fruit in six years will be made to produce in two: they will graft onto it branches that will produce fruit in two years. But that tree will bear fruit for only ten years; it will perish after ten years, and die. In nature, that tree might last for a hundred years while the artificial tree will last only for ten. They will change the nature of things to be artificial. Like this, man's actions will all be harmful actions. His prayers and everything will change in those times of destruction. Those changing times will be the times that danger comes into man's existence. It will be a time when man destroys man.

"During those times there will be famine and pestilence. When man starts trying to feed himself and to protect himself instead of letting God do it, that will be the time of man's destruction. That will be the time of man's destruction."

"Yā Rasūlullāh, how will this end? Will there be no limit to it? Where will this destruction begin?"

"Two sections will emerge in the East to aid the destruction. There will also be two sections in the West that will aid the destruction. The war of destruction will begin between Damascus and Jerusalem; that war will signal the time of destruction. This will occur in the place where Islām once existed, where children of one mother and one father once lived. This war will occur in a place where the children of the same father once believed in Allāhu; it will be a war between brothers.

"Both sides will have forgotten God and the truth; they will have forgotten God, the truth, and justice. When God, the truth, and justice have been forgotten, this war and the destruction will begin in that place of forgetfulness. This war and this destruction will begin in that place. Some people in the West and some people in the East will support this war. Of the two sections from the East, one will be from the Northeast where there is snow and ice. In the West as well, enmity will exist in a similar climate. One of the lands in the West will be a country that was formed possibly two, three, or four hundred years earlier. It is a land where the forests were turned into cities. That is where they will live.

"At that time, they will join the Jerusalem side and the others will join the other side. Of the two sides, one will forfeit justice and the other will forfeit God. One side will forfeit truth and justice. The other side will forfeit God. The two sections in the East will be those who have forfeited God: those in Damascus will have lost God. Those in the West will have lost justice and truth. It is through this that destruction will arise.

"In that destruction, houses might remain but people will not. This war will not be waged with guns, swords, horses, elephant armies, or with any method used in any war that has ever been fought before. Destruction will come from poison and atoms of fire. Atoms of fire. A war of poisons. Poison gas. Everything will be burned to ash by poisonous energies. The trees themselves will shrivel where they stand. If someone falls, he will turn to ash and remain in the same position in which he fell. The forms, the shapes will remain as they are, but they will turn to ash instantly. They will wage this war with such poisonous gases, poisonous vapors, poisonous atoms, brimstone, mercury, and through many different kinds of atoms and toxins.

"At that time they will be able to fly utilizing the energies of iron, earth, gold, copper, and tin. Metals will be able to fly. There will be a certain kind of thick water—heavy water. There is drinking water, there is salt water, and there is heavy water that man cannot drink. You can transform salt water into drinking water but heavy water can never be drunk by human beings. It will never be changed back—it will burn. It is a burning thing. Its energy is similar to brimstone: it can burn. That poisonous rain will fall as icy rain and snow everywhere, whether it is into the ocean, onto land, or into the desert during a sandstorm; it will fall into the ocean and outside the ocean.

"According to the Commandment of God, the earth will be destroyed by fire that comes from the earth itself. At the end times, those fires will manifest at various intervals in various places. Evil lands and evil people will be burned. Those fires will emerge at various times; those countries will be burned to ash and their lands could become oceans of fire. Mountains and entire countries could be turned to ash and end up under water. There could be tidal waves. Countless things like this will occur throughout those times.

"The sun will change; the dusk, the dawn, the stars, the clouds, and the skies will come to a state in which man can change them. With those incendiary things he can travel around the whole world, go out into space and back.

"Many will declare that there is no God, but few will affirm that there is a God. The majority will say there is no God. They will teach their children from the time they are tiny babies to say there is no God. They will avoid the name of God in their churches, their mosques, their schools, their houses, and everywhere. Those who rule the countries and the nations will be turned into gods; their scientific researchers will be turned into gods. They will all be called gods.

"The words of God and the natural things that God has created will be called false, and they will assert, 'It is just nature. It comes all by itself; nature created itself. All the creations created themselves. Nature emerged on its own. It did not come from any one thing, it was not created. Nature appeared spontaneously. It is simply nature.'

"At that time, there will be very few people who trust in God, who believe in God, who realize that state, and who learn the lessons that *insān* must learn. Those who do the research will be many. At that time, they will have instruments enabling the West to hear words spoken in the East, and enabling the East to hear words directly from the West. It will be accomplished through the air. Such marvelous things, such wondrous things will be done through the intelligence of man.

"They will be able to travel into space and to eat concentrated forms of food, atomic forms, and stay alive. They will be able to survive on small portions. Man will build houses in the *dunyā* and in the open expanse of the sky. The wars will be fought in the expanse of the sky and upon the expanse of the earth. There will be enmities and battles in the open expanse of the sky and upon the open spaces of the earth. They will say, 'It is my sky, my world.' and destruction will be the result.

"All that they have discovered through their research will change: all the natural rain, all the natural air, all the natural actions, all the natural things will change. Their poisonous actions will come back to them and illnesses will arise because of them: cancer, dreadful and painful illnesses of the blood, dreadful diseases of the nerves, dreadful diseases of the heart, palsy, defects in vision, trembling of the hands and legs, fibrillation in the heart, congestion in the heart, changes in the heart that will end life, that will stop the *qalb* and deprive it of oxygen. There will be incurable illnesses, illnesses that will cause the skin to itch unbearably. The blood of anyone, no matter who they might be, will change. Their blood will clot, they will suffer from clotting diseases. There will be edema, diabetes, and urinary diseases.

"Like this, the nature in the bodies of men and women will be changed. Brothers will take their sisters and sisters will take their brothers; there will be no morality. They will lose their morality. They will reveal everything that is shameful. They will walk about without clothing. They will show the places that should be hidden and hide the places that should be shown. They will have no shame, no modesty, no respect for others, no sincerity, no fear of wrongdoing, no good conduct. They will not have this section of a human being. They will live without clothing like animals. God has given animals a way to cover themselves. He has given animals tails to cover their shameful places, yet man will not cover those places with his wisdom or with his intellect. He will not even have the hair with which to cover them, everything will be open.

"At that time, they will have intoxicants, alcohol, drugs, and poisonous essences and they will be intoxicated by them. Those substances will change man's wisdom, his abilities, and his qualities. After he takes those substances, he will not know what is happening while he is under their influence. He will have only one thought and he will proceed towards it: if he wants to kill someone, he will do that, pursuing that thought until the end. If he wants to destroy a person, he will do only that. He will intensely focus upon and carry out whatever he is thinking. He will not consider wrong, or right, or wisdom, or capability. If he wants to catch a certain woman, if he wants to kill a woman, he will do that. Man will be like that.

"That is the time of change, the time of destruction. It is then that Damascus and Israel will begin to wage war."

The Rasūlullāh ☮ gave certain other explanations at that time.

"For those who have turned away from Allāh, things will happen in this way. For them, the war will be a great war. There will be two sides. Those in the West who have lost justice, truth, and integrity will help one side, while those [in the East] who have lost God, truth, and compassion will help the other side. Destruction will be the result. At that time, houses might remain standing but there will be no people. Some animals might be left alive and some might die.

"The possessions that the people sought will all remain, but the people who sought these possessions will not be there. The earth will remain, but there will be no people left to rule it; the harvests, the trees, and everything will remain, but they will be unusable. There will be no people to do anything: no one to do the farming, no one to care for the orchards, no one to use the trees. There will be no one left to do anything.

"The war at that time will be a war of poisons, an atomic war. It will be a war waged by man's ignorance and lack of compassion. Some of the buildings will actually melt. Other buildings will be liquefied, and the liquids will then solidify. Like this, what will occur with those weapons of war, with those instruments of war will be very horrible. They will be worse than the poisons of countless snakes. They will make poisons worse than those of vipers.

"At that time there will be opium, marijuana, all kinds of intoxicants, consciousness-changing pills, pills that can destroy wisdom, pills that can destroy awareness, wisdom, and the explanatory processes in the brain. People will be intoxicated by those substances. That is what will happen at the time of destruction. That will be the war of destruction.

"When that war takes place, it will be rare to see a house closer than ten or fifteen miles away. If you are looking for another human being, how far you will be from him! With atomic energy and atomic research, they will be able to fight even without using people. Battles will be fought without people. If one man were here and another man were there, they could destroy the world that lies between them. If there were one man in the East and another in the West, they could destroy the world between them. If there were one in the North and one in the South, they could destroy the world between the two of them. They could destroy it. That state will arise at that time. That war will destroy humanity; that time will come. The roots of that war will be well-established fourteen hundred years or more from now.

"Before that and after I have gone, there will be two other great wars waged by silver-eyed people. They will not be as destructive; they will be nothing like the final one. Those two wars will occur in that way. The characteristics of and the reasons for those wars will be reprisal; they will be wars of revenge, wars of arrogance and never-ending revenge."

Some of it has already occurred.

"A silver-eyed man will start one of the wars." The silver-eyed people are the Germans. "In the East, a short-statured person will start it. It will last for about four-and-a-half years. The silver-eyed man will try to destroy the entire world. His forces will go to Russia, be stopped there, and escape; they will be defeated in the Arab countries. That is what will occur. That war will end like that.

"But the war after that will be a war of destruction, and everything will end within eight years. It will be a war of destruction, a great war of destruction, the roots of which go back over four hundred years. Growing from that time, great destruction will arise. It will be a war in which man will destroy God, truth, and man himself, a devastating war without any justice or compassion," said Rasūlullāh ☺.

Israel ☺, the Angel of Death, arrived after he finished speaking. Everyone was crying. Fātimah ☺ was standing outside the room. Rasūlullāh ☺ had a fever, his body was hot. The Angel of Death had come in the form of an Arab and asked Fātimah's permission to enter. She told him Rasūlullāh ☺ had a fever and that he could not go in to see him. Rasūlullāh ☺ said to those outside, "Let him come in. Let him come in. He came to see me. Let him in."

The Angel of Death approached him and said, *"As-salāmu 'alaikum, yā* Rasūlullāh. Allāh told me to give you His *salāms."*

"All right. Why did you come, Israel? May the peace of God be upon you."

"I came for a reason, Allāh told me to summon you."

"He told you to summon me? That is good."

"All the eight heavens have been decorated; the heavenly beings and the *malā'ikah* have decorated the eight heavens, they have been beautifully adorned and are awaiting your presence. The seven hells have been closed and locked. The *malā'ikah* and the *houris* all await your presence. Allāh has said this. Allāh has told me to say this to you. I have come to fulfill His command."

"Is that so? Good! All right, sit down for a moment, I have about five more minutes of work."

The moment the Prophet ☻ thought of the angel Gabriel ☻, Gabriel ☻ came to him. "*As salāmu 'alaikum, yā* Rasūlullāh."

Rasūlullāh ☻ replied, "*Wa 'alaikumus-salām*, Gabriel. The angel Israel came to speak to me. After I asked him, he told me why he had come. He said to me, 'Allāh told me to inform you that the eight heavens have been beautifully decorated for you, awaiting your presence. All the angels are proclaiming their *dīn* to you, singing *salāms* and *salawāts* that are resonating throughout all the heavens. The seven hells have been closed and locked. The angels are eagerly awaiting you. Allāh has told me to give you His *salāms*.'" This is what he explained to Gabriel ☻.

Rasūlullāh ☻ continued to speak. "Israel also said this to me, but Allāhu ta'ālā had told me I would stay in the *dunyā* for ninety years. Now I am only sixty-three, am I not? That is what Allāh said to me."

"Yes," said Gabriel ☻. "Twenty-seven years passed during the *mi'rāj*. When you went to meet Allāh, twenty-seven years passed in one minute. It was twenty-seven years for you, but it was a minute in the *dunyā*. You were not in the *dunyā* for all those years. Think of what actually occurred: in the *dunyā*, the *mi'rāj* occurred between the night and the day.

"Thus, in the world, it took just a minute, but it aged you twenty-seven years. It was still the same day—the sun had yet to rise again—but twenty-seven years of your life passed by. So now you are ninety. You are ninety years old. Allāh has told me to say this to you."

"Is that what He said? If He said that—"

Gabriel ☺ said, "All right. At the end, Allāh told me that you can come if you like. If you want to stay, you may stay. It is your wish; if your intention is such, you may stay."

"No, I will come because they are all waiting for me."

"The Qur'ān that has been given to you is complete. It has been given to you and now there are certain explanations you must give to the beings in the *ākhirah*. You must come to explain those things to them. Allāh has sent me to say this. You must explain things to those in *'ālamul-arwāh*. The time has come, but if it is your wish to stay, you may stay."

"No, I will come. Please give my *salāms* to Allāh," said Rasūlullāh ☺.

Gabriel ☺ disappeared from there.

Israel ☺ stepped forward and Rasūlullāh ☺ said to him, "O Israel, I am ready. When you take a *rūh* from the *dunyā*, a soul from the world, how do you take it?"

"O Rasūlullāh, I have four faces. With one face, I look at *'ālamul-arwāh*, at the *sidratul-muntahā*, and at *al-lauhul-mahfūz*—the world of pure souls, the leaves of the tree upon which the names of all living beings are inscribed, and the tablet upon which everything is written. I have three other faces: a face of milk, a face of fire, and a face of blackness.

"The face with which I take sinners is the face of blackness. I take the lives of sinners with the black face. My eyes are larger than countless *dunyās*. In my eyes, how many *malā'ikah* and wonders there are! At that time, they will see how many hands I have. The people will shout in fear, wailing and howling, '*Aiyō*, he is coming. He is coming here. He is going there!' They will wail and howl as I strike at them mercilessly. One blow can send them seventy thousand miles deep into the earth. I can reach them no matter where they try to conceal themselves. That is how I take their souls, their *arwāh*. They will wail when they see me and when I take their lives.

"On the other side I have a face of fire to take the souls of *jinns* and fairies. I take the *mu'minūn*, the believers, with my face of milk. Sinners—I take their multitudes with a face of blackness, with a black face, and deliver them to the *adhāb*, the torment.

"But when I take the lives of all good people, I do it in the way a child drinks milk from its mother's breast—so gently do I take the *ambiyā'*, the lights of God, the *aqtāb*, and all the good people. I take their souls in that way.

"I have said I will take your *ummah*, your followers, in that way too, but when I come to them with the face of milk, they will be able to see in my eyes all the faces they have in their hearts. They will see in my eyes all the faces in their hearts, all the thoughts in their hearts, all the differences in their hearts, all the sections they hold in their hearts, everything. They will see everything, all their thoughts, as the *adhāb*. They will see the *adhāb* in my eyes, and they will shout. Most of your *ummah* will experience that because their own thoughts will be revealed in my eyes. They will be looking at my eyes.

"When I go to take them, they will say, 'They are cutting me! They are stabbing me! *Aiyō*, they are cutting me! *Aiyō*, they are killing me! *Aiyō*, they are catching me! *Aiyō*, something has caught hold of me!' They will shout, but it will only be at their own thoughts.

"I have described what the *mu'minūn* will experience; those who are in Islām will see the face of milk in their experience, but I will come to them in the form of their own thoughts. I have four faces."

Then Rasūlullāh ☪ said, "O Israel, please allow me to change the thoughts of my *ummah*. Allow me to change the *adhāb* they might experience."

"I will place my hand upon them, and it will feel as heavy as seven ranges of the Himalayas. Their chests will be crushed, that is how heavy it might be. If their hearts are made of stone, they will be crushed. If I place my hand on them, their bones will be crushed and they will shout."

Rasūlullāh ☮ said, "O Israel, please do not do that to my *ummah*. They might be guilty, but they have not really understood or accepted the truth. Please give all the *adhāb* that is meant for them to me."

The Angel of Death then placed his little finger upon the Prophet's chest and it was as heavy as seven ranges of the Himalayas.

The Prophet ☮ said, "If one finger is as heavy as the seven ranges of the Himalayas, how will it be for my *ummah*? How heavy will your whole hand be?" The Prophet ☮ again asked that his *ummah* be taken as easily and as painlessly as a child drinks milk from its mother.

"*Yā* Rasūlullāh, it is not my fault! They are doing it to themselves—each person has his own section. It is not anything that I do. They will experience only what they bring. For your sake, I will take the lives of those who say your name, those who accept you and Allāh, as a child takes milk from its mother's breast. I will take their lives in that way," said the Angel of Death to Rasūlullāh ☮. After that, he took his life.

That is what has been related in the reported sayings and actions of Rasūlullāh, in the *ahādīth*. I do not know anything beyond that.

Those are the times in which those things will take place. I do not know, I am simply saying what I was directly told to say at that time. I heard a lot, and I was there when they asked him those questions. The words that came to my *qalb* are the words I heard then. I am telling you the section I heard at that time.

Allāh knows best. He gave so many more explanations to those who had wisdom, to those who placed their intentions upon Him, to those who spoke with Him, to those who had a connection to Allāh and the Rasūl ☻. He explained the truth.

Āmīn. As-salāmu 'alaikum wa rahmatullāhi. It is a long story.

CHAPTER 19

A'ūdhu billāhi minash-shaitānir-rajīm.
I seek refuge in God from the accursed satan.

Bismillāhir-Rahmānir-Rahīm.
In the name of God, the Most Compassionate, the Most Merciful.

JESUS ☉ & THE ANTICHRIST

Wednesday, July 7, 1982, 10:30 A.M.
Colombo, Sri Lanka

My memories are coming back...the more I speak, the more I remember. There is a little more about destruction I did not tell you previously that I will tell you now. I left out a little.

The war will occur in that way and then end. After the war, all the destruction will come, and the people who oppose the word of God—the few who remain after the war—will rule the world. It is then that they will do all those things. At that time—I do not really understand very well whether it will be at the Ka'bah [in Mecca], at the old Ka'bah in Jerusalem, al-Baitul-Muqaddas, or in Damascus, I have forgotten. While things like that are happening, they say Jesus ☉ will come at the *waqt* of *'asr*. When the prayer is over, Jesus ☉ will come down to pray there.

The Rasūlullāh ☉ has said this. It has appeared in the *ahādīth* and in the Qur'ān.

"When Jesus prays there, all the destruction will be changed, the actions in which the people were previously engaged will change, and those with *īmān*, absolute faith in God, will gather together—all will gather in one congregation. Some will call Jesus, 'Mahdī.' A short period of time after this, dajjāl, the antichrist, and the group called ya'jūj and ma'jūj, gog and magog, will arise." This is in the *ahādīth*. This has been described there by Rasūlullāh ☾.

"Jesus will come only to kill dajjāl. No one else can kill dajjāl. Jesus himself must kill dajjāl. The reason for this is that when Allāh created Jesus, He created him as light, without the semen of a father. He had no bones in his body. There was no semen, it is semen that becomes the bones. When you touch his body, it will give way. Jesus did not have anything of the male section within him. The section of the male is bones and semen; the section of the mother is flesh. Jesus was created without bones in order to kill dajjāl. If he had bones, and if dajjāl were ever to seize him, all his bones would break in his grip.

"The name for dajjāl was jāhil, the one who has gone astray. His mother's name was jadda, his father's name was badda. A mantra was said when he was born, and it was predicted that when he stood on the earth he would reach the sky.

"He will have so many mantras. In one hand he will show hell to be heaven and in the other hand he will show heaven to be hell. He will say, 'I am God. I am God.' He will be able to show everyone their thoughts, describing all that they think. He will be able to make everything seem heavenly and good. In that state, everyone will come forth to accept him. They will call him god. He will say, 'There is no other god, worship me. I am God, I am your lord.' " It has been related that Rasūlullāh ☾ has said this.

At that time, Allāh told him to say, "O *mu'minūn*! O true believers! Dajjāl will promise to take those who have faith in him into heaven, and to use a sword to cut apart those who do not have faith in him. He will subject them to *adhāb,* intense *adhāb.* Dajjāl will torture them, and cause them severe pain. He will cut out their tongues. He will dig out their eyes. He will cut off their ears. He will cut their bodies into pieces, he will split apart their chests.

"However, you must not forget Allāh who is One. You do not exist. Only Allāh, who is One, does exist. Accept Him with certitude.

"At that time, dajjāl will try to cut you apart and say, 'Go into hell.' But the hell of which he is speaking will be heaven for you; the heaven he bestows will be hell for you. He will do this with magic. Do not renounce your *īmān*," said Rasūlullāh ☺. "Do not deviate from *īmān*. Do not renounce your faith for all the magic that he performs, for all the wealth, the gold, the houses, and the properties. All that he shows you is merely the magic of hell. It is only a display. He cannot truly create a heaven." That is what he said.

When dajjāl comes, he will first come to Russia, to the land of snow. He will come to Russia and control everyone in that manner. He will first influence the regions where there is snow and ice. At that time, all those groups of ya'jūj and ma'jūj and those of ruined *īmān* who follow them will be short in stature. A sixty *mulam* man will become forty *mulams,* a forty *mulam* man will become twenty *mulams,* a twenty *mulam* man will become ten *mulams,* a ten *mulam* man will become a six *mulam* man, a six *mulam* man will become a six foot man—a man of four *mulams.* That is what will occur then. Four *mulams* are six feet. Men will only be six feet tall. At that time, at a time in the future, all of that could happen; it will happen.

When that occurs, the entire world will call dajjāl god. The groups of ya'jūj and ma'jūj will swim in the sea like little fish and fight in the oceans. They will be so short that they cannot be confronted in battle. They will be only this high, about a foot high, so short that they will be able to conceal themselves under all kinds of thorn and eggplant bushes. Trees will all change and become smaller. If you look at how they are grafting and grafting and grafting plants in science now, you can see them making the trees smaller. Previously, there were huge trees, and now they have made dwarf trees. Man will become smaller in the same way. They will be so small that a stem from a pepper bush and a stalk from an eggplant bush will seem like a huge pole. That is how small they will be.

At that time, the ya'jūj and ma'jūj groups will take over the whole world. When they come, in the end, Jesus ☺ will appear in the old Ka'bah in Jerusalem, or else in Damascus. It will be Friday there, and they will be giving the Friday sermon, the *khutbah*. It will probably be in Jerusalem because he will have to cross the Red Sea.

While they are praying thus, those who are in Islām will still have been praying five times. When Jesus ☺ returns, everyone will accept him, because this is what Allāh has said and what the Rasūl ☺ has said: "He shall return to life." At that time, the Mahdī will come. He will be a light.

That is also when dajjāl will come. "I have come as your lord," he will say. He will come while they are praying in the Ka'bah. Jesus ☺ will be leading the prayers, standing on the *mimbar*, reciting the Qur'ān. The *ashāb* will all be there, the *mu'minūn* will all be there. That is when dajjāl will come, saying, "Your lord is here, come out!" At that moment, the people will all scatter in fear.

His feet will be on the ground and his head will be in the clouds. His chest will be forty or fifty feet wide. If an elephant were to fall into the hollow between his clavicles, it would disappear. If an elephant were to fall there, it would disappear. The hollow in his chest will be that large. His hands will be extremely long. His body will be enormous.

That is why, when he first appeared, the *malā'ikah* were told to bind him with seventy thousand iron chains, to take him to Mount 'Arafāt, to place seven mountains on top of him, and to keep watch over him. He licks at these mountains every day; he is bound, so he can only lick at the mountain to try to escape. By the time of the first light of dawn, *awwal fajr*, he has almost licked himself out. That is why Allāh decreed the *qunūt* prayer, before dawn. After the two *rak'ahs* and the *qunūt* prayer are recited, the mountain again covers him. As soon as the mountain grows above him, he again begins to lick at it. He will lick at it until the time of *awwal fajr*. Just as he is close to getting out, the mountain grows over him again, when the prayer is performed.

However, just before the time that Jesus ◎ returns, the Muslims will abandon this prayer. They will not pray this early prayer anywhere. They will not pray this prayer in even a single place. It is then that dajjāl will be able to emerge; he will be able to cut through the entire mountain and emerge. That is dajjāl.

In the end, he will come to Jesus ◎ when he is praying. He will come to him while he is praying and when the people see them, Jesus ◎ will reach only up to his ankles. He will look up and dajjāl—jāhil, known as dajjāl—will be huge.

Jesus ◎ will say, "Allāh! What a wonder, what a wonder!"

The sound of Allāh will come, "Jesus, I created you to control him. I created you without semen, I formed you within Mary—this is why I created you. This is your responsibility, and you must bring this to an end."

"Allāh, how can I do this?"

"You must say, '*Bismillāhir-Rahmānir-Rahīm, Allāhu akbar!*' and leap towards him with the staff that was once in the hand of Rasūlullāh. You must fall onto his chest, and stab him with this staff."

When Jesus ☺ says those words and leaps up, he will fall into that hollow, stand there, and stab him. Then dajjāl will try to crush him, but his hand will not fit into the hollow in his own chest, so Jesus ☺ will fall into that hollow, stand up, take this staff, and stab him. Then dajjāl will attempt to crush him, but his hand will be too large to fit. He will attempt to crush him and smash him, but even in such a huge pit, he will not manage to do so. Jesus ☺ will stand in the hollow and stab him. When he stabs him, dajjāl will fall like a mountain and topple to the ground. The world, the *dunyā*, will be like a grindstone and he will be like the roller stone.

And then for close to sixteen years afterwards, *īmān* and goodness will grow. Goodness will grow and the world will once again become like a heaven. Mankind will become one family, one group, one *mu'min*, one *dīn*, one section. All will be as one. Then the Mahdī will say, "All right. The work that I came for is done. You must take the responsibility." He will say this and hand over the responsibility. Jesus ☺ will disappear.

The Mahdī will return to the *dunyā*, dedicate himself to his work, pray, and unite everyone. The entire *dunyā* will become good. That is the time of the Mahdī.

Then the sound of Allāh will come, and He will say, "Your time is up, you can return to Me."

While he is there, some of the people might change and leave the path of Allāh, the good path, and proceed on the evil path, the path without faith in Allāh, the path with faith in satan. When they change like that, Allāh will call him. He will go; he will leave the world. That will be a sign.

There is a kind of bird, called Karfatullāh, that will fly day and night for three days, going from the East to the West, from the

East to the North. It has four hands. Its body is fifteen miles long, and its wingspan is thirty miles wide. It will fly from the dawn to the dusk. It will wear the ring bearing the Seal of Solomon ☺ on one hand and hold the Staff of Solomon ☺ in another. When it sees sinners, it will strike them with the staff. When it sees the followers of Allāh, it will stroke them with the hand that wears the signet ring, and with all four of its hands. It will fly three times each day from the East to the West, then from the West to the North, then from the North to the South. Many sinners will be destroyed by it. It will fly for three days and finally fall into the sea of Jiddah, where it too will die. After that, the sun will not rise for three days; there will be absolute darkness.

After those three days, the sun that rose from the East will rise from the West and the sun that set in the West will set in the East, like the moon. That will change. When the Mahdī leaves the earth, the letters of the Qur'ān will fly away. The Qur'ān will not contain any letters. The book will be there, but there will be no letters inside. Then both hell and heaven will be closed because there will be no more good or evil. There will be nothing more left to be written. Only the sinners will remain. Allāh will have taken all the good people before the letters of the Qur'ān fly away. Those who are left will be the evildoers.

Women will not menstruate at that time. Of the 1,448 nerves associated with sexual energy and strength in women, a thousand of those nerves lose their strength every month, while men continuously have the strength of those 1,448 nerves. But at that time, the men will only have the energy of 448 of the nerves and the women will have the energy of the 1,448 nerves. Women will predominate, and live in an extreme frenzy of lust. They will be filled with desire and lust at that time. The number of men will decrease; they will be destroyed in war. There will be more women.

When there are more women, the frenzy of their lust will increase. They will hunt out the men and capture them. They will have no modesty or clothing, not even a shirt. They will wear nothing. They will be frenzied with lust.

There will be forty times more women than men, forty women capturing each man. There will be one man for all forty women. His strength will be diminished. The women will catch him, kill him, hang him up in a tree; desire will be the cause of this. Those times will be like that.

How can women—who at other times ordinarily experience the urges arising from 448 nerves that they can barely control—control the energy of 1,448 nerves? There will be forty times more women than men. When we look at the ratio of men to women at present, it seems there are thirty-eight women to one man. It might be this way at this time. There are definitely fewer men than women. That time is approaching, drawing closer and closer. Those energies are approaching, coming closer and closer.

In the destruction that will result, everything will be obliterated. Nothing will be left. Thus, at that time, there will be three days of darkness; when the dawn arrives, the sun will rise from the West and set in the East. It will rise from the opposite direction. The sun and moon will join together; the sun that used to rise in the East will rise in the West, the moon that used to rise in the West will rise in the East; they will pass close by each other, and set. Three days will be like that. On the fourth day, the sun will never rise again. That will be the time of the destruction of the earth.

There will be fire. This time, it will be a day of fire, destruction by fire. The sun that is millions of miles away will be only a thousand miles away from the earth. It will be only a thousand miles away. Everything will turn to fire. As it approaches, the trees, the grass, the weeds, the bushes, people, and rocks will turn to fire. The waters will boil. At that time, the waters will boil and rise up to the sky. They will boil, and water will become fire. All things in the ocean will be destroyed. Three days will pass in this state. Everything will be destroyed and turned to fire: the mountains, the seas, everything. The ocean will rise higher than any other thing. Everything will be burned.

One hundred years after that, God will again create the world. The ocean will settle down and everything else will arise again. However, we are not looking at that time. Now, we are looking at the time of destruction. We do not understand the time that is to come and we do not need to look at it. But destruction will be like this—we have to know this. If we look at our lives, we can see the changes that are taking place. If we as human beings could understand something from explanations that were given earlier, we would see that these changes are gradually, gradually growing in the world. If we look at it according to this state, we can see what will happen in the future.

The things that have been foretold by the Rasūl ☻ are occurring now. Out of forty-one signs he described, about thirty-seven have already taken place. There are only four more to come.

If we understand the thirty-seven signs, we need not doubt that four more will surely come. They will come. We can tell by simply looking at the world, the people, and the animals. When we look at the state that existed three, four, or five thousand years ago and when we look at what exists now, we can see a vast difference.

You can understand if you look at the time of Adam, Noah, Abraham, Ishmael, Moses, David, Jesus, and Muhammad, the Rasūl, Idris, Isaac, Job, Jacob, Salihu, Joseph, may the peace of God be upon them all, in comparison to the time in which we live now. This is current history. Therefore, we can understand what will happen afterwards. When we understand, we believe that the rest of it will certainly happen. This is the opinion of those who have wisdom.

See how things have changed. However, the opinions of those who have wisdom and their thoughts about destruction still exist. We know what God has said, as well as what He has placed before us. The *ambiyā'* have given many explanations and we understand them. There are also many explanations in the *ahādīth*. We have not seen some of the things that have been described, but we think about them, and we accept them.

The lights of God have given us certain explanations, the Sufis have given us certain explanations, the religions have given us certain explanations, the *auliyā'* have given us certain explanations. We can see that many religions have given us many explanations. There are many explanations. Many learned men tell us these things in many, many ways. Some people say it one way, others say it another way, various people quote various *ahādīth*, but no matter what anyone says, there is only One Truth, One Allāh, and no one other than Allāhu ta'ālā is worthy of worship.

Tawakkul-'alAllāh, al-hamdu lillāh, it is all in God's trust, all praise belongs only to Him, only He knows. *Allāhu akbar,* God is the greatest. In this, there is nothing for us to argue about. But when we look at the natural things that are changing, we can see the difference between the past and the present. We can see every section. Despite what anyone may say, and even though the *ambiyā'* have already described this, if we truly open the truth in our *qalbs,* we ourselves can see that these changes have taken place.

The truth exists, and the changes have taken place. Destruction is approaching. People's *qalbs* are changing. Even though the *dunyā* is still the same, even though the sun and the moon are still the same, even though Allāh's compassionate grace, His *rahmah*, is still the way it always has been, man is not. Man's *nafs*, his mind, his *qalb*, and his desires are all changing. Therefore, we can see that the destruction has arisen because of the wars, the separations, the battles, the destruction, the poverty, the diseases, the eminence of the privileged as opposed to the degradation of the poor. We can see this. If we think with our wisdom, we can see this. Thus, if we did understand some of what the *ambiyā'* and the wise men in ages gone by have described and some of the truth that Allāh has described, we could see that more of what has been foretold can occur. We have to accept this.

No matter what has been said in many kinds of *ahādīth*, in many kinds of words, in many kinds of *kutub*, in the Bible, in Judaism, in the Qur'ān, in Zoroastrianism, in many religions, in many different societies, one truth must remain within man. The truth that Allāh, the Rasūl ☺, the *ambiyā'*, and the lights of God have told us must dawn in our *qalbs*, and we must understand it.

If we reflect with our wisdom when we become aware of this, we will understand the changes that are occurring. We will realize that the One who is changeless does exist, and that which is yet to change will occur. We will realize that man has changed and that the animals have changed. As we continue to reflect upon this with our wisdom, we must understand the truth, do what is right, cherish Allāhu, the One who is the Good One, and try to merge with Him.

In the time to come, in the future, we must know what to do in this *waqt* and in the next *waqt*. We must know what we have done in the previous *waqt*—the *waqt* that is over. We must know what we must do in the *waqt* that is occurring now and in the *waqt* that is yet to come. We must know what to do in each *waqt*. We have to see to that and worship Allāh.

If we bow down before Him and worship Him, doing what is right, if we take in the good qualities, we will obtain good results. Let us do this and obtain the good results before that time comes.

Āmīn. As-salāmu 'alaikum wa rahmatullāhi.

This is how the messengers, the *rusul,* gave us many explanations. We are telling you the explanations we understand. Others speak of what they understand and we speak of what we understand. Everyone speaks merely of what he understands. However, there is only One Truth. Allāh, His Truth, and prayer—that knowledge alone will take us to the shore. If we do *taubah* for the mistakes we have made, if we do *tasbīh* in the way we should do it, giving all responsibility to God, saying *tawakkul-'alAllāh* for the future, praising God by saying *al-hamdu lillāh* for what we have received in the present, and if our state, our *hāl,* continues in this manner, that will be what a good person will do.

Āmīn. As-salāmu 'alaikum wa rahmatullāhi wa barakātahu.

All right. Whether it is to happen today or tomorrow, they have spoken about it. These are the words spoken by the *rusul* and the *ambiyā'* in the *ahādīth,* and we have to know them in the future.

CHAPTER 20

A'ūdhu billāhi minash-shaitānir-rajīm.
I seek refuge in God from the accursed satan.

Bismillāhir-Rahmānir-Rahīm.
In the name of God, the Most Compassionate, the Most Merciful.

WHAT'S GONE IS GONE

Wednesday, November 16, 1977, 1:20 P.M.
Colombo, Sri Lanka

What's gone is gone. All that's gone is gone.
The day has dawned.
It's time for all good people to begin the journey.
Good people, all of you, it's time to begin the journey.

What's gone is gone.
The day has dawned.
It's time now for all good people to begin the journey.
It's time now to begin the journey.

When we count the days, we see the time is here.
When we count the days, we see the time is here.
The time for the reign of the cruel people is here.
The time for a world in which only sinners live is here.
The time for a kingdom of terrible crimes is now here.
The time for a world kingdom of terrible crimes is here.

What's gone is gone.
The day has dawned.
It is time now for all good people to leave the world.
It is time now for all good people to leave the world.

It is now the time of the animal that seems like a man.
The word "Man" has been altered and ruined.
The word "Man" has been altered and ruined.
Man's qualities and actions have all been lost,
they no longer exist.
It is now the time in which man has become an animal.
He is like a dog, a jackal, a tiger, and a bear.
It is now a time in which he seizes other living beings,
drinks their blood, and devours them.

All of our time seems to have lasted for but a moment.
When we look at all the creations,
only the animal, the *hayawān*, lives well.
The one who was born a human being
has turned into an animal, and now he no longer exists.
As a result, terrible crimes, grievous sins, murders,
theft, falsehood, and jealousy have become ordinary events.
Jealousy has become ordinary.
Thus, it is difficult for man to live with truth.
Thus, it is difficult for a true man to exist.

A man with a happy heart,
a man with a perfect heart
who has become so through the actions of God,
who has become so through the actions of God,
will be hard to find.

He will rarely appear.
A man in whom God will be seen
will rarely appear.
Such a man will see only God.
Such a man will see only God.

What's gone is gone.
The day has dawned, and
it's time for all good people to begin the journey.
It's time for all good people to begin the journey.

All the worlds have become like this.
Wherever he has been born, man has become a beast
with demonic qualities, animal qualities,
with demonic qualities, animal qualities, satan's actions,
with the venomous qualities of snakes and scorpions.
Man's life has become like that
of a poisonous being in the world.
Man's life has become like that of a poisonous being.

Accordingly, no one who believes in God,
no one who places his intention in God,
no one who trusts God,
no one who loves God
will have this world any longer.
Thus, they do not have this world any more.
From now on, we will not have this world any more.

What's gone is gone.
The day has dawned.
It's time for all good people to begin the journey.

None of the times have changed in the world.
None of the seasons have changed in the world.
None of the animals have changed in the world.
None of the reptiles have changed in the world.
None of the creations in the oceans or
the creations on the lands have changed in the world.
None of them have changed in the world.
None of the birds, the fowls, or
the species of worms have changed in the world.

He who has been born as a man,
he who wears the face of a man,
he who wears the face of a man,
he who makes the sound of a man—
only he has changed in the world.
Only he has changed in the world.

He intends harm to all living beings.
He intends to kill all living beings.
He intends to torment all living beings.
He considers eating all living beings.
He intends to torment and to destroy all living beings.
He has tried to chew and swallow even God.
Doing that, he has tried to discover Him scientifically,
and he has declared that God does not exist.
His constant declaration is "There is no God."
He is constantly talking about how he himself is God.
He asserts that man himself is the creator of the world.
He proclaims that man was once a monkey.
He proclaims that man was born as a monkey before, and
that man evolved into a human being.

They say that man evolved into a human being.
They call this science.
They say he was born with an utter lack of wisdom.
They call this science.
They say he was born with an utter lack of wisdom.
They say he lived inside an animal.
They say he lived inside an animal.
Yet, it is through these very pursuits
that he did change and become an animal.
Yet, it is through these very pursuits
that he did change and become an animal.

He has turned into a monkey, as described, and
become an animal.
He has turned into a monkey; he has turned into an animal;
he has turned into a worm and an insect;
he has turned into an ass and a horse;
he has turned into an elephant, a tiger, and a bear.

He lives in the world as many millions of animals.
He lives in the world as many millions of animals.
He has changed.
He has changed.
He has forgotten God.
He has destroyed the truth.
He has lost the Only One.
He has lost all his own real actions and qualities.

Man is the only one,
the only one who wears the face of a man.
Only he has changed.

None of the rest of God's creations have changed.
The times have not changed.
The seasons have not changed.
Truth has not changed.
The lights have not changed.
The sun has not changed.
The moon has not changed.
The rain has not changed.
The sunshine has not changed.
The law of time has not changed.
The fruits have not changed.
The trees have not changed.
The creations in the oceans have not changed.
Nothing else has changed in the world.
Only the monkey that is man has changed.
Only the animal that is man has changed.
Only he has changed in this world.

Therefore,
all the people of truth, all the good people everywhere,
all the people of truth, all the good people everywhere,
all who serve God,
all who act with compassion,
all who have mercy towards other living beings,
all who live believing in the One,
all the good people,
all who serve God—
it's time for all good people to begin the journey.
It's time for all good people to begin the journey.

Because this world has become dark,
this world has become dark,
as dark as the mind of man, and
because man has changed,
all that is past is over,
the day has dawned,
it's time for all good people to begin the journey,

Everything will become food for fire, for earth, and for water. Through fire, through earthquakes, through water, through air, through hurricanes, through toxic clouds, through microbes, through lightning strikes, and through the methods we have utilized in science—through those poisons and through their interactions—the destruction of the world is drawing closer. They are heaping the fire onto their own heads. They are destroying themselves in the world, through their own science, their own ignorance, and their own arrogance. The time of that destruction is near. It is coming closer and closer.

As a result, human beings will no longer have a place in which to live here. Human beings will not live in this country any more. The ya'jūj-ma'jūj groups who say there is no God are trying to take over. Those groups and all who are on their side will be destroyed by their own actions.

All the good people will be protected by God. God will protect them and rescue them. That day is coming closer and closer now. Human beings cannot live here anymore.

It will be very difficult. Famine, pestilence, poverty, cruelty, and karma will all come, swarm after swarm. Poisons and toxins will taint the food, the drink, and the water. There will be famine and pestilence because of their cruel actions. Famine and pestilence will increase and cause harm to all living beings as a result of the cruel actions of their minds. This is the state that could arise.

War is trying to come to the entire world. In every country, there will be fighting between husband and wife, fighting between father and child, fighting between mother and child, fighting between siblings. There will be fighting between one government and another, fighting between one title and another, fighting between one job and another, fighting between one business and another, fighting between one crop and another.

There will be so many discrete battlefields like this everywhere in the world.

There will be fighting between one religion and another, fighting between one ethnic group and another, fighting between one village and another, fighting between one scripture and another, fighting between one branch of education and another. Each will be fighting the other in the world in this manner. Wars will be fought everywhere in the world, all looking forward to the time of destruction. It is going to occur like this in all parts of the world. Thus, the world seems to be coming to an end very quickly.

Everything is being altered. Even the drinking water is being poisoned. The air is poisonous air. All the atomic energies, the atoms and their energies, are attacking the body and creating cancer, diabetes, asthma, tuberculosis, lung disease, depression, insanity, loss of eyesight, loss of hearing, loss of the sense of smell, the dimming of the light in the eyes. Mental retardation, heart disorders, blood disorders, and skin disorders will all come into being. It is all happening because of these things. Humankind could be destroyed through famine, pestilence, and poverty, through earthquakes, and similar things. The time in which it will have to be destroyed is drawing closer and closer.

Destruction is approaching because of all who endeavor to rule God's kingdom without God, because of all who say, "There is no God." As a result, destruction is drawing near.

It is God's kingdom. He is the Protector, He is the Owner. Those who try to do it without Him will not do His duty. It is God's kingdom, His will, His food, and His protection. He is the Watcher. He is the Servant and He is the Owner. He is the Trustee. He is the Poor Person and He is the Rich Person. He is the small Atom and He is the large Atom. He is the Creator and He is the Protector.

One who tries to rule God's kingdom without God will not accomplish even one of the kinds of work that He does.

God will exist within the atom. He will exist within the smallest thing and He will exist within the largest thing. Therefore, a person in that state will not be able to do it. Since he will not be able to do it, the moment he attempts to take over God's kingdom, the instant he tries to rule it, he will not rule it. However, in the attempt to do so, other lives can be destroyed and he too can be destroyed. This is the reason these evils are going to come. This is what will occur.

Fathers kill their sons and sons kill their fathers, even now. Daughters kill their mothers and mothers kill their daughters; elder brothers kill their younger brothers and younger brothers kill their elder brothers. Many things like this will occur and there will be a deluge of blood everywhere. It is going to occur. I am not saying it will happen today, but it will come.

Part Four
IN GOD'S KINGDOM

CHAPTER 21

A'ūdhu billāhi minash-shaitānir-rajīm.
I seek refuge in God from the accursed satan.

Bismillāhir-Rahmānir-Rahīm.
In the name of God, the Most Compassionate, the Most Merciful.

THE NIGHT IS FINALLY OVER

Thursday, February 19, 1976, 12:57 P.M.
Philadelphia, USA

All that is past is over,
the night is finally over, and
now we can start on the journey.
All that is past is over,
the day has dawned, and
now we can start on the journey,
now we can start on the journey to our Father.

All that is past is over,
the day has dawned, and
the act of our existence here is over,
the act of our existence is done.
All that is past is over,
the night is finally over, and
now we can start on the journey to our Father,
now we can start on the journey to our Father.

Wherever we look, there are actors.
Wherever we look, there are actors.
When we look into the distance and
when we look nearby,
there are actors on stages everywhere,
actors everywhere, actors everywhere.
There is no reward in this,
no reward in this for us.

Leave the actors' groups,
leave the artifice of the actors,
leave the visions of the actors behind.
All that is past is over,
the night is finally over, and
now we can start on the journey,
now we can start on the journey to our Father.

When we look ahead, there is darkness.
When we look south, there is satan.
When we look east, there is maya.
When we look at the mind, there is the world.
When we look at desire, there is the dog.
When we look at the sights we see with our eyes,
they are all acts.

Because of this,
O you who have wisdom,
because of this,
O you who have wisdom,
please analyze and look at,
please analyze and look at your body,

please analyze and look at your body.
All that is past is over,
the night is finally over, and
now we can start on the journey,
now we can start on the journey to our Father,
now we can start on the journey.

Wherever we look, there is business.
when we look ahead, we see the business of acting.
Wherever we turn, everywhere we look,
they are like elephants, tigers, bears, and lions,
elephants, tigers, bears, and lions,
snakes, scorpions, and tarantulas,
birds and animals.

Everywhere we look,
everywhere we look,
they are closing in and glaring at us.
They are thinking about sacrificing us,
drinking our blood,
killing our bodies and our lives, and
trying to eat us.
Because of this,
let's escape with wisdom and leave,
let's escape, leave, and
go to our rightful Father.

All that is past is over,
the night is finally over, and
now we can start on the journey,
now we can start on the journey to our Father.

To secure our birthright from our beloved Father,
to secure our birthright from our beloved Father,
we must search with wisdom.
To secure our birthright from our beloved Father,
we must act with wisdom.
To attain to our birthright from our beloved Father,
we must act with wisdom and blissful qualities.

Let's search for our Father with blissful qualities.
Come, let's search for our Father!
Please come! Please come!
Everyone, gather together, unite,
and focus on that One.

All that is past is over,
the night is finally over, and
now we can start on the journey,
now we can start on the journey to our Father.

The truth has flown off and
man's good conduct has run away.
The truth has flown off and
human conduct has been driven out and chased away.
The goodness has been hidden,
all the goodness has been forgotten.

Falsehood, hypocrisy, arrogance, and
jealousy have become abundant,
jealousy has become abundant.
They have become enemies to God,
in love with ignorance, in love with ignorance.

This world, these people, this creation,
all of them, have begun to act in that way.

Because of this,
O you who have wisdom,
O you who love God,
O you who have grace
must look at and examine yourselves.
Let's search with wisdom,
focus on His grace,
focus on His grace, and
go with love.

All that is past is over,
the night is finally over, and
now we can start on the journey,
now we can start on the journey to our Father,
now all of us can start on the journey.

There is no reward for us on this stage.
The dog of desire does not display
even the slightest gratitude.
In the dance of the monkey mind
there are only delusions, nothing else.
In the dance of the monkey mind
there are only delusions, nothing else.

Wherever we look, there are animals.
When we look at the body, it is a demon.
When we look into the body, there are malignant spirits.
It is hell inside and maya outside,

hell inside and hell outside.
Wherever we look—demons!
When we look into the distance—ghosts!
When we look nearby—animals!
No matter where we look,
there are demonic bloodsucking animals,
demons, ghosts, poisonous creatures, and
malignant spirits playing everywhere in the world.

There is no reward in it at all.
Please realize this with wisdom.
Please see this clearly with wisdom, and
look closely at the body.
Please understand and see the truth, and
search for goodness.
Let's go to our Master.
Let's go to our Master.

All that is past is over,
the night is finally over, and
now we can start on the journey,
now we can all start on the journey,
now we can start on the journey to our Father.

O you who have wisdom,
now you can start on the journey,
now you who have wisdom can go
on the journey to our Father.

CHAPTER 22

A'ūdhu billāhi minash-shaitānir-rajīm.
I seek refuge in God from the accursed satan.
Bismillāhir-Rahmānir-Rahīm.
In the name of God, the Most Compassionate, the Most Merciful.

TAKING THE CHILDREN TO HEAVEN

Monday, May 12, 1986
Philadelphia, USA

[Bawangal is describing a vision. Taping begins after he has started to speak. Only the translator's voice—in italics—is recorded in the beginning.]

"In his meditation, he saw that he was going from this dunyā, *which is hell. He was taking a lot of his children along with him on his way to heaven. And while they were going along, even from a distance, Bawangal could hear and see heaven. And he could see the people there, anxiously awaiting his arrival, anxiously waiting to welcome him, and all kinds of festivity and happiness in anticipation of Bawangal's arrival."*

I was extremely happy. I wept and wept with bliss. However, when I was bringing the children out of hell, and when I looked back happily, I saw that they had divided into three groups, one after the other, after the other. Of the three groups, only one group was in the forefront; the other two were further back and falling behind, as if they were going to pull away. We were getting close to heaven. One group was near me; the other two were separate. Only that one section was following directly behind me.

I spoke to God, "O God, please accept all my children. Accept them all. Gather them together as one. Unite them. Give them all heaven. Give them the *malā'ikah*, the earnings, the invitation, the welcome, and the beauty, and accept them into heaven."

There were three groups: the first moved continuously, the second started and stopped, and the third group was gradually falling behind and drifting away.

I spoke to God again, "O God, please gather them together and take them unto Yourself. They are indeed my children. Please gather them together. They are ignorant and lack wisdom. The creations You have created have so many kinds of ignorance and foolishness. They have arrogance, karma, maya, and a certain amount of obstinacy. You must dispel those things and accept them as Your children. You must gather them together as one and accept them, Father. You must accept them into Your kingdom. You must do this, make them one, and help them." I cried and cried and cried. I wept and wept as I spoke.

Some of the children who had been separate then joined the first group, but others still lagged behind. It was a little difficult for them. They had stopped and were falling further back. Little by little, they were becoming more separate.

"They are all good, good, good, good! They just possess some kind of section. O God, they are all good. O God, they just have that one section—please dispel it from them and accept them. They are good children. They are my children. They are Your children. One people," I said.

Appā, Rahmān! I saw this. I saw a lot. That is what I said as I wept. Heaven was indescribably beautiful and lovely. It was a beautiful place.

"You must forgive my children, O God. Please pardon them. Please forgive my children's faults. May You accept them all, Allāh. O God, protect them."

I was pulling them out of the hell known as the *dunyā*. O God, please accept them.

A'ūdhu billāhi minash-shaitānir-rajīm.
I seek refuge in God from the accursed satan.

Bismillāhir-Rahmānir-Rahīm.
In the name of God, the Most Compassionate, the Most Merciful.

WHAT FORM, IF ANY, WILL HE TAKE NEXT

Sunday, October 26, 1986, 10:25 A.M.
Philadelphia, USA

CAROLYN ANDREWS

This is a big question. You said that you came to many peoples in many forms because they asked for you to come in that form. I believe that we asked for you to come in the form of oneness, and I believe that you have—I know that you have.

At some point this form will leave us. Two questions: What form, if any, will you take next? And what are we to do here in the future without this form? How can we keep this Treasure in this world?

M. R. BAWA MUHAIYADDEEN

Where will it go? When a fish dies, it is turned into a dried fish. If a man dies, the smell is terrible; the smell is unbearable. If a man dies, he stinks, and cannot be used for anything. If a fish dies, at least it can be turned into a dried fish, a dried fish that is worth something. Do you understand? When a man dies, he stinks. When a fish dies, you can have dried fish that is worth something. But the smell will always be simply the smell.

We smell whether we die or whether we live. Are you living depending on this smell? Do not depend on this smell. It is something that can leave at any time.

But there is another matter. If you disappear and if you change before the body disappears and changes, if you turn into That and if you prepare in yourself the state in which you can change, then That is what will remain. Whatever is going to go, will go.

The Treasure you are looking for does exist, does it not? There is an unchanging Treasure. This smell is going to change. There is a Treasure that does not change, a Treasure that does not smell bad. The body will change, but before it changes, you must change into That, or else That must change into you. That will never leave, will it? That will never leave, and That is what you need. Endeavor to search for it.

All right, Secretary, my child, all the things that live in the ocean are there. Let us look at them. Let us speak about fish. The fish are in the ocean; they will not survive without water. They will die. Have you seen this? They will die. Without water they will die. They must live in the water.

The fish need water in order to live, yet it is also in water that they are turned into curry. It is in water that they are turned into curry, that they are made to taste good, and that they are put into the stomach. Which one is the wonder? Without water, they will die, and with water they are turned into curry. Is that a wonder? How can that be?

We need to live in our water, but it is in the same water that we are cooked and turned into curry. That is the wonder. That is the wonder! Child, it is similar to how we take on the body of the five elements in this world and how we live in it; we think we are going to continue living in it. However, there is no actual wonder in this. We just think we are always going to live in the world.

We think like fish amidst the water of our blood ties, our scriptures, our races, our religions, and our ethnic groups—we think we are going to live here in all that surrounds us. "Without this, we will die. Without that, without this, without that, we will die," we say. We continue to live like this. In this life itself, we cannot live without these things: without the world, we cannot take a form, we cannot exist, we cannot live.

But inside, there is a secret, a wonder. Within this body there is another body, a body that exists as the pure soul. Without that body we are dead. We must enter into that body in order to disappear. We must disappear into that body, and then we must disappear into God's body. The secret is to disappear into the body of Allāh. Then we will die without dying.

It is not about dying in this. This is the house of the senses, and that is the house of the soul. Just as the fish disappears after we taste it, we have to experience the taste of our soul in that house. Within it, we can experience the taste and happiness of life. We need to know it while we are still alive. Just as a fish that lives in water is also cooked in water, we have to enter the house of God and disappear while living in the body as human beings. Then we can know the taste.

That, child, is the wonder. Secretary, doing it like this is the secret, it is the wonder. No matter how long we live, there is no other wonder. Find the clarity within it.

If you go into it, find the Taste, and become the Taste, then that individual will be gone. My love you. *Anbu. Anbu.*

CHAPTER 24

A'ūdhu billāhi minash-shaitānir-rajīm.
I seek refuge in God from the accursed satan.
Bismillāhir-Rahmānir-Rahīm.
In the name of God, the Most Compassionate, the Most Merciful.

CAN HE STILL INSTRUCT US

Sunday, January 21, 1978, 8:30 P.M.
Colombo, Sri Lanka

QUESTION

In the case of a *Gnāna Guru* who is being adored and followed by some disciples, could those who really wanted to, meet him or see him or approach him, after his demise?

Can they get the spiritual instruction also after that?

M. R. BAWA MUHAIYADDEEN
(speaking to the people in the room)

Tell us!

ARABY, NOORUL AMEENA MACAN MARKAR
(laughing in anticipation of what Bawangal will say)

Yes, they can!

M. R. BAWA MUHAIYADDEEN

They can?

ARABY

For someone like that, someone with those qualities—

M. R. BAWA MUHAIYADDEEN
(speaking to the people in the room)
She said they can. You tell us.

TRANSLATOR
Araby says it can be done.

ARABY
In shā'Allāh, it can be done.

M. R. BAWA MUHAIYADDEEN
(to the people in the room)
Do you accept Araby's statement? *(then he turns to Araby)* Tell us why they can.

ARABY
(laughing even harder now)
Bawangal has to tell us.

M. R. BAWA MUHAIYADDEEN
How can I do that? You are the one who has to answer for what you say!
(everyone laughs along with Araby)

QUESTION
We are here, followers of Bawangal, listening to him and receiving *gnānam* from him. Specifically, could our children or grandchildren in later years, after the demise of the Shaikh, derive *gnānam* from him?

M. R. BAWA MUHAIYADDEEN
All right. You are following a Guru now. All right. If you truly have been following a Guru, that is good.

However, if you had actually been following the Guru, you should have disappeared into the Guru. If you had disappeared, there would be no duality. You and the Guru would be one.

When it is like that, the Guru is not gone. The Guru is with the one who disappeared. When it is like that, when there is a person who has not met the Guru and a person who has disappeared into the Guru—into that authority—the person who has not met the Guru could receive the benefit of meeting the Guru through the person who has disappeared. If the Guru is there with him, he could meet the Guru through him and obtain the benefit. Then the Guru will be there. He will not have left. There will be another Guru, the Guru who lives as the Guru. He might exist like that.

Is there a Guru like that in the world, in the *dunyā?* Do you live like those disciples?

You must find a Guru like that. You must disappear into that Guru and the Guru must disappear into you. If that occurs, it will not matter if you have sat in front of the Guru or if you have not sat in front of the Guru.

Until then, you will not actually have met the Guru, and neither will the person who has not seen him. Then, neither of you are able to see him, are you? If neither of you sees him—*(Bawangal laughs)*—you have wasted your time and he has wasted his time. Neither of you has seen the Guru. Neither of you has benefited.

There will be a Guru in the world. You must search for him and catch him. After you have searched for him and caught him, you must disappear into him. All your responsibilities must be given to him with determination, faith, certitude, and *īmān*. If your state is like that, the Guru will be within you and it is possible that you will be within the Guru. Then he will not have left. He will not have gone. If there is a Guru who is not gone, the person who has not seen the Guru will see the Guru there. He will be there and he will definitely see him. It is possible that he might obtain a benefit.

Otherwise, you have not seen him and that person has not seen him. Both of you will be the same.

QUESTION

If instead of Guru, you put Allāh, then is the whole, same story valid as well?

M. R. BAWA MUHAIYADDEEN

I do not understand.

ANOTHER PERSON IN THE ROOM

If you put Allāh where the Guru is, will the result be the same? She sees the Guru as Allāh. Can we see Allāh as the Guru?

(the people in the room join in to debate the question)

TRANSLATOR

(to the person who asked the question)

Please, can you come forward?

QUESTION

If instead of giving the devotion to the Guru, you give that to Allāh, then still the story is the same—what he just explained—it is only towards Allāh that you...

M. R. BAWA MUHAIYADDEEN

How can firewood burn without fire? A fire is necessary. Only if there is fire can the firewood catch fire. And when the firewood burns, you can cook something. You cannot cook otherwise. Similarly, you must catch fire from the Guru. The point is there. After that, if you disappear into it, the fire will take hold. You will have light. You can reach the light only through that. You cannot get it otherwise. You cannot go directly. There is a point—there is a point that is the Guru.

Let us look at the word "guru." Everything is called guru, guru. You read books and you talk of gurus. Everything is a guru. Everything in the world is a guru. However, no matter what book you read, the book will just be describing it.

The book will burn only if it is put into a fire. The book will not start the fire. There is no power in it—no power. That is just an academic lesson, knowledge for the intellect to take in. It is for intellect to take in. There is no power in it.

The words of a Guru are direct and there is a power in them. That power must go through you like the electric current that comes from a battery. If you accept it and open your *qalb*, it will enter. That is the current. That is its power.

Therefore, you must endeavor to obtain that power from a Guru. It is not an academic lesson. You must be open, let the words he speaks get through to you, and accept them. They must go inside. You must take them in, take them in, take them in, take them in, and charge the motor. You must take them into the motor. The current must create the charge. Your heart, your *qalb*, must be a fully charged battery. You must take in the current of the Guru. You must take in each word. You must go to him to get charged. That charge is the light. That is the power. There is no benefit in the places that hold no charge: the academic lessons you have learned, the words you have heard. They hold no charge and no light will come from them because they bear no current.

It is for this reason that it is said a Guru is needed. The charge is drawn from him. The current creates the charge. That is why it is said that a Guru is needed. You cannot find it in books. You cannot find it in anything else. The charge must be received directly. To do that, you must connect the wire directly to the battery through a focused mind. One wire must be connected to you—the wire must be connected to the battery. The other wire must be connected to the Guru. The charge must go from this to that. It will be correct only when it is like that. The life will come into it only in that way. If you do not take it in the correct manner, there will be no charge. This is the reason it is said that a Guru is needed. When you speak of a Guru, it is a charged light. A motor! When the motor works, the battery is charged. This is how it works. If it does not, it does not.

GNĀNIYĀR, NOORUL KAREEMAH MOHAMED
It cannot be just any guru, it must be a true Guru.

M. R. BAWA MUHAIYADDEEN
What kind of truth is that?

GNĀNIYĀR
Every guru can't give the charge of the battery like a true Guru such as Bawangal.

M. R. BAWA MUHAIYADDEEN
Where is it? Where is the truth and where is the Guru?

GNĀNIYĀR
The *qalb* understands it, Bawangal.

M. R. BAWA MUHAIYADDEEN
It understands? That must be why you left, went around, and came back. You went home that way and then you came back this way.
（everyone laughs）

GNĀNIYĀR
Wherever we go, the charge brings the benefit.

M. R. BAWA MUHAIYADDEEN
It is not like that. The man who meditated for twelve years lost the fruit of *gnānam* in two seconds. He left for two minutes to wash his face and brush his teeth thinking, "Now I can eat it." And that is when the fruit fell.

It is not like that, Gnāniyār. If you can stay on the correct point, it will be good. Your mouth must remain open. The oyster that grows the pearl must keep its mouth open so that when the rain known as the compassionate grace of God, the *rahmah,* falls, the pearl will be formed from the silvery raindrops. The oysters know from the temperature, the cool wind, "*Ah,* today it is going to rain," and they come to the surface. "*Ah,*" they all come to the surface. The moment the rain falls onto the ocean they take in one or two drops. As soon as the raindrops fall into the oysters, they close their mouths and sink back down to the sea bottom. Your mouth must be open like that. If you keep your mouth open and try a little, the pearl will develop—the pearl. After that, you must stay closed. You must go to the bottom, and hold on to it until the pearl matures. Then the oyster will die on its own and the worth of the pearl can be appraised. That is what it is like.

You are speaking like the turtle that laid its eggs, left them behind, and said, "I am going to the ocean," not realizing the eggs would hatch in the meantime.

GNĀNIYĀR

No, Bawangal, that is not what I said, I said I got a true Guru.

M. R. BAWA MUHAIYADDEEN

That Guru is not in the world. In the world, they are all gurus, saying, "*Viru, viru, vir.*" But they are not the Guru who will give you what you need. They will just say, "*Viru, viru, vir, viru, viru, vir, virupam*s—whatever you want." They are just there for what you want.

Something has happened. I too am searching for a Guru but I still have not found one.

QUESTION

We are following Guru Bawa.

M. R. BAWA MUHAIYADDEEN

You are? I do not know anything about that. I am searching for a Guru. I do not know what you are coming for. I know nothing about that. I am also looking for a Guru. I am searching. I do not know what you are coming for.

Everyone comes to the marketplace. How they search for their villages when the sun goes down, look. Everyone comes to the marketplace. When the sun goes down, they go back to their own homes.

(Bawangal begins to sing)

Everyone comes to the marketplace.
How they search for their villages
when the sun goes down, look.
Do these villages belong to us?
Believe that there is a true and good Friend,
O people of the world.
Believe that there is a true and good Friend,
O people of the world.
Everyone comes to the marketplace.
How they search for their villages
when the sun goes down, look.

All of you come to this market, but then all of you leave when the sun goes down. No one is left at the market. You stop. You all leave. Thus, all of you go back and forth, to and from the market. So I will also sing this song:

You come and you go because of me.
Someone is looking on from above.
I am going to die because of you, and
you are going to perish because of me.

You are coming and going because of me.
That is fine. Come. Go.
You come and you go because of me.
Someone is looking on from above.
The Angel of Death, Israel ☺ is watching from above.
I am going to die because of you, and
you are going to perish because of me.

I am going to die because of you. I am going to die because of you, because of the issue of my entanglement with you. You are going to perish because of me. Are you going to live after both of us have been ruined? Now I am also saying what Gnāniyār said.

At other times I say, "You come and you come and you leave, and it's making my stomach burn. It's burning. You come and you come and you leave. My stomach is burning. Why? What are you coming for? What are you leaving for? Where are you going? What is it that you come for? What is it that you go for? My stomach is burning, *appāh*." This is what I say. This is what it is like.

What Gnāniyār was describing is what the worm on the hook said to the fish. "You come and you go. What are you coming for?" Ah?

All of you go on so many different paths. Many of you are stone worshipers. Many of you are bone worshipers. Many of you are light worshipers. Many of you are sun worshipers. Many of you are prayer worshipers. Many of you are earth worshipers. Many of you are gold worshipers. Many of you are property worshipers. Many of you are inheritance worshipers. Many of you worship your children. Many of you worship your own birth. *Ah?* Many of you worship animals. There are limitless kinds of worship. They are all worship.

Yet only when you truly comprehend what is truly real will your rebirths be cut off. Your rebirths will be cut off when you truly see Reality and then worship. Until you truly see Reality, you will not cut off your rebirth. After all, you worship everything. You worship stones and become a stone. You worship earth and become earth. You worship animals and become an animal. You worship fire and become fire. You worship air and become air— you become the *nafs*. You worship water and become liquid. You worship each thing one after the other. You worship a monkey and become a monkey. You worship a bull and become a bull. You worship a lion and become a lion. You worship a dog and become a dog. You worship an ass and become an ass. You are changing and becoming one thing after another.

CHAPTER 25

A'ūdhu billāhi minash-shaitānir-rajīm.
I seek refuge in God from the accursed satan.

Bismillāhir-Rahmānir-Rahīm.
In the name of God, the Most Compassionate, the Most Merciful.

WHAT WILL HAPPEN TO THE FELLOWSHIP

Thursday, June 5, 1986, 7:10 A.M.
Philadelphia, USA

RABIA MILLER

Bismillāhir-Rahmānir-Rahīm. At the time of the Rasūl ☪, a follower asked the Rasūl ☪ what would happen to Islām after he left, and my question is what will happen to this Fellowship and to these children after Bawa leaves? *Astaghfirullāhal-'azīm.*

M. R. BAWA MUHAIYADDEEN

(laughing)

She is asking pardon for her sins and for her question at the same time! *Astaghfirullāhal-'azīm.* What kind of answer can possibly be given?

(everyone laughs and there is a short pause)

This has a good meaning. The sun will not leave the sky. It has to stay there. The moon will not leave the sky. It has to stay; it is an essential thing and it will not leave. The sun will stay, but you will need a magnifying glass to start the fire.

If you make your *qalb* clear, it will be a looking glass. You can look into it, make yourself presentable, wash, and make yourself clean. Then the understanding will come.

According to faith, certitude, and determination, it will not leave. It is a Light and that is a light as well. *Al-qadā' wal-qadar.* It depends on what you are looking for. Because of your faith, it will stay with you.

No one has seen God, has he? Yet He dwells with everyone. If our intention is God's intention, if we keep our Father in our *qalbs* like that, we can think of Him whenever we need, and the memory will come immediately.

As for the Fellowship—when each *qalb* is right, the Fellowship will be right. If you have hatred in your *qalb,* and if you give your *qalb* to satan, there will be hatred.

If each of you, each child, can remain just as you were in the presence of the Shaikh, having that same *qalb,* and if you continue to nourish your wisdom, the Fellowship will grow.

However, if one person says to another, "I am great! You are great! He is different! He is different!" heads will be split open. *Al-qadā' wal-qadar*: your state will determine what will happen.

If you, the Fellowship members, live as good people and act accordingly, if you are children of wisdom, you will invite your brothers and sisters and you will embrace all of them: the angry child who is burning with rage, those who are jealous, and children bent on revenge will definitely be amongst them.

How should we live? In the same way that we have been calming them, here and there, here and there, bearing it all, and comforting them. The children who are here in the Fellowship should not show any pride, they should not show what is known as the "I." They should be small children to the small children, learned children to the learned children, while constantly calming and comforting everyone. If you do this, it will be all right. It will continue to grow.

The Fellowship has to be God's house. It has to be God's kingdom. If you are God's children, it will never be destroyed, it will always exist. It will always be here for you. If you are not those children, satan could come to take over.

This is in the hands of each one of you, in your *qalbs*. You must be in that state. Allāh is the One who is responsible. If you are the servants doing the duties, then it will be all right. If you are His children, that is how you will do your duties.

Āmīn. Allāh is sufficient. May He protect us. May He protect you, may He protect this, His house.

The Fellowship house is His Mosque—it is a house that is a mosque. He must protect it. You who do duty here can also pray for this.

If you are to sow wisdom, you will have to obtain grace, you will have to obtain His *rahmah.* If you plant those flowers and nurture them, you will have to get the grace, you will have to get the bountiful harvest of His *rahmah,* will you not?

If you take your good qualities and your wisdom and your prayers and use them in the sowing, you can obtain His grace, His treasures, His *gnānam,* His *mubārakāt,* and His qualities.

If you lose your wisdom, only mistakes will be made.

A'ūdhu billāhi minash-shaitānir-rajīm.
I seek refuge in God from the accursed satan.

Bismillāhir-Rahmānir-Rahīm.
In the name of God, the Most Compassionate, the Most Merciful.

HOW CAN WE HELP

Saturday, December 8, 1973, 8:15 P.M.
Philadelphia, USA

M. R. BAWA MUHAIYADDEEN

Loving *vanakkam* from a very small person to all of God's children. Love and *vanakkam* from someone who is very lacking in wisdom. Loving children, what shall we speak about now? What do you want me to speak about? What should be said? What should be spoken about?

QUESTION

Guru Bawa is going back to Ceylon soon. How can we all, in each section, for whatever length of time he is gone, best help him and carry on our own work?

M. R. BAWA MUHAIYADDEEN

My loving child, my child, you are asking an appropriate question. This is the world. In it, we can sow many kinds of plants. Indeed, we can sow any plant acceptable to our minds. We can plant wheat, fruit such as apples, and little bushes such as peanuts. We can plant anything. God has created a section in the earth for everyone to sow whatever they please, no matter what they sow. We can plant. Everyone can sow any seed. Everyone has the right to sow seeds according to his intention and wish. This is something that is outwardly visible. Everyone who looks can see it.

How must the plants be grown? They need water. There is water in the earth. What must be done? The water is there. The earth does not lack water. There is a place for the plants that must be sown, and there is water.

However, can we pour ocean water onto them? The plants will be burned by the salt. Some plants will grow with salt, some plants such as coconut trees, palmyra trees, and sea grasses will grow. Some plants will grow with things opposite to what other plants require.

We cannot do that for the other plants, they need good water. That good water exists in the earth. Water exists in all places at a certain level. If a well is dug to that level, the spring water will flow into it. Then we can install a pump, draw out the water, and grow the plants. The water is there underneath. It will not be absent.

Similarly, if you want to grow your plants and you work hard, the water will not be absent. You must undergo a little difficulty to dig down to the water table. The ocean is all around us. This world is in the middle. Therefore, there will be water. We cannot say there is no water just because it is at the level of the water table; the water is there. If you work hard and dig, you can grow your crops. You cannot say there is no water; the water is where it should be. You must know the place.

Similarly, your Father, your Guru, your wisdom, and the truth are within you, exactly where they should be. The truth is in that dot within your *qalb*. You must open the church. If you open the wisdom and dig to the depth where the wisdom exists, the grace that is the explanation will flow from there. Then you can draw it out and use it for anything you want.

You can draw it out and use it to free the souls of all lives. You can draw out the water known as love for all lives. You can draw out the three thousand divine qualities of God. You can give those lives the grace of God. You can give them the plenitude of God. You can draw out the truth. You can bring the coolness to all the plants everyone in the world has planted. You can comfort their minds. You can end their suffering. You can teach them wisdom.

You must not think there is no water. It exists at the level of the water table. The truth of God does exist. It will be there.

If you truly have the Guru who must give it to you, what he gives you will be the truth. Still, you must dig for it because it is within you. If you take in and keep the wisdom he gives, you can endeavor to dig with that.

If you dig, it will not be far away.

Although the ocean may be far from here, and although you are about sixty-five miles away from Atlantic City, there is water flowing right here beneath you. This water will be filtered by the earth, and if you dig until you reach the water table, that water will be here. However, the salt water will not be here. If you dig in the proper section, the good water will come; it will be filtered. Then you can water the plants as needed.

Like this, no matter where the Guru may be, if you have the truth and the certitude that there is nothing other than God, if you are convinced that there is no father other than that Father, if you know with determination, faith, and certitude that everything visible will change and that He alone will never change, you will know that one day God will cut down and harvest all the plants He created in creation, that there is an agreement for everything that grows, and that it will all come to an end.

There is a rule for all flowers that bloom: they must fade even as they bloom. As soon as every fruit matures and ripens, it must fall to the ground. Every seed has an agreement: it will mature, be cut down, and fall. It must be reaped.

There is an agreement like that for everything in God's creation, for the sun and the moon and everything. They will all change one day. The oceans can become lands and the lands can become oceans.

Except for God, all else will change.

What grows must be cut down. It is a harvest. It is God's *sifah*, God's harvest, God's creation. These things all originated from earth. They are earth's *shaktis*. They are earth's maya. They are earth's glitters. They are earth's powers. They are air's powers. They are fire's powers. They are water's powers, they are ether's powers, the powers of the sun, the moon, and the colors. These powers are connected to the earth. Creation is connected to earth.

Only the soul known as the *ānmā* does not have that connection. It is connected only to Him.

No matter what container we might construct of the five elements, no matter what celestial world we might fly to in it, it will have to come down. That container will have to descend because it is connected to earth. It cannot stay in the sky.

Where did the soul come from? It came from God. It is a magnetic-power, one of His rays of Light, Light that came from Him. It cannot be discovered through any science. Nothing here is connected to it. It belongs to the glory of God. It is mysterious. Whatever God is, it too is like Him.

The soul will never be destroyed and He will never be destroyed. It is Reality without beginning or end, complete Reality. It is called Perfection. The soul is called Nūr. We say, "*Lā ilāha illAllāhu wa inni 'Isā Rūhullāh*. There is nothing other than You,

O God! Only You are God and indeed I am Jesus, the Soul of God. There is another prophet to come." The soul is called Light, Nūr. It is called Perfection. It has been given ninety-nine Names. It has been described as Allāh's three thousand divine blessings.

A thousand of God's three thousand compassionate qualities were given to the *malā'ikah*, to the heavenly messengers, to the *jinns* and the fairies, and a thousand of those blessings were given to the *ambiyā'*. The scripture of Zabūr was given three hundred, Jabrāt was given three hundred, Injīl was given three hundred, and Furqān was given ninety-nine. Only One remains in His own hand. He rules with that One. All powers are within it. All might is within it.

He gave three hundred blessings to the Hindu scripture, to Adam ☙, to the first creation. Then after creation, He gave three hundred to the Hanal scripture—such as to those in Japan who worship the sun and the moon. To the Injīl scripture, the Christian scripture, He gave three hundred. He gave ninety-nine to the scripture of Furqān, to Islām. This is what is called the ninety-nine Names, the *Asmā'ul-Husnā*. There are ninety-nine blessings within it.

He kept One, the resonance, "Allāhu."

Bismillāhir-Rahmānir-Rahīm—creating, protecting, nurturing, judging, giving food, the Inquiry, the Resurrection. He kept these qualities of nurturing and judgment. He took all these powers and placed them within Himself as One Attribute.

Thus, He took the power of these three thousand divine qualities, placed them into the ninety-nine holy Names, and placed the ninety-nine into the One. He took the thousand given to the *malā'ikah*, He took the thousand given to the *ambiyā'* along with all might, and made them into ninety-nine. Then He made the ninety-nine powers into One and He made what was within the One into Allāh.

He exists as Allāh. There is no one as near to us as He is, there is no one as patient or compassionate as He is, there is no tolerance and peace like His. There is no one who performs selfless duty like Him. There is no one else who performs duty without hunger, illness, old age, or death. There is no one else who serves without haste, without impatience, without the differences of "I" and "you."

He rules without ethnic group, religion, division, color, or anger. He feeds. He protects, He sustains, and He creates. Only He has these divine qualities. No one else has them. Realizing this, He took all those powers and placed them within Himself. That is God, He is flawless.

You must have certitude of faith in this God, knowing that all powers exist within Him, being aware that He is the Almighty One who can create or destroy, being certain that there is no God other than Him. Know His Might—that without Him not even an atom will move. Know with certitude that without Him not the earth, nor the sky, nor the sun, nor the moon, nor anything else will be able to move. You must remember that Allāh is the only Might. Have certitude in Him. Have total confidence in Him. Have faith in Him.

If you realize that Allāh is the Truth, if you accept the statements of the Guru with that awareness, and if you place them there when you use that Truth to examine what is there, you will see that all the magic is maya and that Truth is God.

If you know this with total confidence and dig the well with wisdom, if you dig there and look, the water that is the grace, the *rahmah,* and the divine blessing will come. When it emerges from you, it will not be far from you. It will be inside. It will be right there.

If you see a true Guru like that, if he really is a Guru, if his teachings are true, if he is really a messenger of God, if he is really a slave to God, if he is really an unselfish being, if his teachings are God's teachings, if his will is God's will, and if he has dedicated himself to God, he will dwell where God dwells.

If you look closely, you will see. God is within you. That Truth will be within you. His statements will be within you and He will be within those statements. This is what you will have to see within yourself.

If you think God is far away from you, it will not come to you in all its power. How can God be within you but a great distance away? He is closer to you than your own life. When you understand the God who is within you, He will be within you. Therefore, if he is the true Guru, he will not perform magic. You will be able to see him as the Soul that is with your soul. You will be able to see him as a Light that is within God. You will be able to see him as a ray of Light. It will not be far.

Dig that well. Have that certitude. Look at it as truth. The understanding will come from within it. There will be no duality. If you see it as dual, it will be a double. And a double is a double. If you and the Guru are one, there will be only one Soul.

This is the world, this is earth, fire, water, air, and ether. This is the world. There is one Truth. The Soul is One and God is One. Therefore, that is the one and only Thing. If your Truth is One, it is the Guru, it is the Soul, it is God. Then there is no duality. Then all is One.

A disciple and a Guru must be One.

Their bodies might be separate. The body belongs to the demons; it is an elemental body, an illusory body, an earth body, a water body, a fire body, an air body, a color body, a body for religions and colors. It is a power of earth, maya power. We do not want that connection.

The Soul's connection is One. The Truth is One. Wisdom is Light. God is Light within light. Thus, it is definitely One. We cannot see it as dual. When the child is there, the Guru will be within the child. When the Guru is there, the Grace known as God will be there. They will be in the same place, and they will be One, not two. When you look, you will not be there, only the Guru will be there, and then the Guru too will not be there, only God will be there. Instead of you, the Guru will be there; instead of the Guru, God will be there. It is simply One. It is not far. It is not separate. You yourself must understand this. It is actually easy. It is not very far.

There is one sun, and the sunlight is coming from it now. The light is here no matter where the sun may be. The rays of light are coming here. Similarly, when true wisdom is there, the rays of light will emerge from it. Similarly, my child, this is not a great matter. It is a small matter.

We talk on the telephone to Colombo from here. Ten thousand miles! If we wait, the sound is heard here in a little while. The sound that is there is heard here, and what we say here is heard there. If the telephone is working properly like that, the sound of God will be heard here, and the sound of the Guru will also be heard here. You can speak to them directly. However, the wire must be right. If you install the wire and use the mike, it will be right. Hold the receiver and then you can speak. It is a telephone, after all. You do not need to actually go anywhere, you can speak directly.

The aerial must be correct. It must be raised correctly. The aerial is faith, certitude, and determination. Wisdom is the current. If you can correctly aim the aerial of faith, install the motor that is wisdom, and make it work properly, as soon as you activate the switch of discerning wisdom, *pahut arivu,* you can turn the dial; every station will come and you can speak. For this, you have to learn about the stations. You have to learn how to turn the dial. You have to learn a little engineering: where to put the aerial, where to aim it, and where each thing plugs in.

If you want to hear the sounds coming from the earth, you must insert the plug in the earth. Then you can understand it. If you want to understand what comes from water, from creation, how creation comes from semen, you must insert the plug there. If you put the plug into the spot from which the air is coming, that is what will come—the sixty-four arts and sciences will come. Where does fire come from? All the sections of hell will be within it. As you insert each plug, each sound will be revealed. Then you can understand. Then you can change the plugs, and listen to each of the seven heavens.

In the heart of man, there are eighteen thousand universes like this. God's secret and all of His creation are within this heart. All of God's *hikmah* is within it. God's Bible is here. God's Qur'ān is here. Man's secret is here. God's secret is here. God's mystery is here. The eighteen thousand universes are here. The fifteen realms are here. The eight heavens are here and the seven hells are here. The truth is here and falsehood is here. Satan and darkness are here and Allāh is here. Maya is here and the monkey mind is here. Each *shakti* is here like this. There is nothing that does not exist within man.

God gave man the section of wisdom so that he would have the ability to understand everything. Above all creations, God has given man the wisdom to examine everything atom by atom. He has given man the wisdom to understand right and wrong, to understand *halāl* and *harām*, to understand good and evil, to understand truth and falsehood, to understand wisdom and ignorance, to understand the "I" and the "you." He has given man the wisdom to understand who is a human being and who is an animal. He has given man the wisdom to understand all powers, to understand all qualities, to understand love, support, and everything.

"Therefore, Man is My secret and I am his secret. Man is not just a wonder. Do not think that Man is a simple thing. Man is My secret. He contains all My secrets. I am a secret to him. I am his secret. He is My secret. If My history is to be made known, he is the one who must make it known. If his history is to be made known, I am the One who must make it known. If man is to be praised, I am the One who must praise him. No one else can praise him. Only I can praise Man. Only Man can praise Me. Only he has the tongue to praise Me. Only I have the tongue to praise him.

"Therefore, he is My secret and I am his secret. He is My treasury, *khaznah,* and I am his *khaznah.* I have everything he needs. He has everything I need. Thus, man is not a simple thing. I have given him My wealth, the *rahmah* that is the seven kinds of wisdom. Through these seven, he will understand the qualities and the powers of the eighteen thousand universes.

"He can become My representative or he can become a satan. He can become one of My *ambiyā'* or he can become a monkey of maya. He can become either Allāh or satan's maya. He can become My *rahmah* or he can be an heir to hell. He can become *insān* or he can become an animal. He can become any of these things. It is up to him.

"However, I have given him all My wealth. I have placed all the wealth of My *rahmah* into his hands. He will obtain the benefit depending upon the way in which he manages it. I have given him beautiful food. I have given him a beautiful tongue. I have given him beautiful eyes of three colors. I have given him beautiful ears.

I have given him a beautiful *qalb*. Through them, he can know all there is to be known. He can understand right and wrong, he can understand the taste. It is his responsibility to understand and to be aware.

"It is up to him to understand the beautiful taste on his beautiful tongue. It is also up to him if he wants to eat *najis,* unclean things, with his beautiful tongue. It is his work. If he cannot tell the difference, he will become a dog or a monkey or a satan or a demon or an heir to hell. It is his work. I have given him everything. I have given him the wisdom with which to perceive this. I have given him the beauty to make him clear. I have given him the awareness to understand. I have given him the *qalb* to be clear about what each substance is.

"He must be able to understand with his eyes, nose, *qalb*, mind, and ears. He must be able to understand with perception, awareness, intellect, assessment, subtle wisdom, discerning wisdom, and Divine Luminous Wisdom. If he does not understand in these seven ways, he will have become an animal, a satan, or an heir to hell. This is not My responsibility. I have given him everything. I have given him all My earnings. I have given him My wealth.

"How he spends it is entirely up to him.

"However, after he spends My wealth, he will have to account for it to Me. This is what is called the Day of Judgment. These are not his treasures; I have loaned them to him from My bank. I will need an account of the money he has spent, and if he is to bring Me the account correctly, he must show Me the profit and loss statement.

"Moreover, he must return My capital. He can keep the profit he obtains. The profit he obtains is goodness and I will give it to him, but he must return My capital. He can keep the profit he earned from My capital. I do not want it. He must simply return the capital I gave him. Everything else is his profit. If he does not pay Me back, if he does not return My capital, if he incurs a loss, then there will be punishment for him, there will be Judgment for him. He will be a debtor. A debtor is punished in many ways." This is what God has said.

"I have given Man everything. Do not waste My capital; use it to do business. Run your business in a good and beautiful way. Let him have My qualities. He must have My qualities in order to operate My business. He must take on My tolerance. He must take on My peace. He must take on My patience. He must take on My *tawakkul*. He must take on My compassion. He must take on My love. He must take on My conscience. He must take on My justice. He must take on all My three thousand divine qualities.

"If he takes them on like this and runs the business, loss will never come to him. Trouble and sorrow will never come to him. Insufficiency and lack will never come to him. Harm will never come to him. Satan will never affect him. Complaints about his business will never come.

"My capital will benefit him, and he will be able to return My capital to Me. He can keep the profit. If this is what occurs, I will give him a palace in accordance with the profit he earns. He will be given a place according to the amount of profit he brings in— that is where he will dwell.

"It is not My fault. It is the result of the business he has operated. If it is not good, he will receive the Judgment. He must return My capital. He can keep his profits.

"He had nothing. Everything was Mine. His body was Mine. His food was Mine. Everything in his section was Mine. Nothing belonged to him. Therefore, he must return My capital. He must return My justice. He must return My earnings.

"His earnings are goodness, the profit that comes from what he was given to use. That belongs to him. If he becomes evil, the punishment will come to him." This is what Allāh has said.

If each child understands the meaning of this capital, he will know that there is no belonging other than what belongs to Allāh. "I belong to Him. My soul belongs to Him. My eyesight is His eyesight. My speech is His sound. My heart is His heart. My *qalb* is His *qalb*. Everything in the *dunyā* is His. Everything that moves and everything that does not move belongs to Him. The food and the nourishment are His belongings. The earth and the sky are His belongings. The sun and moon are His belongings. Everything belongs to Him. Nothing belongs to me. What belongings do I have? Only Allāh! He is my only belonging. Everything else is His."

If you can have that certitude and that determination, we will not be very far away from Him. We will be in Allāh and Allāh will be in us. Then we will not exist and it will all be His. When that occurs, that is what will be there. He will be within it. He will be inside what belongs to Him.

If you look at it with this certitude, you will see it directly. When you understand truth, you will see the only One who is Truth here. This is Truth. This is what we must know. This is what we must understand, children. Then it will not be far.

It will be with you and within you. The Truth will be within you. When you filter it out, it will not be far. It is within you. You need this wisdom. Then you will understand. Child, do you understand?

If you look at this path, if you cut this road, if you dig this well, if you drink in His taste that is His grace, His honey of wisdom, and if you give it to others to drink as well, it will be good. Then all the plants will benefit. Give everyone a drop. If even a drop of a drop is given, the taste will be there. Do it in this way. Enough?

May God protect us all. May He sustain us. May His grace be upon us. May He forgive our sins.

O God, may You pardon the sins we might have committed unknowingly, the sins we might have committed in the past and the sins we might commit in the future. May You grant us the good way on the straight path with Your grace.

May You protect and sustain us, O God, O the One who is the Qudrah, O the One who is the Rahmah, O the Rahmatul-'ālamīn, O the One who is able to rule the eighteen thousand universes, O God who is Love within love, O Allāhu ta'ālā who is the meaning of the explanation of Grace within grace, O Rare and Great Effulgence, O Ripe Fruit of Wisdom, O Looking Glass of the *Qalb*, O IllAllāhu, the God who is the Ultimate Unique One who makes us understand the meaning.

May You cut off the evils of our karma by the roots. May You open our *qalbs*. May You dispel the darkness in our hearts. May You drive out jealousy, vengeance, and satan's qualities from our *qalbs*. May You give us the grace and the compassionate love that is Effulgent Light. O God, may You establish the state of Your tolerance and peace.

May You dispel the darkness and fill us with grace. May You dwell in the hearts of these children who have been born with me and resonate from there and fill them with wisdom and grace. May You be the *Qalb* within their *qalbs*, the Grace within their grace, the Meaning within the meaning, the Wisdom within the wisdom and resonate from there, explaining the meaning, and filling them with grace.

O God, may You Yourself protect these *qalbs* from satan and from evil. May You Yourself accept these *qalbs*. May maya, satans, glitters, mantras, and magic never approach them or harm them. May suffering, sorrow, and adverse circumstances never come to them. May You protect and sustain our *qalbs* with Your grace so that our wisdom and our sense of judgment are not mesmerized.

May You always be the Rabb who is the Protector of our *qalbs*. May You make our *qalbs* eternal in the outer realm and the inner realm, and be our Protector and our Sustainer. O Allāh, fill us with Your grace and make us complete. Make our *qalbs* into abundant Light, abundant and absolute Light and Grace.

Āmīn. Āmīn. Yā Rabbal-ʿālamīn. O God, You are the One to whom the grace belongs.

EPILOGUE

A'ūdhu billāhi minash-shaitānir-rajīm.
I seek refuge in God from the accursed satan.
Bismillāhir-Rahmānir-Rahīm.
In the name of God, the Most Compassionate, the Most Merciful.

PROTECT MY MOSQUE AND MY WORDS

Wednesday, August 20, 1986, 3:55 P.M.
Philadelphia, USA

[Bawangal⊕ had been in the hospital and was now home at the Fellowship, very ill and very weak. He had not spoken in days and it seemed as if he could leave this world at any moment. Suddenly, he sat up on this day and addressed Carolyn Andrews, the Executive Secretary, and began with great intensity to exclaim the words in the following talk.

The beginning of this talk was not taped. The italicized section comes from notes taken at the time.]

M. R. BAWA MUHAIYADDEEN
The way you looked at me that day...

CAROLYN ANDREWS
I thought you had left us.

M. R. BAWA MUHAIYADDEEN
It could have happened like that. The ship has not yet come in.

CAROLYN ANDREWS
(to the translator)

Our ship or his?

M. R. BAWA MUHAIYADDEEN

I am the ship.

Do your duty until you draw your last breath. Protect my Mosque and my words until your last breath! Protect my Mosque and my words until your last breath! Even then, provide for this before you leave. You must do this!

CAROLYN ANDREWS

I know. I will! I will!

M. R. BAWA MUHAIYADDEEN

I will not leave you. I will be with you here, helping you. (pause) Kelly... Carl... Michael.

Some pray in the Mosque; some do not, but they do their duty well. Some will drift off. Do not reprimand them. I do not.

Make sure the Mosque progresses when I am not here.

This Mosque is not just a building of two stories—the eight heavens are in this Mosque. This Mosque was being fashioned long before I came to this country. Even before I arrived here, it was in the making.

It was built with the hands of the children; their own hands were building their prayers and their houses—the house they build here is the house they will be given in heaven.

No one else could have built a mosque like this. It extends past the seven heavens, into the eighth heaven, to the highest jeweled balcony of heaven, and has been adorned by the angels, the *malā'ikah*. How many years it took to build! They were building it for so many years, making it more and more beautiful. It is not yet finished. The domes need to be installed and other details need to be completed. It is something no one else could have done.

Each person has been building the Mosque within himself at the same time.

After a certain amount of time passes, when wisdom dawns within them, when understanding comes, they will know. Now, some people are finding fault with it, some people are opposed to it.

I do not reprimand them. Each one of them can do as he wishes. Each person has to make his own choice. Each person has a right to make that choice.

Yet, it has been directly indicated. All the prophets have described it. When the proof has been so directly revealed, we can go straight ahead. There is a single path leading away from the intersection. It can be confusing at the intersection, and people can take the wrong road and lose their way. Only those who have wisdom, faith, certitude, and determination can follow that path.

The children of Adam ☺, God's followers, those who love their neighbors as themselves, those who came before, and those who came later are all one people. This is God's command.

Jesus ☺ has said, "Love your neighbor as you love yourself. Your neighbor's father and his mother are not different; he is your father as well. Love other lives as your own. Do not regard other lives as separate from your own. Even if you do not come, let the little children, those with beautiful qualities, the qualities of God, lead you." That is what he said.

Some accepted the mother, others accepted the son. Some—the Catholics—accepted Maryam ☺, the mother. They were known as Jews. Other Christians accepted the son. They were the same Jews. That is why Jesus ☺ said, "The Light was brought to the Jews." Yet, in the end, some accepted him, others did not accept him. This is the way of the world.

Love your neighbor as you love yourself—love the children of Adam ☪, the tribe of Abraham ☪, the *ummah,* the followers, of Muhammad ☪. *Ummah* is unity, harmony, family.

There is no more time to speak, I am tired. Children, every child, do your duty until the very end, for as long as you are still alive. Say this to every child, to Sonia *pillay,* and all the other children.

There may be some who will not accept this, but as time goes by, there may be some who will. You must never go backward.

Go forward. *Anbu.*

GLOSSARY

GLOSSARY

The following traditional supplications in Arabic are used throughout the text:

- ﷺ *sallAllāhu 'alaihi wa sallam,* may the blessings and peace of Allāh be upon him, is used following the name of Prophet Muhammad.

- ؑ *alaihis-salām,* peace be upon him, is used following the name of a prophet or an angel.

- ؓ *radiyAllāhu 'anhu* or *anhā,* may Allāh be pleased with him or her, is used following the name of a companion of Prophet Muhammad ﷺ, the *aqtāb,* wives of the prophets, and exalted saints.

Unless otherwise noted, the following words are Tamil, a Dravidian language whose origins in antiquity are unknown.

Note: Arabic and Tamil words that have become common usage in the English language are not italicized. Also, proper names have not been italicized.

Although the Glossary has been assembled by the editor and/or translator, a majority of the explanations and definitions have come directly from Bawa Muhaiyaddeen ؓ.

Pronunciation Key

The non-Arabic and non-Tamil reader of this book will encounter strange words and names. We have tried to make them as simple as possible to pronounce.

While there are standard ways of transliterating Arabic letters into Roman script, there is no standard system of transliterating Tamil. Thus, we have not adopted any system in its entirety, but are indebted to many.

We have simplified the consonants—for the typical English speaking person, it would not be particularly helpful to distinguish between the two types of s or h or t in Arabic or the two types of t or the three types of n or l in Tamil.

> gn is pronounced like the ng in king or like the ñ in the Spanish word *mañana*.
>
> k has been variously transliterated as k or g or j, depending on whether it has a hard, medium, or soft sound in Tamil.
>
> th (a confusing and inconsistently applied legacy transliteration that has come down to the Tamil from the German) has been simplified throughout as t or d, depending on the hardness or softness of the sound.

We have adopted the phonetic spelling of Tamil words, such as *shari* and *meecham*, that have been incorporated into common usage here at the Fellowship in Philadelphia.

Both Arabic and Tamil have long and short vowels: the long vowels have been indicated by long marks in most cases. Thus, in Arabic and Tamil,

> a is pronounced as in agree,
> ā is pronounced as a long ā in father;[1]
> i is pronounced as in pin,
> ī is pronounced as a long ī as in pique;
> u as in pull,
> ū as a long ū in rule;
> o is pronounced as in opaque,
> ō is pronounced as a long ō in ore;
> e is pronounced as in end,
> ē is a long ē in they;
> ai is pronounced as in aisle except at the end of a word, where it is generally pronounced as in day.[2]

---

1 In Arabic the long ā is generally pronounced with a flatter vowel sound, more like man than father, except after r and six emphatic consonants.

2 However, in Arabic the *ai* is pronounced as the *ay* in day, except after r and six emphatic consonants when it is pronounced like the *ai* in aisle.

Any good transliteration system, of course, needs to be logically consistent. However, the idiosyncrasies of both languages must be considered; a few well-placed exceptions serve to clarify a sound that would otherwise be mangled. For instance, *nāi* (dog, pronounced like high) could not be spelled *nāy* without causing confusion, even though that is what the Tamil spelling would seem to indicate.

The following words are Tamil, unless otherwise indicated.

A

aday (inter.) hey! an exclamation used to call an inferior; an exclamation of contempt

adhāb (Arabic n.) the torment

ādi (n.) the beginning, the primal beginning, the source, the origin

Adonai (Hebrew n.) God

ahādīth (Arabic n.) reported deeds and actions of the Prophet ﷺ

aiyō (inter.) oh, oh no

ākhirah (Arabic n.) The kingdom of God; *ākhirah* is where the soul proclaims the First Kalimah to Allāh. "There is nothing but You, O Allāh!" This is the ultimate and final realization, it is the soul's exclamation as it perceives who it is, and with this final realization and expression, the soul that is a ray of God's Light returns to the One Omnipresent God. The soul returns to the Source from which it came. There is only One—Allāh. Where this occurs is called *ākhirah*.

[Lit. The *ākhirah* is also the place where evildoers will be punished, *Sūratul-Baqarah*, 114:

And who is more unjust than he who forbids that in mosques of Allāh, Allāh's name should be remembered?—one whose zeal is to ruin them? Such people should not enter them except in fear. For them there is disgrace in this world, and in the ākhirah, *an exceeding torment.*]

'ālamul-arwāh (Arabic phrase) the world of pure souls

al-Baitul-Muqaddas (Arabic n.) the Holy House, the Temple of Solomon in Jerusalem; also known as the al-Aqsā Mosque

al-hamdu, al-hamdu lillāh, al-hamdu lillāhi (Arabic phrase) all praise is to Allāh

alif (Arabic n.) (|) The first letter of the Arabic alphabet, equivalent to the English letter "a" and to the Arabic numeral "1," which represents Allāh, the One who stands alone.

Allāh, Allāhu (Arabic n.) God

Allāhu akbar (Arabic phrase) God is greatest. [Lit. "God is greater than anything."]

Allāhu ta'ālā (Arabic n.) God, the High; God, the Exalted

Allāhu ta'ālā Nāyan (combined Arabic n. & Tamil n.) Almighty God; God, the Exalted, is the Ruler. Allāhu—the beautiful, undiminishing One; ta'ālā—the One who exists in all lives in a state of humility and exaltedness; Nāyan—the Ruler who protects and sustains.

al-lauhul-mahfūz (Arabic phrase) the preserved tablet upon which everything has been written

al-qadā' wal-qadar (Arabic phrase) Because Allāh knows everything, His justice is perfect; Allāh knows and has decreed everything in al-lauhul-mahfūz—the tablet upon which everything has been written—regarding the relationship between this life and the hereafter, free will and destiny. Allāh, knowing everything, measuring and judging perfectly, will give to us in the hereafter the house we build in this life through our qualities and deeds. We are accountable to Allāh for the trust, the amānah, that He has given us.

[Lit. al-qadā': divine will, perfectly ordained, executed, and judged; al-qadar, divine knowledge, the apportionment and sustenance for every created thing]

amānah (Arabic n.) trust property, a trust, the treasure given in trust by God to man which must be returned to God in full

ambiyā' (Arabic n.) prophets; (sing.) nabī

āmīn (Arabic n.) may it be so

Āmīn. As-salāmu 'alaikum wa rahmatullāhi (wa barakātahu) (Arabic phrase) May it be so. May the peace and compassion (and blessings) of Allāh be upon you.

anbu (n.) love

Āndavā, Āndavanay (inter.) O God

Āndavan (n.) God who is One

ānmā (n.) soul, life

Appā, Appāh (n.) Father, God

appam (n.) cake

aqtāb (Arabic n.) those beings who have attained the power of the light of discerning wisdom; (sing.) Qutb; *see also* Qutb

'*arsh* (Arabic n.) The throne of God; the plenitude from which God rules; the place on the crown of the head is the throne that can bear the weight of Allāh. Allāh is so heavy that we cannot carry the load with our hands or legs. The '*arsh* is the only part of the human being that can support Allāh.

arwāh (Arabic n.) souls; (sing.) *rūh*

ashāb (Arabic n.) the companions of Prophet Muhammad ☾

asmā'ul-husnā (Arabic phrase) The ninety-nine beautiful Names of Allāh. The plenitude of the ninety-nine duties of God; the manifestations of His essence, the *sifāt* of His *dhāt*. His qualities are the manifestations that emerge from Him. When God performs His duty, these manifestations of His essence are brought into action; His qualities become His *wilāyāt* or duties.

'*asr* (Arabic n.) the afternoon prayer; the third of the five daily prayers in Islām

as-salāmu 'alaikum (Arabic phrase) May the peace of God be upon you.

as-salāmu 'alaikum wa rahmatullāhi (wa barakātahu) (Arabic phrase) May the peace and beneficence (and blessings) of God be upon you.

astaghfirullāhal-'azīm (Arabic phrase) I beg forgiveness of Allāh, the Supreme.

a'ūdhu billāhi minash-shaitānir-rajīm (Arabic phrase) I seek refuge in God from the accursed satan.

auliyā' (Arabic n.) the friends of Allāh, the saints; (sing.) *walī*

avatār (n.) a manifestation of a liberated soul in bodily form on earth; an incarnate divine teacher

āvi (n.) breath, exhalation; vapor; spirit

awwal (Arabic n.) the beginning; the state in which forms begin to manifest [Lit. *al-awwal*, the first]

awwal fajr (Arabic phrase) The pre-dawn prayer, the first *fajr* prayer. This refers to the prayer of *ash-shaf'i wal-witr*, the last prayer of the night before the *fajr* prayer.

B

badda (Arabic n.) father of dajjāl, the antichrist

Bawangal (n.) Father, referring to M. R. Bawa Muhaiyaddeen ☾. In the Tamil language, respect is indicated by adding the suffix *gal* to a name or pronoun. Bawa thus becomes Bawangal. The "n" is added for ease of pronunciation here and the emphasis is placed on the first syllable.

Bismillāhir-Rahmānir-Rahīm (Arabic phrase) In the name of God, the Most Compassionate, the Most Merciful.

brimstone (n.) an element used in making gunpowder, matches, and fireworks; sulfur

D

dajjāl (Arabic n.) the antichrist

daulah (Arabic n.) Wealth, the wealth of the grace of God. The wealth of Allāh is the wealth of *'ilm*, divine knowledge, and the wealth of perfect *īmān*. [Lit. good fortune]

dhāt (Arabic n.) the essence of God's grace, His treasury, His wealth of purity

dīn (Arabic n.) purity of faith; perfect purity, its light and its truth; the resplendence of perfectly pure *īmān*, absolute faith, certitude, and determination; the light of truth for *dunyā*, the world, and *ākhirah*, the hereafter [Lit. path, faith, religion]

dunyā (Arabic n.) the world

F

Furqān (Arabic n.) (A) Islām. This is the fourth step of spiritual ascendance, the teachings revealed to Moses☮ and Muhammad☮. Bawa Muhaiyaddeen☮ included Judaism in this step, explaining that Judaism and Islām are like two brothers descending from one father, Abraham☮.

In the body of man, Furqān corresponds to the head, to the element of ether, and to the Angel Gabriel☮.

[Lit. Furqān is the criterion which distinguishes between good and evil, right and wrong, lawful and unlawful, truth and illusion.]

furūd (Arabic n.) The five *furūd* refer to the five pillars of Islām: absolute faith in God, prayer, charity, fasting, and pilgrimage to Makkah.

G

Gnāna Guru (n.) the spiritual teacher or master who has attained the state of *gnānam,* grace-awakened wisdom; the divinely illumined spiritual guide; the one who can point the way to God

gnānam (n.) knowledge, wisdom, divine wisdom, grace-awakened wisdom

Guru (n.) the Shaikh, the Teacher who awakens the truth within the disciple; the Guide who takes the disciple to the shore of the heart where liberation of the soul takes place

gurus (n.) worldly teachers

H

hāl (Arabic n.) state

halāl (Arabic n.) allowed by God; permissible; that which conforms to the commands of God

Hanal (n.) The religion of fire worship.
>In the body of man, this relates to the region of the stomach, to the element of fire, and to the Angel Israel ☺.

harām (Arabic n.) forbidden by God; impermissible; forbidden; that which does not conform to the commands of God

hayāh (Arabic n.) life; lifetime

hayawān (Arabic n.) animal

hikmah (Arabic n.) wisdom

houris (n.) the beautiful qualities that a person displays during his life in the world become the children that serve him or her in paradise; the children who serve the inhabitants of paradise

I

'*ibādah* (Arabic n.) worship and service to God performed with a melting heart

iblīs (Arabic n.) satan

illAllāh, illAllāhu (Arabic phrase) Only You are God.

imām (Arabic n.) the leader of the congregation in the five times prayer in Islām

īmān (Arabic n.) absolute and unshakable faith that God alone exists; the complete acceptance by the heart that God is One; faith, certitude, and determination; absolute faith in God

Injīl (Arabic n.) Christianity, the third step of spiritual ascendance.
>In the body of man, this relates to the region of the heart which is filled with thoughts, emotions, spirits, vapors, many tens of millions of forms, the five elements, mind and desire, and four hundred trillion, ten thousand types of spiritual worship. In the body of man, Christianity corresponds to the area of the chest, the heart, to the element air, and to the Angel Isrāfīl ☺.
>[Lit. the Gospel]

insān (Arabic n.) man, a human being

Insān Kāmil (Arabic n.) a perfected man; a perfected human being; one who has realized Allāh as his only wealth, cutting away the wealth of the world and the wealth sought by the mind; one who has acquired God's qualities, performs his own actions accordingly, and immerses himself within those qualities; one in whom everything other than Allāh has been extinguished

in shā'Allāh (Arabic phrase) If God has willed.

Islām (Arabic n.) purity; unity; the state of total and unconditional surrender to the will of God; the state of absolute purity; the acceptance of the commands of God and His qualities and actions and the establishment of that state of purity within oneself, when He alone is worshiped

J

Jabrāt (Arabic n.) The religion of Fire Worship or Zoroastrianism, the second step of spiritual ascendance.

In the body of man, this relates to hunger, disease, and old age, corresponding to the area of the stomach, the element fire, and the Angel Israel ☺.

jadda (Arabic n.) mother of dajjāl, the antichrist

jāhil (Arabic n.) dajjāl, the antichrist, the one who has gone astray [Lit. an ignorant one]

jinn (Arabic n.) a being created from fire

jubbah (Arabic n.) a robe, a long outer garment worn by men

K

Ka'bah (Arabic n.) The place where the earlier prophets and the Final Prophet, Muhammad ☺, gathered together in prayer. The fifth obligatory duty is the *hajj*, the pilgrimage, to the Ka'bah in Makkah.

The place where *insān*, the human being, meets Allāh face to face. Whoever brings his heart to that state of perfection and prays to God from that heart will be praying inside the Ka'bah.

Kadavul (n.) God.

In Tamil, when this word is deconstructed, *kada* means to transcend, to cross over, and *ul* means within. *Kadavul* means to transcend the world and go within.

kāli (n.) Hindu goddess of death and destruction

Kalimah (Arabic n.) *Lā ilāha illAllāhu:* There is nothing other than You, O God. Only You are Allāh.

The recitation or remembrance of God that cuts away the influence of the five elements of earth, fire, water, air, and ether, washes away all the karma that has accumulated from the very beginning until now, dispels the darkness, beautifies the heart and causes it to resplend. The *Kalimah* washes the body and the heart of man, making them pure, making man's wisdom emerge, and impelling that wisdom to know the self and God.

kali yuga (n.) The present age, the fourth and last *yuga*. The four *yugas,* two hundred million years, represent one cycle of existence for the universe.

kāmil (Arabic n.) Perfected, completed or finished, thus perfect. When the eradication of the *nafs* is complete, and Allāh alone subsists, then the human being (*al-insān*) is perfect.

Karfatullāh (Arabic n.) The bird that will appear after Destruction and that will fly day and night for three days. It has four hands. Its body is fifteen miles long, and its wingspan is thirty miles wide. It will fly from the dawn to the dusk. It will wear the ring bearing the Seal of Solomon ☺ on one hand and hold the Staff of Solomon ☺ in another. When it sees sinners, it will strike them with the staff. When it sees the followers of Allāh, it will stroke them. It will fly for three days and finally fall into the sea of Jiddah, where it too will die. After that, the sun will not rise for three days; there will be absolute darkness.

karma (n.) The qualities of the connection to hell. There are two kinds of karma: inherited and acquired. Inherited karma is made of the qualities formed at the time of conception by the qualities in the minds of the parents. Inherited karma is dispelled when the Gnāna Shaikh accepts a disciple as one of his children. Acquired karma is formed as the result of our good and evil deeds. Acquired karma must be dispelled by the children themselves.

khair (Arabic n.) that which is right or good; that which is acceptable to wisdom and to Allāh, as opposed to *sharr,* that which is evil or bad

khaznah (Arabic n.) treasury

khidmah (Arabic n.) service, duty

khutbah (Arabic n.) the Friday sermon at the mosque

kiriyay (n.) The second step of spiritual ascendance; Zoroastrianism.
 In the body of man, this corresponds to the region of the stomach, the element of fire, and the Angel Israel ☮.

kutub (Arabic n.) books; (sing.) *kitāb*

L

lā (Arabic adverb) no, not or there is no [followed by a noun in the accusative]; a particle in Arabic expressing negation

lā ilāha (Arabic phrase) There is nothing other than God.

lā ilāha illAllāhu (Arabic phrase) There is nothing other than You, O God. Only You are God. There are two aspects. *Lā ilāha* is the manifestation of the *sifah,* creation. *IllAllāhu* is the *dhāt,* the essence of grace. All that has appeared, all creation, belongs to *lā ilāha.* The One who created all that, His name is *illAllāhu.*
 To accept this with certitude, to strengthen one's faith until it is absolute, and to affirm this *Kalimah* is the state of Islām.

lā ilāha illAllāhu wa innī 'Īsā Rūhullāh (Arabic phrase) There is nothing other than You, O God! Only You are God and indeed I am Jesus, the Soul of God. There is another prophet to come.

lām (Arabic n.) (ل) a letter in the Arabic alphabet, corresponding to the English consonant "l," which represents Nūr, Light, the Light of wisdom

M

madi (n.) assessment, estimate; the fourth of the seven levels of wisdom

Mahdī (Arabic n.) the directed or rightly guided one

malā'ikah (Arabic n.) angels; (sing.) *malak*

Manu-Īsan (phrase) Man-God

ma shā'Allāh (Arabic phrase) Whatever God has willed.

maut (Arabic n.) death

maya (n.) Illusion; the unreality of the manifest world of form; the glitters seen in the darkness of illusion; the 105 million rebirths. Maya is an energy, a *shakti*, that assumes various forms and shapes, causes man to forfeit his wisdom, and confuses and hypnotizes him into a state of delusion. It can take many, many millions of hypnotic forms, and although he "sees" those forms, he will never catch them. Whenever man tries to grasp one of these forms with his intellect, it will elude him by taking yet another form.

mīm (Arabic n.) (م) a letter in the Arabic alphabet, corresponding to the English consonant "m," which represents Muhammad ﷺ, and the fact that nothing could have been created without him

mimbar (Arabic n.) the pulpit in the mosque where the *imām* stands to deliver the Friday sermon

mīn (n.) fish

mi'rāj (Arabic n.) The ascension through the heavens during the night journey of Prophet Muhammad ﷺ when he went to meet with Allāh. The name of the night journey is the *Isra'*, and *Al-Isra'* is the name of the seventeenth chapter of the Qur'ān that begins with its description. [Lit. ascent]

mīzān trās (combined Arabic n. and Tamil n.) justice, the scale that weighs good and evil [Lit. balance-scale]

Mount 'Arafāt: A granite hill east of Mecca where pilgrims to Makkah ask to be pardoned for their mistakes. In the text, Mount 'Arafāt does not actually refer to this hill in Makkah but to the corresponding mystical mountain in the body of man.

mubārakāt (Arabic n.) The supreme, imperishable treasure of all three worlds, *awwal, dunyā,* and *ākhirah*. Allāh's wealth is the wealth of the soul, of wisdom, and of His grace, which is the resplendent wisdom of the Nūr.

Muhammad Mustāfār-Rasūl ﷺ (Arabic n.) Muhammad ﷺ, the Chosen, the Messenger of God

mulam (n.) a forearm's length, approximately eighteen inches

mu'min (Arabic n.) true believer; (pl.) *mu'minūn*

munivar (n.) a worker of miracles (real or feigned)

N

nabī (Arabic n.) prophet; (pl.) *ambiyā'*

nafs, nafs ammārah (Arabic n.) man's base desires; the seven kinds of desires, that is, desires meant to satisfy one's own pleasure and need for comfort

[Lit. person, spirit, personality, inclination, or desire that incites one towards evil]

najis (Arabic n.) impurity, filth

najjām (Arabic n.) the ancient astronomers

niyyah (Arabic n.) intention

nupa arivu (phrase) subtle wisdom; the fifth of the seven levels of wisdom

nuqtah (Arabic n.) dot, point, a drop of water

Nūr (Arabic n.) Light; the resplendence of Allāh; the plenitude of the Light of Allāh that has the resplendence of a hundred million suns; the completeness of Allāh's qualities. When the plenitude of all these becomes One and resplends as One, that is His Light, His Nūr. It is Allāh.

Nūr Muhammad (Arabic n.) one of the nine aspects of Muhammad ﷺ; the aspect that is wisdom, *see above*

P

Pādishah (Persian n.) Emperor, Ruler, great King

pahut arivu (n.) Discerning wisdom; divine analytic wisdom; the sixth of the seven levels of wisdom. Muhaiyaddeen☺; the wisdom of Allāh that explains His mysteries to the soul. This explanation is the Qur'ān.

pār (n.) world, earth

parisutta āvi (phrase) the pure spirit, breath, exhalation, vapor

pārungal (v.) look

pērarivu (n.) Divine Luminous Wisdom

pillay (n.) child

pūja (n.) Hindu ritual worship

pūjari (Hindi n.) a priest in a Hindu temple

Purānas (n.) Hindu scriptures. The seventeen *purānas* are the seventeen worlds: arrogance, karma, maya, *tārahan*, *singhan*, *sūran*, lechery, hatred, miserliness, greed, fanaticism, envy, intoxicants, lust, theft, murder, and falsehood.

putti (n.) intellect; the third of the seven levels of wisdom

Q

qalb (Arabic n.) the heart; the heart within the heart of man; the inner heart

There are two states for the *qalb*. The first state is made up of four chambers, corresponding to Hinduism, Fire Worship, Christianity, and Islām. The second state is that of the flower of grace, *rahmah*. This flower that is the *qalb-pū* grows inside these four chambers as the divine qualities of Allāh. God's fragrance exists within this inner *qalb*.

Qiyāmah (Arabic n.) the standing forth; the Day of Reckoning

Qudrah (Arabic n.) power of God

qunūt (Arabic n.) a supplication performed before the pre-dawn prayer

Qur'ān (Arabic n.) The words of Allāh that were revealed to His Messenger, Prophet Muhammad ☪. Those words that came from Allāh's power are called the Qur'ān; Allāh's inner book of the heart; the Light of Allāh's grace which comes as a resonance from Allāh; the Tiru Maray, the Hidden Treasure, the Divine Book

Qutb (Arabic n.) One who has attained the power of the light of the grace-awakened discerning wisdom that dawned from the throne of God and that investigates, understands, and analyzes everything in the eighteen thousand universes and beyond. Through this inner analysis, the darkness of evil is dispelled and the beauty of goodness is made clear and radiant. The Qutb is sent by Allāh, through His grace and mercy, to reawaken mankind's faith in God and to establish certitude in our hearts. He is the wondrous embodiment and illustration of *īmān,* absolute faith in God, in all three worlds. (pl.) *aqtāb*

Qutbiyyah (Arabic n.) the state of discerning wisdom, or *pahut arivu,* the sixth level of wisdom, the state that explains the truth of God to the wisdom of the human soul

R

Rabb (Arabic n.) God, the Lord, the Creator

Rahīm (Arabic n.) God, the Most Merciful

rahmah (Arabic n.) compassion, grace, mercy

Rahmān (Arabic n.) God, the Most Compassionate

rak'ah (Arabic n.) the bowing; also a set of prescribed movements and words performed while offering prayers, consisting of standing, bowing once, prostrating twice, and then sitting

Rasūl, Rasūlullāh ☪ (Arabic n.) Prophet Muhammad ☪, the Messenger of Allāh [Lit. messenger]

rizq (Arabic n.) nourishment given by Allāh

rounding: traveling in a circle; going out and coming back to where you started

rūh (Arabic n.) The soul, the Light-Ray of God, the Light of God's wisdom. Bawa Muhaiyaddeen☉ explains that the *rūh* is life, *hayāh*. Out of the six kinds of lives, the soul is the Light life, the human life. It is a ray of the Nūr, the Light of Allāh, a ray that does not die or disappear. It comes from Allāh and returns to Allāh. (pl. *arwāh*)

rūhānī (n.) The spirits of the elements. There are six kinds of lives within man. One is human life, the light-life that is the *rūh*, the soul, and it is pure. The physical body is formed from the lives of earth, fire, water, air, and ether. Their spirits constitute the *rūhānī*, and are impure.

When all the four hundred trillion, ten thousand intentions and thoughts take form, they are called *rūhānīs*. All the things to which the mind roams in its thoughts are called *rūhānīs*. Even after a person dies, his desires bring him back. It is those desires, those *rūhānīs*, that bring him back to be reborn again and again.

rusul (Arabic n.) messengers; (sing.) *rasūl*

S

sabūr (Arabic n.) Patience; inner patience; to go within patience, to accept it, to think and reflect within it. *Sabūr* is that patience deep within patience which comforts, soothes, and alleviates the suffering caused by the mind. [Lit. *sabūr* is the intensive form, meaning a patience more intense]

saivam (n.) purity; veganism; to exist in a state of not killing or eating others, not causing pain to others

salām (Arabic n.) greeting of peace, peace

salawāt (Arabic n.) prayers or blessings; usually used for the supplications asking God to bless the prophets and mankind

sarihay, kiriyay, yōgam, and *gnānam* (n.) the four parts of the body, corresponding to the elements earth, fire, air, and ether; the four steps of spiritual ascension, Hinduism, Zoroastrianism, Christianity, and Islām

Shaikh (Arabic n.) the Guru; the Teacher who takes the disciples to the shore of the heart

shaikhs (Arabic n.) teachers

shaitān (Arabic n.) satan

shakti (n.) the energy or force of creation arising from the five elements

shānti (n.) peace

sharr (n.) that which is evil or bad

shukūr (Arabic n.) gratitude; contentment with whatever may happen, realizing that everything comes from Allāh; contentment arising from gratitude

siddhan (n.) one who has attained supernatural powers and can perform miracles

sidratul-muntahā (Arabic n.) the tree of paradise that bears the fruit of grace

sifah (Arabic n.) form, creation, manifestation

subhānAllāh (Arabic phrase) All glory and exaltedness is to God.

Sufi: A genuine Sufi is in (a state of) *maunam*, silence, within God. He prays with God as God. He performs forty-three thousand, two hundred and forty-two prostrations in prayer each day. His every breath goes out to unite with God. His every intention goes to Him and unites with Him. His every idea goes to Him and unites with Him. His every thought goes to Him and unites with Him. A Sufi establishes the state of the ninety-nine meanings of the ninety-nine beautiful Names of God, the *asmā'ul-husnā*, in his *qalb*.

sūrah (Arabic n.) form

swāmi, swāmiar (n.) teacher, ascetic

T

tambi (n.) brother, specifically younger brother

tantra (n.) trick

tārahan, singhan, and *sūran* (n.) the three sons of maya; the beastly and hypnotic aspects of the sexual act

tasbīh (Arabic n.) a *dhikr* containing the words "*SubhānAllāh*—all glory and exaltedness is to God;" prayer beads

tattwa (n.) the strength or vitality inherent in the qualities of the creations manifested through the actions of those qualities

taubah (Arabic n.) to repent, to do penance

tawakkul, tawakkul-'alAllāh, tawakkulun 'alAllāh (Arabic n. & phrase) absolute trust in God; surrender to God; handing over to God all responsibility for everything

tiyānam (n.) meditation

U

ummah (Arabic n.) followers, people, community, nation

unarchi (n.) awareness; the second of the seven levels of wisdom in man

unarvu (n.) feeling, perception; the first of the seven levels of wisdom in man

V

vairavan, vairavar (n.) a fierce Hindu dog god, associated with annihilation

vanakkam (n.) a respectful greeting acknowledging the presence of God; prayer, worship

W

wa 'alaikumus-salām (Arabic phrase) May the peace of God be upon you also.

walī (Arabic n.) saint, friend of God; (pl.) *auliyā'*

waqt (Arabic n.) Time of prayer. In Islām, there are five specified *waqts*, times of prayer, each day. But in reality, there is only one *waqt*—the prayer that never ends, wherein one is in direct communication with God and merged with God.

wilāyah (Arabic n.) the miraculous Names and actions of God; God's Power; that which manifests through God's actions; the ninety-nine beautiful Names and actions of God; (pl.) *wilāyāt*

wudū' (Arabic n.) ablutions

Y

yā (Arabic inter.) O! an exclamation of praise, a title of greatness or praise

Yahweh (Hebrew n.) God

ya'jūj and ma'jūj (Arabic n.) Gog and magog. This evil group is referred to in the Qur'ān in *Sūrah Kahf*, xviii, verses 83-98.

yā Rabbal-'ālamīn (Arabic phrase) O Creator of all the universes

yoga rishis (n.) yoga masters

yuga (n.) fifty million years

Z

Zabūr (Arabic n.) Hinduism, the first step of spiritual ascendance.
    In the body of man, Hinduism corresponds to creation, to the area below the waist, to the element earth, to form, and to Adam ☪.

INDEX

INDEX

Passim denotes that the references are not to be found on all of the listed pages; e.g., 24-29 *passim* would be used where the reference is on pages 24, 25, 27, and 29. Numbers in **bold** denote major references (e.g. **83**).

abilities *(tattwas)*, ninety-six, 28-29
Abraham☺, 106, 188
accidents, causes of, 147-153 *passim*, 197, 200-201, 211
act of our existence, 333-337 *passim*
actions
   of man, 109-110
   and qualities of God, 42, 120, 129, 133, 135-136
actor(s)
   man as an, **99-103**, 108-115 *passim*
   in the world, 277-278
Adam☺, 28, 30
   and Eve☺, the light forms of, **45-67, 69-92**
adhāb (torment), 306-307
ahādīth (traditional stories), 309-317, 318-320
air, 70, 173-174, 178
   good and bad, **231-236**
ākhirah (the kingdom of God), 4-6, 66-67, 294
'ālamul-arwāh (the world of the souls), 209, 245-249 *passim*, 294
alcohol
   affects conception, 254
   effects of, 281-282
   and war, 261-262
Allāh, the One. *See* God, Allāh the One
al-qadā' wal-qadar (divine will), 358
alteration of conception, **246-255** *passim*
amāna (trust property), 12-13, **19-21,** 25

ambiyā', 101, 154, 175, 191-192
   given one thousand of God's qualities, 365
   God's explanations given through the, **xv-xviii**
   insults against the, xvi-xix
   See also prophet(s)
America, 181-182, 191-194
angel(s), 175, 188
   of Death, 303-307, 355
   Gabriel☺ greets the Rasūlullāh☺, 304-305
   three thousand, 180
   See also malā'ikah
animal(s)
   destructive, 278
   eat man in hell, 127-133 *passim*
   forms, 56-57
   have faith in God, 105
   human beings are, 97, 104, 110-114 *passim*
   live in peace, 186, 239
   man does the work of, 238, 285-286
   man has become an, **322-326**
   meditate upon God, 185
   qualities, **56-57,** 272, 275
   serve man, 104
   switch roles with man, 295-296
   try to eat us, 335-338 *passim*
ānmā. *See* soul
antichrist (dajjāl), **310-314**
appams (cakes), 157-158

407

aqtāb, 101. *See also* Qutb ☺
arrogance of the "I," 236-237, 240-242
'arsh. See God, throne of
artificial
　food, 240-241
　means of creations, 245-253 *passim*
　things become natural, 255-296
ascent of man. *See* man, ascent of
ash, all turned to, 298
atomic
　energies, 236, 238, 298, 301, 328
　research, 264
atrocities of man. *See* man, atrocities of
attachments
　separating from, 123-124,
　　130-134 *passim*
　of the world, 146-153 *passim*
attack
　of animals, 56-57
　the story written by man will, 100
auliyā' (saints), God's explanations given
　　through the, xv-xvi
awakening of essence in conception, 254
awareness, we must have, 125,
　　132-136 *passim*
awe, state of, 135
awwal (the beginning), 67, 294

baby
　conceived without a father, 251-253
　mind as a, 199, **203-209** *passim*
bad and good within man, 288, 291
balance
　of a human being, 99, 113-114
　must be achieved, **147-160** *passim*
bar, man will not find peace at the, 10,
　　102, 110-114
battles. *See* wars
Bawa Muhaiyaddeen('s) ☺
　asks God, xv-xix
　bathes in a pond, 140-143
　begs God to accept his children,
　　339-341
　can—instruct us after he leaves the
　　world? 347-356 *passim*

Bawa Muhaiyaddeen('s) ☺ *(continued)*
　and the form he will take next, 243-245
　how can we best help, 361
　protect—words, 379-382
　searches for a Guru, 353-354
beautiful qualities of God. *See* God,
　　beautiful qualities of
beginning, what man saw in the, 202-203
benefit from what God creates,
　　260-263 *passim*
Bible, 190
bird called Karfatullāh, 314-315
birth, **33-44** *passim*
　human, **17-26**
　passageway of, 159, 202-203
　right, secure our, 336
　state of natural, 251
　See also rebirth
Bismillāhir-Rahmānir-Rahīm, the One
　　Attribute, 365
bliss, wealth of—in the heart,
　　206-211 *passim*
blood
　changes in, 211
　high—pressure, 147
　ties, 34-36, 177
body, **33-37** *passim,* 41
　analyze your—with wisdom,
　　334-338 *passim*
　as a container, 227
　changes, **344-345**
　creation of the, 246
　elemental, 173-175, 367
　harm to one's own, 284
　of man, 13-15, 69
　microorganisms in the, 234-236
　secret, 197
bomb, time—of destruction, 290-291
bones
　Jesus ☺ had no, **310**
　microorganisms in the, 234
book
　man is a, 287-288
　no power within a, **350-351**

brain
   changes from intoxicants, 281
   of small children, 257-258
   used to gain money, 193-195
burial in the earth versus cremation, **233-236**
burn(ing)
   corpses, 234-236
   heavy water will, 298
   of the mind, 70
business, 181-195 *passim*
   God's, 372

cancers, 238
candles, lighting for statues, 51
cannibalism, 243
capacity and balance, **148-156** *passim*
Catholics accepted Maryam☺, 381
cat, 154
   man is like a, 96, 99
cattle are vegetarians, 163-164
change(s)
   are taking place, 317-319
   before the body changes, **344-345**
   everything in the world, 121-122, 131-134 *passim*
   everything will, 363-364
   from intoxicants, 281
   in nature, 231-244 *passim*
charge the motor of the heart, 351-352
chemicals
   bring destruction, 261-262
   the effect of—on maturity, 257-258
   in food, **238-241** *passim*
   of intoxicants bring destruction, 254-255, 261-262, 280-281
   put in animal's food, 249, 256-258, 261
   released in conception, 246, 248, 251, 254
chicken
   artificial conception of—eggs, 249, 252
   magnetism in a, 247-248
   mother—trains her chicks, 247
   pecks for food, 5-6

child(ren)
   ask unanswerable questions, 240
   become a—of God, 40
   grow large from chemicals, 257-258
   Kalimah will create qualities of a young, 211
   of the mind, 206
choice
   between justice and injustice, **81-93** *passim*
   between natural and artificial, **245-267** *passim*
   between positive and negative, **137-143** *passim*
   between story of God and story of world, **33-44**
   of pots, clay or copper, **21-26**
Christian
   church, worship in a, **50-53**
   scripture given three hundred of God's qualities, 365
clarity
   few people choose, 29-30
   people of—disappeared, xvi-xvii
clay and copper pots, **21-26**
climbing up is the only true miracle, **161**
clothing
   of God's truth, 286
   man will live without, 300
colors and hues, 52, 101-110 *passim*, 115
"come alone," 28-29
comfort
   from God's words, xvii
   in life, 66
Commandments of God, 78, 179-181
compass points, eight, 177, 181
compassion, women have, 77
conception, 246-255 *passim*, 264
   artificial—of eggs, 249, 252
   of a baby must be between a man and a woman, 245-261 *passim*, 283
   embracing during, 246-249, 251-252
   essence created during natural, 245-251 *passim*
   harmed by chemicals, 254-255, 262

conception *(continued)*
  preventing, 256
  time of, 198-199
conditions that result from organ replacement, 258-259, 266
connection(s)
  between man and God, 11, 13
  to the earth, **125-134** *passim*
  of the mind, 198-199
conscience, 65-66, 110, 185, 271, 275-279, 291
  speaks to man, **85-90**
consciousness
  during conception, 246-255 *passim*
  effect of chemicals on, 257-258, 261
cook, do not say there is nothing to, 139
copper and clay pots, **21-26**
corpses, burning of, 234-236
cow(s), 163-164
  and bulls mate, 254
  meditates, 185
  sent to the supermarket, 164
creation(s), **27-28**
  artificial—is of no benefit, 260-264
  energy of. *See* creation, energies of
  of God and of man, 245-267 *passim*
  ideal structure of God's, 248-252 *passim*, 258, 262
Creator, God the. *See* God, the Creator
cremation versus burial in the earth, **233-236**
crimes, five, 57
crops of good or evil, 274
current
  of the Guru, 351-352
  man can become a, 250-251

dajjāl (the antichrist), **310-314**
Damascus, war between—and Israel, 293, 297-303
danger(s)
  of imbalance, **148-157** *passim*
  man's happiness is a, 167
darkness
  of the earth, 51

darkness *(continued)*
  has dispelled light, **272-274**
day
  good or bad, 137
  of Judgment, 371
  the Last, 278, 280, 287
death
  Angel of, 303-307, 355
  brings the body back to the earth, 123-125, 159
  of man, **343-345**
  from man's enmity, 48
  and the one span stomach, 240
  wrapped in cloth at time of, 286
deception of women by men, 77
demon(s)
  called forth by words, 139-140
  inner—and conscience argue, **86-90**
desire(s)
  disabled by the *Kalimah*, 212
  dog of, 204-206
  and mind, went to steal, 157-159
  sexual, 177-178, 188
destruction, 79-80, 85-86, 250, 255
  avoided, **289-292**
  causes of, 261-264
  of good people, 272
  of harmful things by earth, 232-236, 239, 244
  has increased in the past hundred years, 280, 284, 287, 290, 291
  man has caused, 243
  man's research and, 235-242
  progress of, **280-287** *passim*
  ruling the world through, 279-280
  signs of, 317
  since the year 1914, 91
  will come, 309, 316-319
  within, **289-292**
  in the world, 45, 50-59 *passim*, 64-67 *passim*
  of the world, **75-93** *passim*, **185-195**, 239-244, **269-292** *passim*, 295-303, **327-329**
  can be averted, 192

devils. *See* demons
Dhikr, say the, **207-212**
  See also Kalimah
dictionary of God. *See* God, dictionary of
die
  everyone will, 354-355
  without dying, 345
  See also perish
differences
  among mankind, 48
  between what God and man create, **253-266** *passim*
  God has no, 265
difficulties, 97-100 *passim*
  that come from choosing the clay pot, **22-25**
dignity lost in the bar, 111-112
disciples, 195
diseases, 185-186, **232-243**, 300
  caused by chemicals, 257
  cured by *lā ilāha, illAllāhu,* **210-211**
  pleasures are, 146
  remove, 131
Divine Luminous Wisdom. *See* wisdom, divine luminous
doctors need God, 265-266
dog(s)
  of desire, 204-206
  have many germs, 154
  meditate, 185
dream(s)
  demons speak to man in his, 87-88
  of Rasūlullāh's ☺ disciple, 294
drugs
  affect conception, 254
  effects of, 280-281
  taking—and alcohol, 110-114
drunkards in a bar, we are like, 10
duality, no, 367
dunyā, **5-6**, 67, 294
  is hell, 339, 341
  the Mahdī returns to the, 314
  weight of the, 71
  See also world
duty(ies), 163-164, 291

duty(ies) *(continued)*
  do your, 359, 380, 382
  done by the prophets, 76
  of God. *See* God, duties of
  in heaven, 133

earth, 173-174
  Adam ☺ and Eve ☺ created from, **46-51** *passim*
  as a mother, 239
  connection to the, **125-127, 131-134** *passim,* 364
  darkness of the, 51
  destroyed by fire, 298, **316-317**
  destroys harmful things, 232-236, 239, 244
  destruction of the, 243
  element of, 69-73
  given the *Kalimah,* 61
  is a beautiful woman, 76-77
  kissed by Nūr Muhammad, 61
  man lives between sky and, 240, 243
  man made from, 28
  transforms all things, 234-236
  water in the, 362-363
  we return to the, 159
earthquakes caused by man, 57, 283-384
eat, all that we nurtured will—us, **124-134** *passim*
echo between two mountains, 155
education will change, 281-283, 287
electricity, 283
elements, 175
  destroy the world, 327
  five, 69-73 *passim*
  food for the, 182
  powers of the, 364
  waves of the, 177
embryo(s)
  connections of the mind in the, 198-199
  God protects all, 217, 219
  why the womb sometimes cannot hold the, 255
enemies, pleasures as, 146, 150-151

energy(ies)
  atomic, 328
  of creation, 249-253
  destructive, 236
  in the heart, 174
enmity, **47-48**
escape
  the destruction, 191-195 *passim,* 290
  from hell, 132
  from our thoughts, **130-136** *passim*
Essential Principle. *See* God, the
      Essential Principle
ether, the mind exists as, 175-176
ethnic groups, 99, 103-104, 107-110,
      115-117
everyone, all that belongs to, 109
evil(s)
  mountain standing against, 192
  path of, 281-282
  qualities, 4
  staring down, 142-143
explanation(s)
  given, 318-320
  of God, given to the prophets, **xv-xviii**
  of God's story, 43-44
  within our hearts, 227

faces, four—of the Angel of Death,
      305-306
fairies, 27-30 *passim*
faith
  aerial of, 368-369
  certitude and determination, 143
  creations have—in God, 105
  in the scriptures, 274, 277
  tree of, 205-206
  See also īmān
family, one, 265
famine, 193, 327-328
Father (father)
  God the. *See* God, the Father
  journey to our, **333-338**
  no—during conception, 251-253
fats released by burning a body, 235

fear
  comes to Bawa Muhaiyaddeen ☺,
      141-142
  in the mind, **218-229** *passim*
Fellowship
  help the, 4
  what will happen to the, 357-359
female and male must conceive, 250
fertilizer, 233-234
fighting. *See* wars
fire(s), 173, 192
  caused by man, 57
  of cremation, 234-235
  of the Guru, 350-351
  in the heart, 49-50
  of hell, 30, 132-134, 277
  will destroy the earth, 298, 316-317
fish in comparison to man,
      122-136 *passim,* **343-345**
flower
  garden of the heart, 80
  happiness of a, 166-167
food, 237-238, 242
  bioengineered, 240-241
  chemicals in, 261, 280-281
  diseases within, 240-242
  for the earth, 125-130 *passim*
  effects of cremation on, 235
  of God, 171, 181-183
  for hell, 127
  how a chicken pecks for, **5-6**
  tainted, 327-328
forgotten, man has—God, 181, 184-186.
      See also man, forgets God
form(s)
  and qualities of animals, **56-57**
  of truth, 65
  what—will Bawa Muhaiyaddeen ☺
      take next? 343-345
fragrance of God. *See* God, fragrance of
freedom
  meaning of, **131-136**
  needed for peace, 201-202, 212
fruit, 237
  beaten with a stick, 145-146

fruit *(continued)*
  of *gnānam,* 352
  must fall to the earth, 64, 125-127
  the nature of—will change, 296
Furqān (Islām), 175

Gabriel☮, angel—greets the
       Rasūlullāh☮, 304-305
  See also angel(s)
garden, flower—of the heart, 80
gnānam. See wisdom
God('s)
  Allāh, the One, 365-368, 373-375
  animals have faith in, 105
  attain peace through, 189
  Bawa Muhaiyaddeen☮ asks, **xv-xix**
  capital of, 371-373
  child of, 40
  commandments of, 78, 179-181
  commit our lives to, 119
  controls all creation, 75, 231
  created
    Bawa Muhaiyaddeen☮ to
      remind the people, **xvii-xix**
    nature, 260
  creates many seeds from one seed, 181
  creations of, 245-266 *passim*
    change, **121-122,** 134
  the Creator, 27-28, 35-38,
      218-221 *passim*
  dictionary of, 178-180, 183, 194
  doctors need, 265-266
  duties of, 109, 110, 120
  the Essential Principle, 269-270, 274
  everything belongs to, 372-373
  explanations of—given to the prophets,
    xv-xviii
  the Father, 37-38, 42-44, **333-338**
  few trust in, 271, 278
  food of, 171, 181-183
  fragrance of, 58, 153, 157-162 *passim*
  gave man wisdom, 10-13 *passim,*
    369-371
  goodness of, 282

God('s) *(continued)*
  grace of, 10-14 *passim,* 119-120,
    182-183, 222-229, 359, 373-375
  See also grace
  hidden in man, 96
  history of, **40-44** *passim*
  ideal structure of—creations,
    248-252 *passim,* 258
  if one in ten million meditates on,
    190-192
  is natural, 243
  journey to, **321-327, 333-338**
  the justice of, 81-82, 291-292
  keep your intention on, 193-194
  kindness of, 58
  kingdom of, 19-25 *passim,* 80, 153,
    183, 264, 328-329
  know, 18-20
  love of, 153
  man
    can become, **96-117** *passim*
    of—hard to find, 322-323
    is subordinate to, 232-233
  the Master, 225-228 *passim*
  the mind has not seen, 206
  Mosque of, 359
  mystery of, 18-23 *passim,* 264
  nothing other than, 207
  the One, 14-15, **34-44,** 81-82, 119-121,
    125-127, 132-136 *passim,*
    217-229 *passim,* 269-274 *passim,*
    367-370 *passim,* 373-375
  path to, 96-99 *passim,* 107, 244
  the Peaceful Witness, 135
  the Point, 267
  possession of, 29-30
  the Power, 264-265
  power of, 173, 232-233, 236
  prayer to, 189
  provides, 80-81
  quality(ies), 3-6 *passim,* 19, 25, 65,
    97-98, **102-117** *passim,* 120,
    129-136 *passim,* 180-181
    earth embraced, 55
    keeps one—for Himself, 365

God('s) *(continued)*
  quality(ies) *(continued)*
    lock—in your heart, 207
    make man beautiful, 116-117
    reach, 189
    representatives of, 12, 25
    the Researcher, 260
    safeguards, 81-82
    search for, 193-195
    secret(s) of, 18-19, 171-172, 370
    share that which belongs to, 160
    son of, 103, 114
    speaks within, 95-96
    state of, 59-64 *passim*
    story of, **18-21** *passim*, **34-44** *passim*
    surrender to, 274
    take everything from, 266-267
    takes half of our difficulties, 73-74
    man says there is no, 92, 299, 324
    title given by, **285-286**
    treasure of, 20-21, 25, **29-30**, 166-167
    the Truth, 168, 263-264, 366-368, 373
    understand, 18-20, 172
    wealth of, 3, 38-42 *passim*, 55-56, 115-117, 370-371
      given to Earth, 61
    will be forgotten, 297, 299
    will create the world again, 317
    will know man, 172
    will never change, 363-364
    will of, 215-227 *passim*
    within man, 292, 367-373 *passim*
    words of, xvii-xix, 60
    worship of, **50-64** *passim*
god(s)
  many, 55
  world calls man a, 97-98, 102
good and bad
  are both within man, 288, 291-292
  in man and nature, **231-239**
goodness, 41, 289, 292
  of God, 282
  has been forgotten, 336
  within, 292

grace *(rahmah)*, 61, 248
  of God. *See* God, grace of
groups, three—go to heaven, 339-341
guide, God's qualities as a, 107-108
guru(s), 153, 193-195
  as a saint, 180
  disappear within the, **347-352**
  the disciples of a—and karmic burdens, 71-73
  false, 193-195
  follow a true, 347-354
  is within, 362-368 *passim*
  words of a, 351

halāl (permissible), 5-6
happiness
  of a flower, 166-167
  man's—is dangerous to other lives, 167
harm(ful)
  to one's own body, 284
  things in man and nature, **232-239**, 243-244
hayawān, 104, 114, 265. *See also* animal(s)
heart
  all is within the, **174-175**, 369-375
  animals within the, 49
  as a battery, 351-352
  filter the, 225
  fire in the, 49-50
  God will know man through his, 172
  heaven exists in the, 270
  innermost
    fragrance of the, 43
    is the kingdom of God, 80-81
  lock God's qualities in your, 207
  and lungs, 232
  open your, 145, **153-162** *passim*, 208, 220-227 *passim*
  of a person with wisdom, **58-59**
  scale is in the, 149
  turns into light, 51
  See also qalb
heaven(s), 6, 108, 133-136 *passim*, 153, 160-161, 264

heaven(s) *(continued)*
   Bawa Muhaiyaddeen ☮ takes his
      children to, **339-341**
   described by dajjāl, 310-311
   eight—decorated for the Rasūlullāh ☮,
      303-304
   in life, 66
   Mosque extends into the eight, 380
   will be closed, 315
   world of, 208-212 *passim*
heavenly beings, 30
hell(s), 102, 108
   escape from 132-136
   fire of, 30, 277
   food for, 127
   heir to, 370-371
   is the world, 339, 341
   kingdom of, 24, 26
   will be closed, 303-304, 315
Hindu
   scripture given three hundred of
      God's qualities, 365
   temple, praying in a, **54-55**
history of God. *See* God, history of
honeybee takes honey, 140
horse
   of the mind, 152
   when a—mates, 246-247, 254
houris (heavenly maidens), 208
house(s)
   of the body, 20-21
   for our life, 5-6
human
   birth, **17-26** *passim*
   kind, 265
human being(s), 85-86
   are animals, 97, 104, 110-114 *passim*
   balance of a, 99, 113-114
   Bawa Muhaiyaddeen ☮ is a—created
      by God, **xviii-xix**
   becoming a, 168-169
   cannot live in the world, 327
   changes, 104
   food for, 182-183
   has two parts, 69

human being(s) *(continued)*
   needs of a, 261
   one in ten million is a, 190-192
   perfected, 3, 180
   true, **46-47, 65-67**. *See also* man, true
   with wisdom, 153-156
hunger, 34
   God satisfies your, 182
   of the soul, 46
hurricanes caused by man, 57
hurt
   feel the—of others, 242-243
   to the mind, 128
   world will—man, 97-98

"I," 79
   arrogance of the, 74-75, 233,
      236-242 *passim*
   ideal structure of God's creation,
      248-252 *passim,* 258
idols, **54-55**
ignorance, the glitters of, 4
illness. *See* diseases
illusion (maya), 99-100, 150-151
   oceans of, **176-178**
   tārahan, singhan, and *sūran,* the three
      sons of, 57, 100, 153, 174, **253**
īmān, 43, 102, 106, 114, 128,
      310-314 *passim*
   See also faith
immersed in the world, 122-123
Indian *swāmi,* 193-194
infertility, 256
injustice. *See* justice
insān. See man
insān kāmil. See man, true
insane(ity), 87-88, 147
   becoming, 113
   caused by chemicals, 261
insults, teachings that arose between—
      and explanations, **xvi-xix**
intellect, 30
intention, 223
   on God, 193-194
intersection, path leading from the, 381

intoxicants, 184
  bring destruction, 261-262
  changes in the brain from, 281
  harm conception, 254-255
  will change man's wisdom, 300-302
Islām, **59-64**
  given ninety-nine of God's qualities, 365
  is the *dīn*, 5-6
  state of, 293
Israel☉, the Angel of Death. *See* death, Angel of
Israel, war between—and Damascus, 293, 297-303

jail of life, 199-203
Jesus☉, 365, 381
  will come, **309-315**
  will kill dajjāl, **312-314**
Jews at the time of Jesus☉, 381
jinns, 27-28
Job☉, 188
journey,
  good people begin the, **321-327**
  start on the, **333-338**
judgment,
  Day of, 371-372
  is within us, 135-136
justice
  of God, 81-82, 291-292
  has changed, 76-79 *passim*
  and injustice, **80-92**
  learn, 9-14 *passim*
  loss of, 183-185, 276-281, 289-292 *passim*
  scale of, 151-153
  will be forgotten, 297, 301

Ka'bah, 63
  Jesus☉ will pray at the, 312
Kalimah
  given, 61-63
  See also Dhikr; *lā ilāha illAllāhu*
kali yuga (the last age), 231-244 *passim*
karma, 34, 36, 44, 99-100, 224-225

karma *(continued)*
  burdens of, 71-73
  connections of, 198-199
  and maya, springs of, 150-151
killing
  after taking drugs, 261-262
  in families, 329
kingdom(s)
  of creation, **18-26** *passim*
  of God. *See* God, kingdom of
  of heaven, 133
  ruler of your own, 9-10
know oneself, 274-275, 288
knowledge
  scientific, 186
  worldly, 281

lā ilāha illAllāhu, 61-63, 226
  say, **207-221**
language(s), 178-180, 194
Last Day, 278, 280, 287
lawyers and the poor, 83-84
leave everything behind, **122-136** *passim*
liberation of the soul, 164, 264
life(ves)
  all—are one, 13-15
  boat we call, 123
  commit our—to God, 119-121
  conjugal—of a cow, 164
  of darkness, 273-274
  free the souls of all, 362
  house for our, 5-6
  how should we conduct our, 358-359
  look at our, 243-244
  prisons of, **199-203**
  see all—as one's own, 81-82, 381
  state of our, 149-153 *passim*, 157-161 *passim*
  witness in every, 66
  in the world, **21-25**
light
  Adam☉ and Eve☉ as, **45-67, 69-92**
  dispelled by darkness, 272-273
  Divine Luminous, 39-40
  in a dream, 294

light *(continued)*
   of the Guru, 351-352, 367-368
   known as Nūr Muhammad, 60-61
   the soul is, 364
   transformation into, **51**
   while reciting *dhikr,* 208-212
limit
   Bawa Muhaiyaddeen's ☺, xix
   everything has a, **147-161** *passim,* 269-270
   to karma and sin, 64
love
   form of, 65-66
   of God, 153
   lost, 47-49
lungs and heart, 232
lust, frenzy of, 315-316

Mahdī, 310-315 *passim*
maidens, heavenly, 208
majority denies God, 271-282 *passim*
ma'juj and ya'jūj (gog and magog), 310-312, 327
malā'ikah, 133, 303-305
   are in the body, 175
   given one thousand of God's qualities, 365
   leaders of the, 27
   See also angel(s)
   male and female must conceive children naturally, 250
   See also conception
man (men)
   acts as if he were God, 74-75
   alters creation, **246-267**
   animal qualities in, 79-80 *passim,* **322-326**
   as an actor, **99-103**, 108-109, 115
   ascent and descent of, 30, 101-104
   bad and good within, 288-292 *passim*
   become like women, 238
   becomes satan, 97-105 *passim,* 110, 114-115
   body of, 13-15, 69
   burdens carried by, 71-73

man (men) *(continued)*
   burial of, **233-236**
   can become God, **96-117** *passim*
   causes destruction, **57**
   changes in, 233, 241-243
   deceives women, 77-78
   destroys himself and the world, 269-274, 277-287, *passim*
   dictionary of God within, 178-180
   does the work of an animal, 285-286
   exaltedness of, 171-173
   exemplification of, 28
   fighting among, 241-242
   forgets God, 57-58, 92, 181-186 *passim,* 238-239
   forsakes the path, 210-212
   freedom for. *See* freedom
   God created, 11-15
   of God, hard to find a, 322-323
   -God, man must become, 167-168
   grows large from chemicals, 256-261 *passim*
   harmful things in nature and, **232-239**
   harms other lives, 166-168
   has no peace, 239-242 *passim*
   hidden in God, **96**
   is a book, 287-288
   is God's secret. *See* God, secret of
   joined together with woman, 283
   the justice of, **81-92**
   live as a, **99-117** *passim*
   lives between the earth and sky, 240, 243
   made the world ill, 241
   madness in man, 87-88
   and man joining together cause destruction, 283
   meditates on satan, 185
   must see God through wisdom, 172-173
   must understand what God has given, 370-373
   power given to, 173
   prayer of, 172-173, 192
   punishment for, 372-373
   qualities of, 101, 233-239, 243-244

man (men) *(continued)*
  secret of. *See* God, secret of
  secrets—will know, 28
  sections in, 262-265
  state of, 45
  story of, **99-103** *passim,* **108-109, 113-115**
  subordinate to God, 232-233
  switches roles with animals, 295-296
  thinks he is correct, 237
  thinks he is God, 74-75
  true, 3, 180. *See also* human being, true
  trying to do women's work, 238
  what—saw in the beginning, 202-203
  who has qualities of a woman, 78
  who meditated for twelve years, 352
  will become short in stature, 311-312
  and woman must conceive, 250
  and women join together, 283
    See also conception
mankind, majority of—deny God, 271-274 *passim*
mantras, 34, 173, **179-195** *passim*
  of dajjāl, 310
marketplace, everyone comes to the, 354
Maryam ☪ accepted by Catholics, 381
maut. See death
maya. *See* illusion
meaning(s)
  inner and outer, 101
  that is clearly evident, 226-227
meditation, 72, **179-190** *passim,* **201-212** *passim*
  of one in ten million on God, **190-192**
  twelve years of, 352
menstruate(tion)
  blockage of, 254-255
  women will not, 315
mesmerized, do not be—by anything, 220-221
messengers of God, 12
microorganisms, 234-236
milk
  cow gives—to others, 163-164
  face of—of the Angel of Death, 305-307

mīm, the letter, 129
mind(s)
  as a baby, 199, **203-209** *passim*
  as a monkey, 154-160 *passim,* 212
  as a rock, 156
  burning of the, 70
  connections of the, 198-199
  and conscience, **86-92** *passim*
  controlling the, 187, 209-212
  ether of the, 69-73 *passim,* 175
  four sections of the, 178-179
  has fear, 218-229 *passim*
  is in the heart, 173-178 *passim*
  mire of the, 150-152
  monkey, 154-160 *passim,* **199-207** *passim,* 212
  pain to the, 128-130
  peace of, **177-189, 199-212** *passim*
  rounding by the, 152
  sleep of the, 209-212 *passim*
  the two mountains of—and desire, 155
  two sides of the, 287-288
  went to steal, 157-159
  world of the, 197-198
minority of people trust in God, 271
miracles, 126-127, 150, **154-155, 161**
mi'rāj (ascent), 304
miscarriage, causes of, 255-256
mīzān trās (balance scale), Rasūlullāh ☪
  will be met at the, 295
modesty will be abandoned, 277-278
money
  charged for mantras, 193-195
  when someone comes into, 115
monkey mind. *See* mind, monkey
moon, 176-177
  and sun will join, 316
morality will be lost, 300
Mosque
  of Bawa Muhaiyaddeen ☪, protect the, 380
  each person builds the—within himself, 381
  of Islām, **59-63**
  pray in the, 3-4

Mother
   bird protects chicks, 247
   and Father to all creatures,
      46-50 *passim*, 61. *See also*
      Adam ☺ and Eve ☺
motor, charge the—of the heart, 351-352
mountain(s)
   icy, 236
   of mind and desire, 155
   standing against evil, 192
   top, living on a, 289-290
mouth(s)
   must be open for grace, 353
   speaking with their, 279
Muhammad ☺, 63, 137-138
   followers of, 106-107
   Mustāfār-Rāsul ☺, xvi
   Nūr, 60-61. *See also* Nūr
   predicts the future, 293-311 *passim*
   See also Rasūlullāh ☺
murder
   becomes commonplace, 186
   men make women commit, 77
   the poor are accused of, 82-85
mystery of God. *See* God, mystery of

nabī (prophet), man becomes a, 101
naked
   we are born, 286
   worshipping, 273
natural
   that which is, **282-287** *passim*
   things become artificial, 295-296
   things will change, 300
nature
   altered, 255
   changes in, **231-244**, *passim*
   created by God, 260
   man will believe in, 299
   positive and negative in, 231, 237
needs
   of a human being, 261
   of people, **28-29**
neighbor(s)
   love your, 381-382

neighbor(s) *(continued)*
   we and our, 242-243
   nerves, the 1,448—of men and women,
      315-316
night is finally over, **333-338**
1944, meditation techniques since, 184,
   186, 205
niyyah. *See* intention
Nūr, 225
   Muhammad, 60-61
   soul called the, 364-365
   See also Muhammad, Rasūlullāh ☺
nurture
   everything we—will eat us, **124-134**
   God's qualities, 133-135

ocean
   all around us, 362
   building a shore for the, 187
odors, 233-235
   of death, 343-344
organ replacement, 75, 258-259, 266
oyster grows a pearl, 353

pahut arivu. *See* wisdom, *pahut arivu*,
   discerning
pain
   to the mind, 128-134 *passim*
   of others, 242-243
   See also suffering
pairs of opposites are natural, 282
paradise, 80, 108-109, 115
past is finally over, **333-338**
path
   of good or evil, **106-113** *passim*
   leading from intersection, 381
   to peace, 203
   of truth forsaken by man, 210-212
patience, 11-12
peace, 92-93, 105-106, 177-194 *passim*,
   239, 241-243, 264-265, 270, 283
   attainment of, **110-117**, 167-169, 283
   brought by a true human being, **46-47**
   find, 9-14 *passim*, 289
   from God's words, xvii-xix

peace *(continued)*
    man has no, 239-242 *passim*
    of mind, **177-189, 199-212** *passim*
    state of, 173
pearl in oyster, 353
people
    clear—disappeared, xvi-xvii
    destruction of good, 272
    differences among, **60-64** *passim*
    a few good, 50, 58-59
    good—begin the journey, **321-327, 333-338**
    have changed, 185-190 *passim*
    insults against the *ambiyā* by, xvi, xix
    killed by atomic war, 301-303
    remind the, xvii-xix
    silver-eyed, 302-303
    three—who know God, 29-30
perish
    all will—except God, 131-134 *passim*
    man's creation will, 249-250
    See also die
pestilence, 327-328
place(s)
    correct, 97
    obtain a good, 100-117 *passim*
    of prayer, **51-64** *passim*
plants, sow, 361-373 *passim*
point(s)
    enter the zygote, 251
    of God, 267
    when man gets to the correct, 97-98
poison(s), 145-146, 154, 236, 327-328
    destruction from, 298, 301-302
    of a snake, 47, 154
    in words, 139
    in the world, 280
pollution, 231-236 *passim*
poor
    degradation of the, 319
    do not say "I am," 138
    people and lack of justice, 82-85
    See also poverty
positive and negative, 137-143 *passim*, 237

pots
    bring your own, 28
    copper and clay, **21-26**
poverty, 185-186, 327-328
    See also poor
power(s)
    of the elements, 364
    in the heart, 174
    ninety-nine, 365
    that exists in man, 96
    in the words of the Guru, 351-352
praise
    do not accept, 4
    taking the—that belongs to God, 74-75
pray(er)
    doing quick, **59-60**
    to God. *See* God, prayer to
    of man, 172-173, 192-193
    in the Mosque, 3-4
    in the past, 270
    in unity, 51-52, 59-63 *passim*
prejudice, 82-84, 109
prices, rising, 193
Principle, Essential. *See* God, the Essential Principle
prison(s)
    are filled with the innocent, 84-85
    of life, **199-203**
profit
    from God's capital, 371-373
    opportunists for, 276-277
proliferate, man's creation cannot, 249-254 *passim*
prophet(s)
    God's explanations given through the, **xv-xvi**
    man rejected the, 233
    Muhammad ﷺ. *See* Muhammad ﷺ
    words of the, **187-195** *passim*
    See also ambiyā'
proportion, balance must be in, 147-149
protection
    by a mother for her chicks, 247
    of the qualities of God, 180-181

punishment for man, 372-373
Purānas (ancient scriptures), 174
purity
    absolute—is *saivam*, 166-169
    of the *dīn*, 5-6

qalb(s), 43, 63, 67, 115, 216-221, 227
    the flower of the, 167
    make your—clear, 358-359
    must stick to the Shaikh, 140
    open our, 318-319
    spring that flows from the, 151
    truth within the, 362-363, **371-375** *passim*
    See also heart
qualities
    connected to the earth, 126-131 *passim*
    of created beings, 246-247
    dark and light, 282
    evil, 4, 150, 336
        burn up everything, 79
        must be cut by the roots, 153-154
    and forms of animals, **56-57**
    of God. *See* God, qualities of
    God's three thousand compassionate, 365
    loss of original, 272-282 *passim*
    of man. *See* man, qualities of
    of the mind, **197-199**
qudrah (power), 248
Questioning, the, 20
questions, children ask, 240
qunūt prayer, 313
Qur'ān, 190, 216, 309, 312, **315**, 319
Qutb ﷺ, 223
Qutbiyyah, 180

rape, 78-79
Rasūlullāh ﷺ
    and the Angel of Death, 303-307
    answers questions, **293-308**
    is asked how long Islām will last, 293, 295
    speaks of the destruction, **295-320**
    staff of the, 313-314

Rasūlullāh ﷺ *(continued)*
    will be at the *mīzān trās*, 295
    See also Muhammad ﷺ
Reality, see, 356
rebirth, 131, 134, 276, 356
reflection, careful, 242-243
religions, 99, 103-109 *passim*, 115-116, 184-186
    inner meanings of the—will be destroyed, 296
representative of God. *See* God, representative of
research
    atomic, 264
    destructive, 233-242 *passim*
    the difference between God's and man's, **245-267** *passim*
    scientific, 299-300
Resurrection, 365
reward, there is no—in acting, 334, 337
right from wrong, knowing, 163-164
robot
    child will be a, 252
    man as a, 250, 256, 261-262
rock, mind as a, 156
rooster meditates, 185
roots of evil qualities must be cut, 153-154
    See also qualities, evil
rounding, by the mind, 152
rūh, 248. *See also* soul
rūhānī. *See* spirits, impure
ruler of your own kingdom, 9-10
Russia, dajjāl will come to, 311

saint, guru as a, 180
saivam (purity), **163-169**
salāms (greetings of peace), 59-60, 63
satan
    Abu, 27
    as a god to hell, 102
    man can become, **96-106** *passim*, **110-115** *passim*
    meditation on, 184-185
    and the time of destruction, **190-192**

satan *(continued)*
  work of, 105-106
  worship of, 273-274
scale(s)
  of balance, **147-160** *passim*
  of justice, 151-153
science, man believes in, 324-327 *passim*
scriptures, faith in the, 274, 277
seas, seven, 174
seasons, man does not know the, 186
secret(s)
  of God. *See* God, secret(s) of
  man will know, 28
section(s)
  destructive and good, 262-264, 292
  of the mother and father, 252-254, 264
seed(s)
  created by God, 35-36, 70,
    245-249 *passim*, 260
  in a dream, 294
  God created many—from one,
    181-182
  return to the earth, 125
self
  man does not know him,
    274-292 *passim*
  understand your, 12-15
semen, 246, 262
  Jesus ☮ is without, 310
  when extracted, 252-253
separation(s), 271, 276-277, 288
  from attachments, 124, 131
  between men, 105
  man must separate from qualities of,
    168-169
sex(ual)
  desire, 177-178
  games, 34
  shakti arises during, 253
Shaikh
  help the, 4
  wisdom of the 5-6
  of wisdom, 153-156 *passim*
  words of the, **155-162** *passim*
shaktis. *See* energies of creation

shānti. *See* peace
share, remaining—which belongs to
  God, 160
siblings, the elements are, 48-49
sick, do not say you are, 138-139
sickness. *See* diseases
side(s)
  right and wrong, **287-290**
  on the—of God, 283
sidratul-muntahā. *See* tree of life
signs of destruction, 317
silver-eyed people, 302-303
sin(s), 49, 64
  cause natural catastrophes, 57,
    283-284
  may God pardon our, 374
  those who—are taken by the Angel of
    Death, 305-306
sky
  everything in the—returns to the
    earth, 125-126
  open expanse of the, 299-300
  substances in the, 233-238
slavery, we must free ourselves from,
    132-136 *passim*
slaves, making people, 272
sleep, of the mind, 209-212 *passim*
smells. *See* odors
snake meditates, 185
  poison of a, 47, 154
Solomon ☮
  feeding the fish, 182
  seal and staff of, 315
son of God. *See* God, son of
soul
  connected to God, 364-365
  creation of the, 18-20
  cultivation of the, 284-287
  enemies to the, 146
  eye of the, 151
  freedom of the, 101
  hunger of the, 46
  -light, 45
  light of the, 51, 53
  of man is a sun, 172

soul *(continued)*
  when the—is given, 248
  when the—is understood, 165
  will be conscience itself, 65-66
  within the body, 345
  within the soul, 264
sound between two mountains, 155-156
space travel, 299-300
speaking for the sake of the world, 275-276
speech, good, 39
sperm and ovum, merging of, 246-254 *passim*
spirits *(rūhānīs)*
  evil, 255
  impure—will follow a guilty man, 87-90
  malignant, 337-338
spring(s)
  of maya and karma, 150-151
staff of the Rasūlullāh ☪, 313-314
stars, 175-177
state(s)
  of all states, 11-14 *passim*
  altered, 238-242 *passim*
  of awe, 135
  of God, 59-64 *passim*
  of man, 45
  -God, 96, **102-103**
  of peace, 173
  in which we exist, 149-153 *passim*, 157-161 *passim*
statues, **51-56** *passim*
stealing, 72
  by mind and desire, 157-159
stomach
  burning, 355
  enemy to the, 146, 150-151
  hunger of the, 46
  one span, 240
story
  of God. *See* God, story of
  of man. *See* man, story of
  which—shall we tell? **33-41** *passim*
strength, man has no, 241

structure, ideal—of God's creation, 248-252 *passim*, 258
subordinate, man is—to God, 232-233
suffering, 97-98
  of all living beings, 39
  of human beings, 287
  of others as one's own, 243
  See also pain
Sufis give explanations, 318
suicide, 70-78 *passim*
  of women, 77-78
sun, 48, 176, 368
  goes down, 354
  soul of man is a, 172
  will not rise, 315-316
sūrah (form) of truth, 65
surrender
  of earth to God, 55
  to God, 274-278 *passim*
swāmi who came to America, 193-194

talk is easy, 149
tārahan, singhan, sūran. *See* illusion, *tārahan, singhan, sūran*, the three sons of
tasbīh (glorification of God), 63
tattwas (abilities), 28-29
teacher title, 194-195
telephone to God, 368
temple, Hindu, **54-55**
theft. *See* stealing
thoughts, 70
  affect conception, 251
  angels will be in your, 212
  crafted by the mind, 56
  destructive, 64
  devour us, **128-134** *passim*
  have a limit, 147
  of a man who drinks, 111
  swimming in, **122-136** *passim*
  of *ummah*, 306
time
  bomb of destruction, 290-291
  of destruction, **269-292** *passim*
  is going very fast, 240

titles, **285-286, 291-292**
training
  of chicks by the mother, 247
  of the zygote, 251-252
travel, 40-41
tray, golden—brings fruit, 128
treasure, 223-228 *passim*
  of Bawa Muhaiyaddeen ☙, 343-344
  of God. *See* God, treasure of
  held in trust, 12-13
tree(s)
  creation of a, 260
  in a dream, 294
  of faith, 205-206
  the nature of—will change, 296
troubles cause man to change, 97-98
truth, 49, 65-67
  enemies to, 146
  exists in a few people, 75-76
  God is. *See* God, the Truth
  and insults of God's words, xvi-xix
  man has forsaken, 210
  one, 202, 319-320
  sūrah of, 65
  try to realize the, 184-185, 194-195
  will be forgotten, 297, 301
  within the heart, 362-363
  the world will hurt those who
    possess, 91
turtle, you are like the—that laid eggs, 353

ummah (followers), 382
  of Muhammad ☙, 106
  will look in the eyes of the Angel of
    Death, 306
*unarvu, unarchi, putti, madi, nupa arivu,
    pahut arivu,* and *pērarivu. See*
    wisdom, seven levels of
understand(ing), 179-180
  God gave man, 172, 369-374 *passim*
  right and wrong, 11
  and *saivam*, **165-169**
  we must, **33-44**
  we must—our state, 151-153, 161-162
  yourself, 12-15, 80

union of a male and female necessary for
    true creation, 249-250
unity, pray in. *See* pray(er) in unity
universes, eighteen thousand, 369-370
universities, 192

vampire, work of a, 105
vapors, 174
vegetarianism of cattle, 163-164
villages
  searching for their, 354
  travel throughout all the, 40-41

waqt (time of prayer), each, 319
war(s), 232-233, 236-243 *passim,* 328
  after—destruction will follow, 289,
    309, 319
  among men, 278-280
  between Syria and Israel, 293,
    297-303 *passim*
  cause of, 261-262
  East and West will join in,
    297-302 *passim*
  the next, 301-303
water, 48, 71, 187, 235
  drinking, 282
  fish live in, **122-130** *passim,* **136,
    344-345**
  heavy, 298
  for plants, 362-363
  poisoned, 327-328
  supply for others, 266-267
waves of illusion, 176-178
wealth
  of bliss, **206-212** *passim*
  of God. *See* God, wealth of
  for our lives, 95, **107-109, 115-116**
  what is not, 121-122
weapons
  developing, 279
  in the time of destruction, 91
weather
  has changed, 186, 190
  and natural disasters, 284
well, dig a, 362

white and black. *See* colors and hues
wilāyāt (attributes), ninety-nine, 133
wisdom, 41-42, 114, **124-134** *passim*
   analyze your body with,
      334-338 *passim*
   animal, 185
   and balance, 147-154 *passim*
   blocked by chemicals, 261-262
   divine crown of, 66
   divine luminous, 124
   God gave man, 10-13 *passim,* 369-371
   is within, 265, 362-363
   limits destruction, **59, 66**
   man of, 153-156 *passim*
   natural section of, 284-285
   pahut arivu, discerning, 104, 114, 150, 203, 368
   person with, 58-59
   seven levels of, 30, 124, 150, 172-173, 370-371
   of the Shaikh, 5-6
   study, 288-289
   sun of, 176-181 *passim*
   and understanding, 163-169 *passim*
   will be changed by intoxicants, 300-302
witness, 61, 66
womb cannot hold the embryo, 255
women
   becoming like men, 238
   conduct of, 272
   deceived by men, 77-78
   and men joining together is natural, 283
   qualities of, **76-77**
   violated, **87-90**
   will predominate, 315-316
   and women joining together cause destruction, 283
words
   Bawa Muhaiyaddeen ☺ was sent to listen to the people's, xvii-xix
   of Bawa Muhaiyaddeen ☺, protect, 379-380
   of God, 60

words *(continued)*
   of a Guru, 351
   old, xvii-xviii
   positive and negative, 137-143 *passim*
   of the Shaikh, 155-160
   the two, **203-212** *passim*
world(s), **33-36**
   actors in the, 278
   attachments of the, 146-153 *passim*
   of creation, **19-26** *passim*
   destroyed if no one remembers God, xviii
   destruction of the, 45, 50-59 *passim,* 64-67 *passim,* 76, 80, 239-244, **269-292**, 295-303, **327-329**. *See* destruction, of the world
   can be averted, 192
   does not see the value of the clay pot, **21-25**
   finding a man of wisdom in the, 155-157
   forgot God's words, xvi-xviii
   God will create the—again, 317
   good state in the, 270
   heavenly—in the heart, **208-212** *passim*
   is an enemy to the soul, 146
   is within, 291-292
   man has changed in the, **323-327**
   of the mind, 197-198
   mind and desire stole from the, 157-160
   saved by one or two people, xviii
   speaking for the sake of the, 275-276
   will try to turn man into satan, **96-106** *passim*
   See also dunyā
worship
   of darkness, 273
   many kinds of, 355-356
   places of, **50-64**
   useless, 189

ya'jūj and majūj (gog and magog), 310-312, 327

year(s)
    destruction has increased in the past hundred, 280-291 *passim*
    two hundred million, 231-232
yugas (age), 148-149, 231

zygote, training of the, 251

ABOUT
M. R. BAWA MUHAIYADDEEN ﴿ق﴾

The teachings of Muhammad Raheem Bawa Muhaiyaddeen ﴿ق﴾ express the mystical explanation, the SUFI path of esoteric Islam; namely that the human being is uniquely created with the faculty of Wisdom, enabling one to trace consciousness back to its origin—Allah, the one divine Being, the Creator of all—and to surrender the self within that Source, leaving the One God, the Truth, as the only reality in one's life. He spoke endlessly of this Truth through parables, discourses, songs and stories, all pointing the way to return to God.

People from all religions and races flocked to hear and be near him; he taught everyone, regardless of origin, with love, compassion and acceptance. An extraordinary being, he taught from experience, having traversed the Path, and returned, divinely aware—sent back to exhort all who yearn for the experience of God to discover this internal Wisdom, the path of surrender to that One.

M. R. Bawa Muhaiyaddeen's known history begins in Sri Lanka. He was discovered in the pilgrimage town of Kataragama by spiritual seekers from the northern city of Jaffna. Begging him to come teach them, he did so for forty years until 1971, when he accepted an American invitation to Philadelphia, from where he lovingly taught until his passing in December, 1986.

In these distressing times, his teachings are increasingly recognized as representing the original intention of Islam which is Purity—the relationship between man and God as explained by all the prophets of God, from Adam to Noah, Abraham, Moses,

Jesus and Muhammad, may the peace of God be upon them — all sent to tell and retell mankind that there is one and only one God, and that this One is their source, attainable, and waiting for the return of each individual soul.

The Bawa Muhaiyaddeen Fellowship is in Philadelphia, Pennsylvania, which was the home of M. R. Bawa Muhaiyaddeen ☺ when he lived in the United States. The Fellowship continues to serve as a meeting house, as a reservoir of people and materials for everyone wishing access to his teachings.

The Mosque of Shaikh M. R. Bawa Muhaiyaddeen is located on the same property; here the five daily prayers and Friday congregational prayers are observed. An hour west of the Fellowship is the Mazār, the resting place of M. R. Bawa Muhaiyaddeen ☺ which is open daily between sunrise and sunset.

If you would like to visit the Fellowship, or to
obtain a schedule of current events, branch
locations and meetings, please contact:
Bawa Muhaiyaddeen Fellowship
5820 Overbrook Avenue
Philadelphia, Pennsylvania 19131
Phone: (215) 879-6300
Fax: (215) 879-6307
E-mail: **info@bmf.org**
Website: **www.bmf.org**

Books by M. R. Bawa Muhaiyaddeen ☾

The Choice

Bawa Asks Bawa Muhaiyaddeen ☾, Volumes One, Two & Three

Life Is a Dream: A Book of Sufi Verse

A Timeless Treasury of Sufi Quotations

The Four Virtues and Their Relationship
to Good Behavior and Bad Conduct

Sūratur-Rahmah: The form of Compassion

God's Psychology: A Sufi Explanation

The Point Where God and Man Meet

The Map of the Journey to God: Lessons from the School of Grace

The Golden Words of a Sufi Sheikh, Revised Edition

Islam and World Peace: Explanations of a Sufi, Second Edition

A Book of God's Love

The Resonance of Allah: Resplendent Explanations
Arising from the Nūr, Allāh's Wisdom of Grace

The Tree That Fell to the West: Autobiography of a Sufi

Asmā'ul Husnā: The 99 Beautiful Names of Allah

Questions of Life — Answers of Wisdom (Volumes One & Two)

The Fast of Ramadan: The Inner Heart Blossoms

Hajj: The Inner Pilgrimage

The Triple Flame: The Inner Secrets of Sufism

A Song of Muhammad ☾

To Die Before Death: The Sufi Way of Life

A Mystical Journey

Sheikh and Disciple

Why Can't I See the Angels: Children's Questions to a Sufi Saint

Treasures of the Heart: Sufi Stories for Young Children

Come to the Secret Garden: Sufi Tales of Wisdom

My Love You My Children: 101 Stories for Children of All Ages

Maya Veeram or The Forces of Illusion
God, His Prophets and His Children
Four Steps to Pure *Īmān*
The Wisdom of Man
Truth & Light: Brief Explanations
Songs of God's Grace
The Guidebook to the True Secret of the Heart (Volumes One & Two)
The Divine Luminous Wisdom That Dispels the Darkness
Wisdom of the Divine (Volumes One to Six)
The Tasty, Economical Cookbook, Second Edition

Booklets
Gems of Wisdom series:
Vol. 1: The Value of Good Qualities
Vol. 2: Beyond Mind and Desire
Vol. 3: The Innermost Heart
Vol. 4: Come to Prayer

Pamphlets
Advice to Prisoners
Come to Prayer: The Wake-up Song
Du'ā' Kanzul-'Arsh (The Invocation of the Treasure of the Throne)
Faith
The Golden Words of a Sufi Sheikh: Preface to the Book
Letter to the World Family
Love is the Remedy, God is the Healer
Marriage
The Opening of the Mosque of Shaikh M. R. Bawa Muhaiyaddeen ☙
The Pond — A Letter to the Fellowship Family
A Prayer for Father's Day
A Prayer for My Children

(continued on next page)

A Prayer from My Heart
Strive for a Good Life
Sufi: A Brief Explanation
A Sufi Perspective on Business
Sufism
25 Duties — The True Meaning of Fellowship
With Every Breath, Say *Lā Ilāha Ill-Allāhu*
Who Is God?
Why Man Has No Peace (from My Love You, My Children)
Why We Recite the Maulids
The Wisdom and Grace of the Sufis

The Instructions:
The Fox and the Crocodile and Do Not Carry Tales
God Is Very Light
Unity
Prayer: Starting Over

A Contemporary Sufi Speaks:
Teenagers and Parents
On the Signs of Destruction
On Peace of Mind
On the True Meaning of Sufism
On Unity: The Legacy of the Prophets
On the Meaning of Fellowship
Mind, Desire, and the Billboards of the World

From Islam and World Peace
Islam & World Peace: Explanations of a Sufi — *Jihād,* The Holy War Within
Islam & World Peace: Explanations of a Sufi — The True Meaning of Islam and Epilogue
Islam & World Peace: Explanations of a Sufi — Two Discourses

Foreign Language Publications

Ein Zeitgenössischer Sufi Spricht über Inneren Frieden
(A Contemporary Sufi Speaks on Peace of Mind — German translation)

Deux Discours tirés du Livre L'Islam et la Paix Mondiale:
Explications d'un Soufi
(Two Discourses from the Book, Islam and World Peace:
Explanations of a Sufi — French translation)

La Paix (Two Discourses — French Translation)

¿Quién es Dios? Una Explicatión por el Sheikh Sufi
(Who is God? An Explanation by the Sufi Sheikh — Spanish translation)

Other Publications

Bawa Muhaiyaddeen Fellowship Calendar

Morning *Dhikr* at the Mosque of Shaikh M. R. Bawa Muhaiyaddeen☺

For free catalog or book information call:
(888) 786-1786 or (215) 879-8604 (voice mail)

For information about books and pamphlets
by M. R. Bawa Muhaiyaddeen☺
and CDs and DVDs of his discourses,
please visit **www.bmfstore.com**

For information about
Muhammad Raheem Bawa Muhaiyaddeen☺,
the Bawa Muhaiyaddeen Fellowship,
the Mosque of Shaikh M. R. Bawa Muhaiyaddeen☺,
and the *Mazār* of Shaikh M. R. Bawa Muhaiyaddeen☺,
please visit **www.bmf.org**

Al-hamdu lillāh!
All praise belongs to God!